D1315449

The Licensure and Certification Mission

D epicted on the cover of this book is the tetradrachma, a coin produced in Athens and circulated in ancient Greece during the sixth century B.C. One side of the coin portrayed the head of Athena, goddess of wisdom and reason; the other side portrayed the owl, an animal sacred to the goddess and often associated with her. To the ancient citizens of Athens, the goddess Athena was their guide and protectress.

Professional Examination Service (PES) has taken a stylized owl as its symbol (shown opposite) to convey its commitment to wisdom and reason as guiding principles of the PES mission. Founded in 1941, PES is a nonprofit organization with a mission to promote the understanding and use of sound credentialing practices. The foundation of PES's mission is the belief that licensure and certification activities benefit the public good. This belief is based on the tenet that credentialed professionals have shown that they possess the knowledge, skills, and abilities required for the attainment of their profession's license or certificate. Credentials, therefore, play a valuable role in helping the public to make informed decisions regarding the selection and use of professional services.

PES achieves its mission by providing services and making contributions to credentialing stakeholders in the areas of assessment practice, educational activities, scientific research, and policy development. Over the years, PES has developed an extensive program of public service activities designed to promote the understanding and use of sound cerdentialing practices. This book forms an integral part of the PES public service mission.

The Licensure and Certification Mission

Legal, Social, and Political Foundations

Edited by

Craig G. Schoon
I. Leon Smith

Professional Examination Service
New York, New York

Professional Examination Service   •   NEW YORK

Library of Congress Cataloging-in-Publication Data

The licensure and certification mission: legal, social, and political foundation/
edit by Craig G Schoon, I. Leon Smith.

    p.cm.
    Includes bibliographical references and index.
    ISBN 0-8281-1450-1 (alk. paper)
        1. Professions—Law and legislation—United States. 2.
    Occupation—Licenses—United States. I. Schoon, Craig G. II. Smith, I. Leon.

    KF2900 .L53 2000
    352.8'4'0973—dc21

ISBN: 0-8281-1450-1

This book is printed on acid-free paper.

Professional Examination Service offers discounts on this book when ordered in bulk quantities.

Professional Examination Service
475 Riverside Drive
New York, NY 10015-0089
mission@proexam.org

Current Printing (last digit):

10 9 8 7 6 5 4 3 2 1

PRINTED IN THE UNITED STATES OF AMERICA

Preface

This book addresses the mission of licensure and certification programs from the perspectives of their legal, social, and political foundations. Although there are a number of books that address the psychometric and procedural foundations of credentialing organizations, few have addressed their mission. The importance of discussing credentialing activities from these perspectives is clear when we look at the critical issues that surround credentialing. Should teachers be certified before they can teach? Should licensed professionals be required to demonstrate their competence on a continuing basis? Is licensing too widespread in the professions? Are state boards doing their job to protect the public? What is the difference between licensed and certified professionals? Is the primary goal of licensure to restrict the right to practice, and therefore to promote the interests of a licensed profession, rather than to protect the public? Should voluntary certification receive more emphasis than licensure for professions? What is the impact on the public of hospitals' increasing use of fewer licensed nurses and more noncertified or unlicensed employees?

Questions such as these—questions of public policy, the politics of credentialing, the economics of health care, and the legal foundations of credentialing—are presented here so that stakeholders in credentialing can engage in an effective dialogue regarding the appropriate mission of credentialing, and the means of accomplishing that mission. This dialogue is important because the nature and structure of professional services are rapidly changing. This rapid change is being reflected in power struggles among professional groups and stakeholder organizations that control or receive services from the professions. By addressing these issues, we hope that this book will enhance and promote productive dialogue regarding the licensure and certification mission.

Our coverage of the credentialing mission is accomplished by addressing (a) the legal, social, and political foundations of certification and licensure activities; (b) actual mission statements of a number of certification and licensure organizations; (c) the role of major educational and/or standard-setting stakeholder organizations in the certification and licensure arenas; and (d) the implications of clear mission statements that are responsive to their perceived stakeholder groups.

We believe that it is crucial to focus on the underlying nonprofit role of most credentialing activity. Most credentialing takes place under the aegis of nonprofit organizations, and most of these organizations are professional associations, independent boards, or membership organizations incorporated as either 501(c)(6) or 501(c)(3) nonprofit corporations. Given the nonprofit underpinnings of credentialing activity, it is expected that such organizations should have mission statements that explicate their purposes, goals, values, and philosophy, and that therefore justify their nonprofit status as beneficial to the profession and/or to the public. Our presentation of the implications of credentialing organizations' nonprofit status is a salient feature of this book.

The intended audience includes policy makers, regulators, educators, accreditors, and board members, as well as program directors and staff members—all those responsible for initiating, developing, monitoring, and enhancing credentialing programs.

We thank the members of the Professional Examination Service Board of Directors for their leadership and guidance, their belief in the missions of nonprofit organizations, and their commitment to the mission of PES and its clients in the credentialing fields. Their emphasis on clarification of the PES mission led to our interest in exploring the mission of PES's clients, our stakeholders. We also wish to thank our clients and colleagues in credentialing for their willingness to discuss their missions and to share their problems, issues, and prospects for the future. It is our hope that our stakeholders can use this book to evaluate their missions with the view to better serving their stakeholders in licensure and certification.

Finally, we express our appreciation to the following members of the PES staff, whose contributions have assisted in making this publication possible: to Angela Cabri, for managing the editorial review process and coordinating communications with the authors; to Karen Cullen, for overseeing the cover design and layout; to Henry Boehm, for consulting on the many production decisions; and to Sandra Greenberg, for coplanning and codirecting the 1996 PES Invitational Seminar on the Credentialing Mission, which served as the basis for the publication.

Craig G. Schoon
I. Leon Smith

Contents

Preface   *iii*

Contributors   *viii*

INTRODUCTION

The Licensure and Certification Mission: Foundations   **1**
Craig G. Schoon and I. Leon Smith

SECTION ONE: THE CERTIFICATION MISSION

1. The Meaning of Tax-Exempt Status in the Work of Certification Organizations   **16**
Bruce R. Hopkins

2. Establishing and Demonstrating the Value of a Credential   **31**
Michael S. Hamm

3. The Governance Structure of Credentialing Programs   **53**
Susan Dorn

4. Missions of Organizations Involved in Certification   **77**

The Mission of the Board of Pharmaceutical Specialties   77
Richard J. Bertin

The Mission of AACN Certification Corporation   85
Melissa Biel

The Mission of the National Commission for the Certification of
Crane Operators   88
Graham J. Brent

The Mission of the Pharmacy Technician Certification Board   93
Melissa M. Murer

The Mission of the National Board for Certification in Occupational Therapy 100
Edna Q. Wooldridge

The Mission of the American Society of Association Executives   108
Gary A. LaBranche

5. The Mission of Stakeholder Organizations in Certification   **114**

The Mission of the National Organization for Competency Assurance
and the National Commission for Certifying Agencies   114
Larry Allan Early

SECTION TWO: THE LICENSURE MISSION

6. Legal Issues in Licensure Policy   **124**
Dale J. Atkinson

7. The Role that Licensure Plays in Society   **145**
Benjamin Shimberg

8. Missions of Organizations Involved in Licensure   **164**

The Mission of the American Institute of Certified Public Accountants and
the Certified Public Accountants License   164
James D. Blum

The Mission of the National Association of State Boards of Accountancy   174
David A. Costello

The Mission of a State Licensing Board   178
Lynda Farrar

The Mission of the National Conference of Bar Examiners   181
Erica Moeser

The Mission of the National Association of Boards of Examiners of
Long Term Care Administrators   183
John H. Hogan

The Mission of a State Testing Unit   186
Barbara A. Showers

The Mission of the National Council of State Boards of Nursing   189
Anthony Zara

9. **The Mission of Stakeholder Organizations in Licensure**   **194**

The Mission of the Council on Licensure, Enforcement and Regulation   194
Pam Brinegar

The Role of Mission Statements in the Work of the Pew Health Professions
Commission   200
Catherine Dower

The Mission of the Federation of Associations of Regulatory Boards   207
Randolph P. Reaves

SECTION THREE: IMPLICATIONS AND CONCLUSIONS

10. **The Meaning and Implications of the Credentialing Mission**   **214**
Craig G. Schoon and I. Leon Smith

Index   *234*

Contributors

Dale J. Atkinson, JD Attorney, Atkinson & Atkinson, Evanston, Illinois

Richard J. Bertin, PhD, RPh Executive Director, Board of Pharmaceutical Specialties, Washington, D.C.

Melissa Biel, RN, MSN Executive Director, AACN Certification Corporation, Aliso Viejo, California

James D. Blum, PhD, CPA Director—Examinations, American Institute of Certified Public Accountants, Jersey City, New Jersey

Graham J. Brent Executive Director, National Commission for the Certification of Crane Operators, Fairfax, Virginia

Pam Brinegar, MA Executive Director, Council on Licensure, Enforcement and Regulation, Lexington, Kentucky

David A. Costello, CPA President and Chief Executive Officer, National Association of State Boards of Accountancy, Nashville, Tennessee

Susan Dorn, JD Managing Partner, Dorn & Klamp, P.C., Washington, D.C.

Catherine Dower, JD Health Law and Policy Analyst, Center for the Health Professions, University of California, San Francisco, San Francisco, California

Larry Allan Early, PhD Manager, Clinical Skills Assessment, and Assistant Professor, Clinical Medical Education, Center for the Studies of Clinical Performance, Northeastern Ohio Universities College of Medicine, Rootstown, Ohio

Lynda Farrar, OD Optometrist, Oregon, and Member, Wisconsin Department of Regulation and Licensing, Madison, Wisconsin

Michael S. Hamm, MHA Principal, Michael Hamm & Associates, Rockville, Maryland

John H. Hogan, MS President, National Association of Boards of Examiners of Long Term Care Administrators, Portland, Oregon

Bruce R. Hopkins, JD Polsinelli, White, Vardeman, & Shalton, Kansas City, Missouri

Gary A. LaBranche, CAE, CMC Vice President, Professional Development, American Society of Association Executives, Washington, D.C.

Erica Moeser, JD, MS President, National Conference of Bar Examiners, Chicago, Illinois

Melissa M. Murer, RPh Executive Director, Pharmacy Technician Certification Board, Washington, D.C.

Randolph P. Reaves, JD Executive Officer and General Counsel, Association of State and Provincial Psychology Boards, Montgomery, Alabama

Craig G. Schoon, PhD Past President/Research Scholar-in-Residence, Professional Examination Service, New York, New York

Benjamin Shimberg, PhD Emeritus Research Scientist, The Chauncey Group International, Lawrenceville, New Jersey, and Board Chair, Citizen Advocacy Center, Washington, D.C.

Barbara A. Showers, PhD Director, Office of Examinations, Wisconsin Department of Regulation and Licensing, Madison, Wisconsin

I. Leon Smith, PhD President and Chief Executive Officer, Professional Examination Service, New York, New York

Edna Q. Wooldridge, MEd, CAGS, NCC Director of Evaluation and Research, National Board for Certification in Occupational Therapy, Gaithersburg, Maryland

Anthony Zara, PhD Senior Director of Testing and Research Services, National Council of State Boards of Nursing, Chicago, Illinois

The Licensure and Certification Mission

Foundations

Craig G. Schoon and I. Leon Smith

Professional Examination Service, New York, New York

Clear mission statements are of critical importance for licensure and certification organizations because they enable these organizations to best serve their stakeholders. Although many in the licensure and certification field may assume that their mission is self-evident, the chapters in this book indicate that there may be disagreement about their respective focus. For example, licensure is widely regarded as the government's means of protecting the public; however, licensure activities are often criticized for promoting the interests of the profession rather than protecting the public. Certification, on the other hand, perceived by most as a profession's means of recognizing professional achievement and thereby promoting the business interests of the profession, is often depicted as a means of public protection. Also, in a society in which the definition of a profession is rapidly changing in the face of technological advances—for example, healthcare reform with its pressure for cost reduction via managed care—we may find that how a profession defined itself in the recent past no longer holds true. Professions that once considered themselves secure and permanent fixtures of our society's healthcare environment find that their skills no longer reflect the advancements in knowledge and technology in the field, or that their services are being performed by others with lesser training, or by those without credentials. In short, the practice or job of a licensed or certified professional is rapidly changing in a rapidly changing society. In the face of such rapid transformation, we believe that a close examination of the legal, social, and political foundations of a profession, leading to a clear and forceful mission statement, will enable professions to better define their role, cope with an ever-changing work environment, and serve their stakeholders effectively.

I. What Is a Credential?

As used in this book, the word *credential* refers to the act of occupational licensure or certification. We shall define *licensure* as the granting of a license to practice a profession by a governmental body. A license is a property right of an individual, and as a property right, a license is backed by the laws of the state in which it is granted.

Certification, on the other hand, is the recognition by the private sector of voluntarily achieved standards. Certification is most usually bestowed by a private sector, nonprofit, professional association or independent board on those members who achieve specified standards. Certification is therefore distinguished from licensure because it is generally nongovernmental and voluntary. Confusion can result when the title *certified* is used for a licensed profession, such as Certified Public Accountant.

Registration, another credentialing term, refers to the keeping of lists of practitioners by a governmental agency. It can be equivalent to licensure but may also be distinguished from licensure in that criteria for registration may not exist, and registration may not be required for practice. In this book, therefore, we will deal exclusively with licensed and certified professions as defined above.

We use the word *credential* not only to denote licensure and certification, but also to connote an affective element inherent in these terms. The word *credential* is derived from the Latin word *credere*, which means to believe, to put trust in; and from the Medieval Latin word *credential*, meaning belief, faith. Credential is a synonym for the word credence, which means primarily "belief, especially in the reports or testimony of another" (McKechnie, 1979, p. 428). Credentialing, then, is closely related to the word *certify*, which is derived from the Latin words *certus* (certain), and *facere* (to make). We see that the word *credential*, which includes by definition the act of certification, also conveys the more affective meaning of belief, putting one's trust in, having faith in that is intended by the act of certification. The word *credential* conveys this sense of belief as well as the act of certification.

Licensure, on the other hand, is derived from the Latin word *licentia*, meaning freedom, liberty, license, which in turn is derived from the Latin *licere*, to practice. *Licensing* means the freedom or liberty or permission to practice something, and leads to our modern definition of "to permit by grant of authority; to remove legal restraint by a grant of permission" (McKechnie, 1979, p. 1043). Licensure is understood as the permission to do something as given by an authority, with the implication that one would not be permitted to do this thing without such permission. To be licensed is more than a statement of qualification, as certification is. It is a statement of qualification, and it is the right to do a thing otherwise not permitted by a given authority. Both certification and licensure, however, carry the connotation of trust, belief, and confidence, for without these attributes, the certification or the license would have little worth.

II. What Is a Mission Statement, and Why Is It Important?

A statement of mission is a hallmark of those institutions and organizations that exist to benefit, directly or indirectly, the public welfare. The government of the United States exists to benefit the public welfare, and this intent is established in the preamble to the Constitution.

> We the People of the United States, in Order to form a more perfect Union, establish Justice, insure domestic Tranquility, provide for the common defense, promote the general Welfare, and secure the Blessings of Liberty to ourselves and our Posterity, do ordain and establish this Constitution for the United States of America. (Bailyn, 1993, p. 968)

The preamble to the Constitution constitutes the mission statement for the government of the United States. It answers the questions *who* (the People of the U.S.), *what* (establish the Constitution), *why* (promote the general Welfare, etc.), and *how* (the articles of the Constitution). All government agencies and departments exist in order to benefit the public welfare in some specified manner, and each of these entities should have a mission statement that indicates how the public will benefit from its activities.

The government also recognizes nongovernmental organizations whose activities are intended to be beneficial to society by exempting such organizations from the payment of taxes. These organizations, called tax-exempt or nonprofit organizations, are not subject to taxation specifically because the government perceives that they are conducting activities that the government would or could conduct itself, and are thereby saving the government the cost of conducting the activity. As stated by the House Ways and Means Committee:

> The exemption from taxation of money or property devoted to charitable and other purposes is based upon the theory that the government is compensated for the loss of revenue by its relief from financial burden which would otherwise have to be met by appropriations from public funds, and by the benefits resulting from the promotion of the public welfare. (House of Representatives Report No. 1860)

The existence of nonprofit organizations in the United States is recognition by the government that its mission of promoting the public welfare can be achieved through the activities of the private sector. Credentialing activities take place under the aegis of either governmental or private sector nonprofit organizations. An effective understanding of the mission of licensure and certification organizations, then, must address the missions of both governmental entities and nonprofit organizations.

A clear statement of mission is essential to obtaining tax-exempt status from the Internal Revenue Service (IRS). This mission statement must indicate the purposes and objectives of the organization, which the IRS will then use to classify the organization's tax-exempt status. The relationship between a credentialing organization's mission and its tax-exempt status are described in this book, particularly by Hopkins (Chapter 1) and Atkinson (Chapter 6).

Mission statements, to be effective, need to address the legal, social, and political foundations of the organization's or agency's purpose and function. In addressing these issues, the organization or agency will address the activities by which it intends to meet the needs of its stakeholders. In terms of licensure and certification, if the needs of those who have a stake in the license or certification are not effectively met, the value of the credential may decline and stakeholders will choose alternative credentials that provide services more responsive to their needs. According to Bryson (1988):

> Ultimately strategic planning is about purpose, meaning, values, and virtue, and nowhere is this more apparent than in the clarification of mission and the subsequent development of a vision of success. The aim of mission clarification is to specify the purposes of the organization and the philosophy and values that guide it. Unless these purposes focus on socially useful and justifiable ends, and unless the philosophy and values are themselves virtuous, the organization cannot hope to command indefinitely the resources needed to survive. (p. 96)

Finally, as we have seen, credentialed professionals want their stakeholders to have credence in the rights implied from possession of the credential. A clear and forceful mission statement will address the question of the belief, confidence, and trust that stakeholders have in the claims of credentialed professionals.

In summary, mission statements for organizations that license or certify are essential because credentialing is carried out by either governmental or by nonprofit entities, both of which exist to benefit the public welfare. Nonprofit organizations must legally state their mission in order for the IRS to approve their status as a nonprofit entity. Governmental agencies must state their mission to demonstrate how their activities are in accord with the Constitution of the United States, the ultimate purpose of which is to promote the general welfare of the public. Mission statements, being essential, are also desirable in that they lay the foundation for the trust, or credence, that the public has in the services and products provided by governmental and nonprofit entities. While credentialing may be based either on governmental or on private, nonprofit activities, both depend for their continuing existence on the belief and trust of their stakeholders.

In addressing the mission of licensure and certification organizations, the authors of this book describe the legal, social, and political foundations of these missions. We will preview this discussion, beginning with the legal foundations of licensure and certification.

III. The Legal Foundation of Licensure and Certification

A. The Legal Foundation of Licensure

The promotion of the public welfare, the mission of the U.S. Constitution, is the basis for the regulation of professions, which is carried out by the states. The states' charge to protect the public through licensure of professional practice has one and only one legitimate goal: the protection of the public. Their power to do so is backed by the police power of the state. Furthermore, a license is recognized as the property right of the individual, and his or her property rights are protected under the due process laws of the Constitution. Chapter 6 gives a full and detailed analysis of the legal basis for licensure and the implications of this legal foundation for the mission of licensure boards.

The legal basis for licensure also extends to the realm of nonprofit organizations. This is because state boards often join together in associations or federations of boards of licensure, which are incorporated as nonprofit entities. As we have seen, nonprofit corporations exist because the government has recognized that private sector organizations that exist to promote the public welfare should be exempt from taxation. An issue arises here, however, regarding the type of nonprofit entity to which licensure boards should belong, given that there are different kinds of nonprofit categories for associations and organizations involved with credentialing. The two common types of nonprofit organizations are the 501(c)(3) and the 501(c)(6) corporations, as designated by the IRS (Chapter 1). 501(c)(3) corporations are known as "charitable" organizations, and their mission is to directly benefit the public welfare through a variety of activities, including education and research. The 501(c)(6) designation, on the other hand, is a designation often given to membership and/or certification associations. Such corporations are known as *business leagues*, and their primary mission is to promote the business interests of their members, which indirectly benefits the public welfare. As Hopkins (1992) says,

> For example, while charitable and social welfare organizations operate to promote the general welfare, trade associations and other forms of business leagues act to promote the welfare of the business and industrial community. Thus, exemption from federal income tax is accorded 'business leagues' under IRC 501(c)(6), presumably on the theory that a healthy business climate advances the public welfare. (p.12)

This point is also addressed by Bryce (1992), who writes:

> Associations do not have to conform to the eight missions for 501(c)(3)s...although they may include any of these in their mission. . . [A]ssociations exist to promote the welfare of their members, but in a manner that is consistent with public welfare. Associations may be viewed as improving public welfare indirectly through their members. (p. 61)

Certification organizations are almost always incorporated as 501(c)(6) corporations (Chapter 4). Many associations of boards of licensure are also so incorporated (Chapter 8). Atkinson (Chapter 6), however, believes that associations of boards of licensure, and any stakeholder organization dealing with licensure activities, should be incorporated as 501(c)(3) entities.

Atkinson suggests that the promotion of professional interests, a primary mission of (c)(6) organizations, is incompatible with a primary mission of public protection. The importance of Atkinson's analysis becomes clear in light of common criticisms of licensure activities in which it is argued that licensure appears to promote the economic interests of the licensed profession rather than the protection of the public.

B. The Legal Foundation of Certification

Hopkins (Chapter 1) and Atkinson (Chapter 6) agree that the legal foundation of certification lies in private sector nonprofit organizations, most usually 501(c)(6) corporations. The primary mission of 501(c)(6) entities is to further the business interests of its members. The IRS has taken the position that the primary purpose of certification activities is to promote the common business interests of those so certified. Hopkins provides several examples of IRS decisions holding that certification organizations' primary purpose is the promotion of their members business interests rather than public protection. Although public protection can be and is a stated mission of many certification organizations, the IRS has held that a public service mission is incidental to the furtherance of the business interests of the profession if the primary activity of the organization is certification.

IV. The Social and Political Foundations of Credentialing, Licensure, and Certification

A. The Social and Political Foundations of Credentialing

The mission statements of nonprofit organizations follow from their incorporation status. Those organizations incorporated as 501(c)(3) entities must address one of the eight approved purposes of charitable organizations, including education and research (Bryce, 1992). Those incorporated as 501(c)(6) organizations recognize that their primary mission is to advance the professional, business interests of their members (Chapters 1 and 6). In addition, mission statements must address some social or political need that they exist to meet. As Bryson (1988) states:

> An organization's mission, in tandem with its mandates, provide its raison d'être, the social justification for its existence. For a government corporation or agency, or for a nonprofit organization, this means there must be identifiable social or political needs that the organization seeks to fill. Viewed in this light, organizations must always be considered a means to an end, not an end in and of themselves. Communities also should not be seen as an end in themselves, but must justify their existence based on how well they meet the social and political needs of their various stakeholders. (p. 49)

In order to identify an organization's social or political goals, they must first identify their major stakeholders. According to Bryson (1988), "A stakeholder is defined as any person, group, or organization that can place a claim on an organization's attention, resources, or output, or is affected by that output" (p. 52). This book examines the mission statements of licensure and certification organizations from the perspective of their social and political goals, as based on their major stakeholder needs.

B. The Social and Political Foundations of Licensure

The primary stakeholder of licensure activities is the public, and the only legitimate goal of licensure is to protect the public. By stating that the public is the primary stakeholder of licensure activities, we must also state who or what is *not* a stakeholder. Included in this group are the members of the licensed profession; the schools that prepare and train these professionals, the companies that provide resources to the profession, or any other group that has any interest in the practice of the profession other than public protection. By asserting that the members of the licensed profession are not stakeholders of the licensure activities of their boards, we mean that a board's activities must be directed solely to those issues that affect the welfare of the public, and not the welfare of the profession. Licensed professionals constitute the majority of membership of most licensure boards. Their duties, however, as expressed in the public service mission of boards, is exclusively to make decisions that are in the best interest of the public that they serve. In order to assure that the public's interests are served, many boards include members of the public as members of the board.

The mission of licensure boards, however, may not be as clear as we might assume. Shimberg (Chapter 7) and Dower (Chapter 9) give ample evidence of problems with the credibility of the stated mission of licensure boards to protect the public. At the core of all these criticisms is the perception that licensure boards act as if their primary stakeholder is the licensed profession rather than the public. Boards may act as if their mission is that of a membership association rather than as a governmental entity whose sole mission must be the advancement of the public welfare. Schmitt (1995) summarizes the conflicts in the mission of professional associations as against protection of the public as follows.

Members of professional associations believe that licensure will:

1. Lead to enhanced economic benefits,
2. Provide practitioners with increased status,
3. Protect the reputation of the profession,
4. Provide a symbol of respectability,
5. Define the professional field more clearly,
6. Provide for the payment of services by third-party payers, and
7. Control the number and geographic distribution of practitioners (pp. 10–11).

Guilds, or associations of workers, have existed from the early Middle Ages, and their activities have been directed at the protection of the interests of guild members as well as making contributions to the towns and cities in which they worked. The nonprofit tax laws recognize that associations will work both to improve the conditions of their members, and that they will also work to improve the image of their profession so that their product or service is appreciated and used by the public. Such associations are tax exempt because, in their efforts to improve the business conditions of their members, they indirectly work to benefit the welfare of the public. Associations do not, however, generally have as their primary goal the protection of the public. Thus, as the critics of licensure activities indicate, licensure should not have as a consideration the improvement of the business conditions of the licensed profession, and hence that associations' influence in the operation and staffing of boards of licensure should be minimized. If the members of a profession make up the membership of a board of licensure, then their mission as members of that board should have no relation to their mission as members of the professional association to which they belong. Any activities of board members to promote the interests of the profession above the interests of the public will provide evidence of a direct conflict of missions.

Many critics of licensure are disturbed by the political nature of licensure activities (e.g., Schmidt, 1995). It is assumed by these critics that an activity whose stated function is to protect the public should not be subject to political and socio-economic influences; that a goal of the high seriousness of public protection should be accomplished by the state without the possibility of professionals exerting their influence through legislators, and by their presence on state boards. In this country, on the other hand, we allow the political process to work in order for the full range of citizens to be able to express their interests. Health care is recognized to be the legitimate domain of private sector for-profit and not-for-profit organizations, and of the political process whereby citizens are able to exert their influence on politicians and professionals are able to lobby for their interests. Our society permits the expression of the social, economic, and political needs of professionals through the activities of their professional associations. These associations, if they are incorporated as 501(c)(6) corporations, are legally permitted to have as their mission the promotion of the interests of the members of the profession. It is the assumption of the government, and apparently of the public, that this expression of self-interest, in the final analysis, promotes the public welfare. Thus, licensure is a political process that allows for the expression of the needs of the professions and of the public.

Our government apparently believes that this competition of interests through the political process will have greater long-term benefits than restricting the ability of groups to lobby for their interests. In any case, our system puts a premium on a clear statement of mission. In the end, licensed professions are expected to have as their primary goal the promotion of the public welfare; a mission statement will specify how the profession intends to serve the interests of their primary stakeholders, the public. This theory of political expression of professional interests may underlie the use of the 501(c)(6) designation of professional associations of licensure boards. However, the strong criticism of boards for their perceived promotion of the business interests of licensed professions suggests that, at the least, this issue should be addressed in the missions of licensure organizations that are incorporated as (c)(6) entities. They should indicate how this designation will not lead to the profession taking advantage of its position to place the profession's interests above those of the public it serves.

C. The Social and Political Foundations of Certification

Most certification organizations are incorporated as 501(c)(6) nonprofit entities. As Hopkins (Chapter 1) indicates, the primary mission of corporations of this kind is the professional advancement of their members. However, this mission is tempered by the implication that attending to the welfare of their members indirectly benefits the welfare of the public (Bryce, 1992). It is the implication of public benefit that justifies the tax-exempt status of certification organizations. If the certification agency existed only to advance the economic interests of their members, then there would be no justification for the government to grant exemption from taxation.

Many certification organizations emphasize that the goal of their certification programs is to measure competence, and that this identification of competent professionals will promote the public welfare (Chapters 2–4). From our analysis of the implications of the legal incorporation status of most certification groups, we see that a mission emphasis on competency assessment is an appropriate mission for certification programs. Atkinson (Chapter 6) and Shimberg (Chapter 7), on the other hand, emphasize that certification does not carry the same public protection implications that licensing does.

The government, therefore, is involved with both licensure and certification activities. It is involved directly with licensure activities in that states conduct and administer licensure; it is involved with certification activities to the extent that nonprofit associations, which must obtain their exemption from taxation from the government, conduct these activities. Licensure, therefore, may be defined as a government-directed activity whose direct purpose is to protect the welfare of the public. Certification is a government-approved activity whose purpose is to promote the business interests of professions and thereby indirectly benefit the public welfare. In terms of their stakeholders, licensure's sole stakeholder is the public, and certification's primary stakeholder is the members of their profession, and incidentally members of the public.

Agencies such as the National Organization for Competency Assurance (NOCA), on the other hand, were established to encourage professions to seek certification rather than licensure as the route for competency recognition on the theory that there was too much emphasis on obtaining licensure in the professions (Chapter 5). The theory under which NOCA operates fits the libertarian perspective of Milton Friedman, who makes the case that licensure almost always results in control of entry into the profession by the members of the profession and therefore leads to a monopoly position. He believes that the public would be served better by the use of certification alone. According to Friedman (1962):

> Certification is much less harmful in this respect. If the certified "abuse" their special certificates; if, in certifying newcomers, members of the trade impose unnecessarily stringent requirements and reduce the number of practitioners

too much, the price differential between certified and non-certified will become sufficiently large to induce the public to use non-certified practitioners. In technical terms, the elasticity of demand for the services of certified practitioners will be fairly large, and the limits within which they can exploit the rest of the public by taking advantage of their special position will be rather narrow.

In consequence, certification without licensure is a halfway house that maintains a good deal of protection against monopolization. It also has its disadvantages, but it is worth noting that the usual arguments for licensure, and in particular the paternalistic arguments, are satisfied almost entirely by certification alone. If the argument is that we are too ignorant to judge good practitioners, all that is needed is to make the relevant information available. If, in full knowledge, we still want to go to someone who is not certified, that is our business; we cannot complain that we did not have the information. Since arguments for licensure made by people who are not members of the occupation can be satisfied so fully by certification, I personally find it difficult to see any case for which licensure rather than certification can be justified. (p. 149)

However, in accord with the current laws of this country, and unless the government delegates its pubic protection duties to the private sector, the missions of licensure and certification organizations must be clearly distinguished. We make the case in this book that this clarification is best facilitated by the conduct of a strategic analysis by the licensure or certification entity, resulting in a mission statement that specifies the meaning of the credential, and the credentialing policies that will ensure that the credentialing mission is met.

V. Organization of the Book

This book is organized into three sections: 1. The Certification Mission, 2. The Licensure Mission, and 3. Implications and Conclusions. The sections on certification and licensure address the legal foundations of the credential, the social and political foundations of the credential, the mission statements of representative groups that license or certify, and the mission statements of major stakeholder organizations that serve the needs of constituent credentialing organizations. By following this format, we intend to analyze the purpose and function of credentialing in our society, and to contribute to the dialogue regarding the credentialing mission.

In the first chapter of Section One, on the foundations of certification, Bruce R. Hopkins presents an in-depth analysis of the legal foundation of certification organizations. Hopkins describes the mode of incorporation of the majority of certification entities as 501(c)(6) corporations and presents the implications of this incorporation status for the conduct of certification activities. He also analyzes the obligation, if any, of certification organizations to have certification missions that involve promotion of the public good vs. promotion of the interests of the profession. Many examples are given of the implications for certification activities of the 501(c)(6) incorporation status.

In Chapter 2, Michael S. Hamm describes the steps involved in conducting a strategic analysis of a certification program, and the steps for implementing and evaluating this strategic plan. Particular emphasis is given to the formulation of a mission statement for certification organizations. Described in detail are the steps for establishing a certification program, marketing that program, and demonstrating the value of the certification to the organization's stakeholders.

In Chapter 3, Susan Dorn describes the implications of an organization's mission on its governance structure. She describes the many considerations that must be taken into account in order to develop and maintain an organizational governance structure that is responsive to the needs of stakeholders and thus to the organization's credentialing mission.

Chapter 4 contains a description of the certification mission of six certification organizations. Each author describes the certification agency's mission, addressing such questions as: Who are we? What are the basic social and political needs we exist to full or the social and political problems we exist to address? What do we want to do to recognize or anticipate and respond to these needs or problems? How should we respond to our key stakeholders? What is our philosophy and what are our core values? What makes us distinctive or unique? The authors also describe how the implementation of the certification mission achieves the goals and objectives of the organization.

These organizations represent a range of certification missions, from health- and non-health–related organizations to professional membership organizations that conduct certification as part of their educational program.

In Chapter 5, Larry Allan Early describes the mission of two major stakeholder organizations in certification, NOCA and the National Commission for Competency Assurance (NCCA). The missions of NOCA and NCCA are described, including their educational and standard-setting mission. NOCA is an organization that attempts to bring standards and expertise to organizations that seek membership. NCCA is the accrediting arm of NOCA. These organizations play a critical role in establishing standards that organizations with a certification mission must meet if they wish to become accredited. It accomplishes the goal of establishing a foundation of necessary procedures that organizations must follow if their certification is to have value.

Section Two, The Licensure Mission, begins with Chapter 6, by Dale J. Atkinson, who describes the legal status of licensure organizations that are incorporated as 501(c)(6) or 501(c)(3) corporations. Atkinson describes the mission of licensure organizations and proposes that organizations with a licensure mission may best be categorized as 501(c)(3) corporations, since their primary mission is to promote the public good by protecting the public against nonqualified practitioners. Examples are given of licensure organizations incorporated as 501(c)(3) entities.

Chapter 7, by Benjamin Shimberg, describes the appropriate mission of licensure activities from the perspective of state governments, professional associations, and the public. The roles and functions of state boards are described, along with a detailed description of their actual procedures, and how these procedures should be designed with protection of the public as the only goal. Examples of exemplary and nonexemplary board procedures are given. Variations in the licensure nomenclature are described. Emphasis is on what the mission of licensure organizations and boards should be.

Chapter 8 surveys the actual mission statements of seven stakeholder organizations in licensure. The organizations cover a range of licensure missions, from health-related fields to accounting and the legal profession. The missions of the state licensure boards themselves are also described.

Chapter 9 examines the missions of major educational and standard-setting organizations in licensure. The missions of these organizations are described in terms of their legal, political, social, and policy goals and purposes. These organizations have a major impact on the missions of licensure organizations in terms of their educational activities, standard-setting activities, and mission clarification activities. Each organization describes its mission with respect to the licensure organizations that are their stakeholders.

Section Three, by Craig G. Schoon and I. Leon Smith, is a concluding perspective on the implications of licensure and certification organizations' tax-exempt status as 501(c)(3) or 505(c)(6) entities, their social and political foundations, and their respective missions. The discussion follows the questions answered by organizations in the formulation of their mission, and the authors make several suggestions regarding the mission of licensure and certification organizations and how they can best serve their stakeholders.

References

Bailyn, B. (Dd.). (1993). *Debate on the Constitution: Part one.* (1st ed., Vol. 62). New York: The Library of America

Bryce, H. (1992). *Financial and strategic management for nonprofit organizations.* (2nd ed.). Englewood Cliffs, NJ: Prentice-Hall.

Bryson, J. M. (1988). *Strategic planning for public and nonprofit organizations: A guide to strengthening and sustaining organizational achievement.* San Francisco, CA: Jossey-Bass.

Freidman, M. (1962). *Capitalism and freedom.* Chicago: The University of Chicago Press.

H.R. Rep. No. 1860. 75th Cong., 3rd Sess. 19, (1939).

Hopkins, B. R. (1992). *The law of tax-exempt organizations.* (6th ed.). New York: John Wiley & Sons.

McKechnie, J. L. (Ed.). (1979). *Webster's new universal unabridged dictionary* (2nd ed.). New York. Simon & Schuster.

Schmitt, K. (1995). What is Licensure? In Impara, J. C. (Ed.), *Licensure testing: Purposes, procedures, and practices* (pp. 3–32). Lincoln, Nebraska: Buros Institute of Mental Measurements.

1

The Meaning of Tax-Exempt Status in the Work of Certification Organizations

Bruce R. Hopkins

Polsinelli, White, Vardeman, & Shalton, Kansas City, Missouri

The current state of the law by which certification organizations are eligible for tax-exempt status is reflective of the dichotomy that is inherent in the rationale for certification programs. That is, one view of certification programs is that they exist primarily for the benefit of the general public, in that they are an integral component of an educational process designed to inform purchasers of the merits of goods and services. The other view is that certification programs are primarily beneficial to those who are certified, in that their professional standing is burnished and the prospects of their employment are enhanced.

16

The Internal Revenue Service (IRS) has adopted the latter view as regards certification programs. This in turn has dictated the category of tax-exempt organizations that are permitted (without revocation of exempt status) to conduct these programs. Thus, the conduct of a certification program by a tax-exempt organization—alone—may mandate the classification of exemption that the IRS will recognize. This, then, is the fundamental meaning of tax-exempt status in the work of certification organizations.

I. The Basics

The focus here is on the federal income tax status of nonprofit certification organizations. For the most part, it may be assumed that the state income tax status of these organizations will parallel the federal-level classification, although that is not always the case.

Tax-exempt status is predicated on the primary purpose of a nonprofit organization (Hopkins, 1998; Income Tax Regulations, § 1.501(c)(3)-1(c)(1)). It is thus not required that an organization be operated exclusively for exempt purposes. For example, a tax-exempt organization is permitted to have some nonexempt activities, such as the provision of an incidental amount of private benefit or one or more unrelated businesses (Internal Revenue Code, § 501(b), §§ 511–514).

However, if more than an insubstantial part of an organization's activities is not in furtherance of an exempt purpose, the primary purpose test is not met and the organization cannot qualify for the pertinent category of tax exemption (*Better Business Bureau v. United States,* 1945; *Nationalist Movement v. Commissioner,* 1994).

Organizations that meet the statutory criteria for a category of tax exemption generally are tax exempt for that reason. It often is not required that an organization receive a ruling from the IRS as to exempt status, although usually it is prudent to obtain such a determination. When the IRS rules favorably as to an organization's tax-exempt status, it *recognizes* that tax exemption. Most charitable organizations, however, are required to obtain this recognition as a condition of tax exemption (Internal Revenue Code, § 508(a)).

In general, to be tax exempt (Internal Revenue Code, § 501(a)), an organization must satisfy both an *organizational test* and an *operational test*. The organizational test focuses on the provisions that must be in the organizational document (termed the *articles of organization*) and on language that should not be there (Hopkins,

1998). The operational test entails an assessment of the organization's activities (Hopkins, 1998).

Federal law provides tax exemption for organizations that are organized and operated primarily for charitable, educational, scientific, and like purposes (Internal Revenue Code, § 501(c)(3)). These are referred to generally as *charitable* organizations. In part, this is because all of these entities may not be operated for a purpose that is contrary to public policy (*Bob Jones University v. United States,* 1983). Also, gifts to these organizations are deductible as charitable contributions for income, estate, and gift tax purposes (Internal Revenue Code, §§ 170, 2055, 2522).

Tax exemption is also available for organizations that endeavor to improve conditions within a line of business. These entities, usually known as associations or societies, are *business leagues* (Internal Revenue Code, § 501(c)(6)). Organizations that work to enhance the welfare of society may also be tax exempt; these are termed *social welfare organizations* (Internal Revenue Code, § 501(c)(4)).

A common characteristic of these three types of tax-exempt organizations is that they may not—as a condition of exempt status—contravene the doctrine prohibiting *private inurement*. Read literally, this doctrine means that the organization's net earnings may not inure to the private benefit of persons who are insiders with respect to the organization (Hopkins, 1998). As applied in practice, the doctrine forbids transactions entailing excessive compensation, unreasonable lending or rental arrangements, sales of assets for less than fair market value, and the like.[1]

An organization interested in a certification program may be any one of these three types of tax-exempt organizations. The applicable category of exemption is a function of the organization's primary purpose.

A fundamental characteristic of a certification organization is that it either has a membership or otherwise serves a defined constituency. A charitable organization, business league, or social welfare organization can have this characteristic. That an organization has a membership is not, itself, a feature mandating a particular category of tax-exempt status. Nonetheless, the IRS often regards this feature as giving

---

[1] As a practical matter, in cases involving charitable and social welfare organizations, in an instance of a private inurement transaction with an insider, the IRS is more likely to impose an intermediate sanctions penalty (Internal Revenue Code, § 4958) on the disqualified person involved, rather than revoke the tax exemption of the organization (Hopkins, 1998, Ch. 19, § 11).

rise to an informal presumption that the organization should be qualified as a business league, particularly where the membership is comprised of individuals.

There are advantages and disadvantages associated with various categories of tax exemption. As noted, contributions to charitable organizations are deductible; this is rarely the case for business leagues or social welfare organizations. There are limitations as to the extent to which charitable organizations can attempt to influence legislation; business leagues and social welfare organizations can have lobbying as the principal (indeed, sole) function (Internal Revenue Code, § 162(e)). All three of these types of organizations generally are obligated to file annual information returns with the IRS (Internal Revenue Code, § 6033).

II. Charitable Organizations

As noted, the concept of a charitable organization includes entities that are engaged in charitable, educational, and scientific activities (Hopkins, 1998).

An organization interested in certification can be a charitable organization—using the term in a more technical sense—as the result of pursuits such as relief of the poor, promotion of health, environmental conservancy, lessening the burdens of government, or promotion of the arts. Educational entities are not simply schools, colleges, and universities; they also provide training for individuals or instruction of the public. Scientific organizations tend to be entities that undertake scientific research in the public interest. An organization can constitute a charitable organization, in satisfaction of the operational test, where purposes of this nature are its primary ones.

For example, the IRS ruled that an engineering society formed to engage in scientific research in the areas of heating, ventilating, and air conditioning to the benefit of the general public qualified for tax exemption as an educational and scientific entity (Revenue Ruling 76-366). Full membership in the society was limited to individuals who had more than eight years' experience in the sciences relating to heating, ventilating, or air conditioning, and who had actively practiced the profession at least four years during which they had been in charge of work consisting of design, construction, research, development, or teaching. Provision was made for associate members, junior members, and student members, all of whom had to meet requirements as to age, training, and experience. The society's dominant activity was research carried on continuously by a full-time paid staff in its own laboratory. Typical subjects of investigation have been solar radiation through various materials, the phenomenon of heat flow and transfer, and the physiological effects of air conditioning on the human body. Research and studies have been conducted on a cost basis for universities and some government agencies. In addition, data from one of the society's annual publications had been assembled into more than a score of model codes of minimum standards for heating, ventilating, and air conditioning. All information was made freely available to the public. The society did not engage in activities directed at or concerned with the protection or promotion of the professional practice or business interests of any of the professions represented by its membership. Moreover, it did not engage in any public relations activities, it did not have a code of ethics, it did not police the profession in any way, and it did not seek to improve the conditions of its members. The society did not have any purposes, committees, or activities primarily aimed at developing good will or fellowship among its members, or fostering a mutuality of interests. It did not have any social or recreational activities, and did not have any facilities for members such as a restaurant, lounge, or clubhouse.

As another example, a court ruled that the benefit to the legal profession was insubstantial in relation to the benefits to the public occasioned by the conduct of its lawyer referral service, the purpose of which was to make legal services available to those who could afford to pay reasonable fees (*Kentucky Bar Association v. Commissioner,* 1982).

Likewise, a court passing on the tax-exempt status of professional standards review organizations (PSROs) (renamed "utilization and quality control peer review organizations") held that the exempt purpose of ensuring the economical and effective delivery of health care services under the Medicare and Medicaid programs predominated over any benefits physicians might derive (including promotion of esteem for the medical profession) (*Virginia Professional Standards Review Foundation v. Blumenthal,* 1979). These benefits were found to have only a "tenuous, incidental, and non-substantial connection with the PSRO scheme" (*Virginia Professional Standards Review Foundation v. Blumenthal,* 1979).

The private inurement doctrine is applicable to charitable organizations. There are limitations on the amount of lobbying in which a charitable organization can engage (Internal Revenue Code, § 4911), and excessive lobbying can lead to special taxes (Internal Revenue Code, § 4912). Moreover, a charitable organization cannot be operated in a manner that serves private interests, unless the private benefit is incidental (Income Tax Regulations, § 1.501(c)(3)-1(d)(1)(ii)).

In relation to the private benefit rule, the IRS considered an organization that was an association of investment clubs formed for the mutual exchange of investment information among its members and prospective investors to enable them to make sound investments. Its activities included the preparation and distribution of teaching aids for the use of its member clubs; the conduct of workshops and seminars and the sponsorship of lectures on various investment subjects; the publication of a monthly newsletter for individual investors; the establishment and enforcement of standards for the operation of investment clubs; and the furnishing of technical advice to member clubs relative to their organizational, bookkeeping, and operational problems. The IRS concluded that this organization did not qualify for tax-exempt status as a charitable entity (Revenue Ruling 61-177). The IRS conceded that some of the organization's activities were educational in nature. However, it also found that many of the activities were directed in whole or in part to the support and promotion of the economic interests of the investments clubs that constitute its membership—activities that are not charitable. Further, by furnishing information to prospective investors to enable them to make sound investments, the association was found to be serving private interests.

III. Business Leagues

A business league is an association of persons having some common business interest, the primary purpose of which is to promote that common interest (Hopkins, 1998). The applicable organizational test requires that its activities be directed to the improvement of business conditions of one or more lines of business, as distinguished from the performance of particular services for individual persons (Income Tax Regulations, § 1.501(c)(6)-1).

The term *business* is broadly construed and includes nearly any activity carried on for the production of income, including trades and professions. The line-of-business requirement means that the organization's efforts must benefit a sufficiently broad segment of the business community, and must include organizations in competition with each other within an industry (*National Muffler Dealers Association, Inc. v. United States,* 1979). Thus, tax exemption as a business league is not available for an organization that endeavors to improve business conditions in only a segment of a line of business (Revenue Ruling 83-164). However, a tax-exempt business league is permitted to represent less than a full line of business in one respect: its constituency can be all components of an industry within a geographic area (*Crooks v. Kansas City Hay Dealers Association,* 1929).

The private inurement doctrine is applicable to business leagues. As far as tax exemption is concerned, there is no limitation on the amount of lobbying in which a business league may engage (Revenue Ruling 61-177). However, lobbying activities by an association or other business league may cause the members' dues to be less than fully deductible as business expenses (Internal Revenue Code, § 162(e)) and may subject the organization to a special tax (Internal Revenue Code, § 6033(e)(2) (A)(ii)).

Typical activities of a business league include annual conferences of members, training and educational programs, publications, research, lobbying, other forms of government relations, maintenance of facilities (*American Plywood Association v. United States,* 1967),[2] enforcement of a code of ethics, and promotion of improved business practices.

In one instance, the IRS held that a medical society, which primarily directed its activities to the promotion of the common business purposes of its members, was tax exempt as a business league but not as a charitable organization (Revenue Ruling 71-504). The IRS noted that many of this organization's activities were charitable and educational, such as monthly meetings where technical papers on medical subjects are presented, maintenance of a medical library, support of medical education at local medical schools, and support of local public health programs. However, there were other activities that promoted the common business interest of the organization's membership, such as a grievance committee to hear complaints and settle disputes between member physicians, a legislative committee to communicate the association's views to state and local government officials on issues germane to its members professional interest, and a public relations program. This latter category of activities constituted a substantial portion of the society's total activities.

The IRS maintained a similar stance with respect to a bar association that primarily directed its activities to the promotion and protection of the practice of law (Revenue Ruling 71-505). Again, the IRS observed that the organization was engaged in a host of activities that were charitable or educational in nature. However, it also engaged in many activities that promoted its members' professional and business interests, such as establishing and promulgating minimum fee schedules, pre-

---

[2] For example, an organization was classified as a business league because it maintained laboratories for testing quality control.

paring papers on the economics of law practice, and establishing and enforcing standards of conduct for members.

In another instance, the IRS reviewed a medical specially board formed by members of the medical profession to improve the quality of medical care available to the public and to establish and maintain high standards of excellence in a particular medical specially. The board's activities consisted of devising and administering written examinations and issuing certificates to the successful candidates in the medical specially. The board determined whether the candidates met established criteria necessary to qualify for the examination. The certified physicians were authorized by the board to hold themselves out as specialists. The IRS ruled that this organization was a business league and not a charitable organization (Revenue Ruling 73-567). The IRS said that, by examining and certifying physicians under these circumstances, the board promoted high professional standards. Although some public benefit may be derived from promoting high professional standards in a particular medical specially, the activities of the board were held to be directed primarily to serving the interest of the medical profession. Under these circumstances, the board was determined to be organized and operated not primarily for charitable purposes. Inasmuch as the activities of the board consisted of certifying physicians who were thereafter authorized to hold themselves out to the public as specialists, the organization's purpose was said to be to promote the common business interest of the physicians.

IV. Social Welfare Organizations

An organization may be tax exempt as a social welfare organization (Hopkins, 1998). This is an entity that has as its primary purpose the conduct of one or more activities that are commensurate with the "common good and general welfare" and that entail "civic betterments and social improvements" (Income Tax Regulations, § 1.501(c)(4)-1(a)(2)(i)). The operational test requires that the activities of the organization must be those that will benefit a community, rather than merely benefit the organization's membership or other select group of individuals or organizations (Income Tax Regulations, § 1.501(c)(4)-1(a)(2)(i)).

The private inurement doctrine is applicable to social welfare organizations. As far as tax exemption is concerned, there is no limitation on the amount of lobbying in which a social welfare organization may engage (Revenue Ruling 71-530). Thus, many social welfare organizations are those that pursue one or more forms of advocacy—to an extent impermissible for tax-exempt charitable organizations. However, illegal activities, which violate the minimum standards of acceptable conduct necessary to the preservation of an orderly society, are not a permissible means of promoting social welfare (Revenue Ruling 75-384).

A social welfare organization may be structured as a membership entity. While uncommon, this type of organization may be interested in a certification program.

V. Anatomy of a Certification Program

An organization is free, within the bounds of reason, to cast the purposes of its certification program in any manner it wishes. Emphasis can be placed on the benefits flowing to the general public, or on the benefits flowing to the profession involved and its members (Revenue Ruling 74-146).[3] The literature generated by an organization reviewed by the IRS reflected the latter approach.[4]

A document adopted by the organization's board of directors stated that the objectives of the certification program were twofold: (1) to support the "professional recognition" of the organization's members and all others in the field and (2) to "achieve universal acceptance, recognition, and professional standing" of the designation reflective of the certification.

It was also stated that the program supported professional recognition by (1) "identifying the body of knowledge and the work experience needed to qualify as a professional" in the field, (2) "stimulating and encouraging the professional development" of all individuals in the field, (3) "defining the criteria for professional recognition," and (4) "developing an accepted examination program which will measure the candidates knowledge and ability with respect to the profession's current state of the art."

Literature prepared by the organization contained the following:

---

[3] Where the practice is one of accreditation and the entities being accredited are tax-exempt educational institutions, the function is regarded by the IRS as a charitable one because it advances education.

[4] All of the material quoted in the remainder of this section is taken from IRS General Counsel Memorandum 39721 (March 31, 1988).

[The individuals] who have attained the [organization's certification] desig-nation have the deep, personal satisfaction of knowing they have reached a recognized and accepted level of competency. They are members of a recog-nized professional group and receive the benefits accorded to professionals. These benefits include recognition by business and professional associates, more rapid career advancement, and greater acceptance in their roles as advi-sors to management.

The organization promoted the certification designation through advertisements in its publications. One example read in pertinent part:

I have become very successful in my chosen career of . . . Why? There are several reasons. But I believe one thing really made a difference. I became a certified . . . Not only does the . . . designation carry with it a great deal of prestige. It also means that I have attained a wide spectrum of business-management skills, which makes me a key resource for senior management. I can see the company from their point of view. They appreciate it. And they've shown me how much.

Another example of how the organization promoted its certification program appeared in its journal. A profile of an individual, a retiring president of a chapter and an incoming director of the organization, had him commenting as follows:

We continually remind our members of the advantages of our professional certification by regular memos in our chapter newsletter. We also encourage them to use the designation on their business cards, and to remind their top-level executives of it by showing the title under their signatures on all [docu-ments]. Chapter officers should themselves set the example by becoming certified, using the . . . designation in all their business contacts and promot-ing it at chapter functions so that all members and visitors truly understand how much the . . . certification can help their careers.

This organization also had a long-standing government relations program and had sponsored a code of standards for the profession. It provided considerable serv-ices in support of its chapters, all of which are business leagues.

One of the purposes of the organization, as stated in its articles of incorpora-tion, is to furnish information regarding the profession and the "practice and methods thereof" to the general public. The activities emphasized in pursuing tax-exempt status as a charitable entity were (1) the presentation of seminars and courses that instruct interested individuals on various subjects and techniques related to the profession and (2) the publication of educational materials to be used in connection with these courses and other books, manuals, and brochures.

As noted, the organization's certification program allows an individual who is certified to designate himself or herself as a certified professional. The criteria for certification includes passage of an examination, at least two years' experience in the profession, and a bachelor's degree from an accredited college. Candidates for certification must subscribe to the organization's code of ethics.

Given facts of this nature, it was not difficult for the IRS to conclude that the principal purpose of the certification program was improvement of the reputation and business interests of the organization's members and the profession of which they form a part.

VI. Analysis

The classification of certification organizations as tax-exempt entities is principally a matter of application of the operational test, which as noted constitutes an assessment of the organization's primary purpose. In the realm of certification, the IRS adheres to its position taken when categorizing organizations such as medical societies and bar associations. That is, the IRS is of the view that the principal purpose of these organizations is the furtherance of the profession involved.

It is the judgment of the IRS that the primary purpose of certification is to improve the reputation and business interests of the members of the certifying organization (or other related constituency) and the profession of which they form a part. In its sole pronouncement on the point, the IRS (technically, its lawyers) stated that a certification program (at least the one they reviewed) is designed and operated to achieve professional standing for the profession involved and to enhance the respectability of those who have been certified.

Usually, an organization operating a certification program also engages in other activities. Some of these activities may be inherently charitable, educational, and the like. However, it is generally the view of the IRS that the primary purpose of a certification organization is the furtherance of the common business interests of its members (or other constituency).

This conclusion is often reached by an identification of activities, other than certification, that are deemed to be noncharitable. These activities usually are (1) establishment and enforcement of a code of ethics and (2) representation of the profession in government affairs. This array of noncharitable activities (including certification) is then found by the IRS to be more than insubstantial.[5]

There is a secondary rationale utilized by the IRS in finding a certification organization not to be a charitable entity by reason of violation of the operational test. This is that this type of organization is operating to promote a private interest. The private interest involved is the enhancement of the respectability of those who have been certified.

Thus, it is obvious that an organization whose sole purpose is certification would not be recognized by the IRS as being a charitable organization. At the other extreme, an organization that had certification (and any other noncharitable activities) as merely an insubstantial amount of program could qualify for tax exemption as a charitable entity. However, as to the latter, it is highly unlikely that the IRS would agree that a certification program is merely an incidental undertaking of an organization.

VII. Structuring Considerations

One of the most common devices used by nonprofit organizations today, usually solely for tax reasons, is bifurcation. Bifurcation, in this context, means creating two tax-exempt organizations where there otherwise would be only one.[6] Usually, one of these exempt organizations controls the other, so that there is a parent–subsidiary relationship. There are many contemporary instances of this practice:

- A charitable organization with a lobbying arm structured as a social welfare organization.
- A social welfare organization with a research foundation organized as a charitable organization.
- A trade association with a related charitable foundation.
- A charitable organization with a related charitable organization, such as a fund-raising arm or a separate endowment fund. The subsidiary charitable or-

---

[5] This flow of analysis is referenced in four of the IRS revenue rulings discussed above: Revenue Ruling 71-504; Revenue Ruling 71-505; Revenue Ruling 73-567; and Revenue Ruling 76-366.

[6] The creation by a tax-exempt organization of a for-profit subsidiary is another example of bifurcation.

ganization in an arrangement of this nature is often structured as a supporting organization, which is the subject of IRC § 509(a)(3).

- A foreign charitable organization with a United States–based fund-raising arm.
- A tax-exempt organization with a title-holding company. Title-holding organizations are tax-exempt by reason of IRC § 501(c)(25).
- A tax-exempt organization with a political action committee. Political organizations are tax-exempt by reason of IRC § 527.

In the bifurcation setting, where both organizations are tax-exempt entities, the parent entity usually controls the subsidiary entity by means of overlapping boards of directors. In essence, this means that the parent entity, by one or a blend of mechanisms, is able to determine who constitutes at least a majority of the board of directors of the parent entity. Another approach is to structure the subsidiary entity as a membership organization and cause the parent entity to be the sole member; the member then selects some or all of the board members of the subsidiary. A third approach is to create the subsidiary entity as a nonprofit organization in a state where the law permits it to issue stock; the parent organization as the sole stockholder then selects some or all of the subsidiary's board members.

It is critical, however, that the legal formalities associated with an entity be respected with both the parent and subsidiary. This includes separate governing instruments, board meetings, and bank accounts. It is also important that the parent entity not be involved in the day-to-day management of the subsidiary entity. If these rules are not properly attended to, the IRS may be successful in the assertion that the arrangement is a sham, resulting in the treatment of the two organizations as one. This consequence, of course, would defeat the tax planning that was the basis for the bifurcation.

The most common type of certification arrangement in the tax-exempt setting involves a single organization: a business league. Thus, the frequent model is a trade, business, or professional association (classified as a business league) with a certification program. However, bifurcation may nonetheless be present in this context, such as where the association has a related educational foundation.

Another fact situation concerns the charitable organization (association or otherwise) that wants to have a certification program. As discussed, this type of program is deemed by the IRS to be inconsistent with charitable status. Still, by means of bifurcation, a charitable organization can maintain a certification program—by housing it in a controlled subsidiary rather than by engaging in the certification activity itself.

This subsidiary organization would qualify for tax-exempt status as a business league.

Although the IRS has not ruled on the point, presumably its position is that the maintenance of a certification program is incompatible with tax-exempt status as a social welfare organization. Thus, this type of organization also could utilize the principle of bifurcation and place the certification activity in a controlled nonprofit subsidiary, qualified as a business league.

The subsidiary organization that has the certification function in it may have certification as its sole activity, or certification can be one of several of its programs.

There is a nontax reason for using bifurcation to place the certification function in a separate entity. When that is done, the seeming autonomy accorded the certification organization can provide the certification program with greater credibility, from the standpoint of both those certified and those relying on the certification. That is, this type of arrangement—where the certification program is in an entity separate from an organization such as the membership association—can cause the certification process to be more objective, or at least be perceived as such.

VIII. Conclusion

This body of law did not have to develop in the manner and direction it did. The IRS could have determined that certification programs are inherently educational in nature—because of their function of enlightening prospective consumers of goods and services—thus allowing them to be conducted by charitable organizations. But the IRS, as it often does in narrowing the range of a category of tax exemption, shepherded the evolution of this law in the other direction. The IRS's views in this regard have become considerably entrenched, so that—absent an unanticipated intervention by Congress or the courts—it must be assumed this perspective will continue to inform the meaning of tax-exempt status in the work of certification organizations.

References

American Plywood Association v. United States, 267 F. Supp. 830 (W.D. Wash. 1967).
Better Business Bureau v. United States, 326 U.S. 279 (1945).
Bob Jones University v. United States, 461 U.S. 574 (1983).

Crooks v. Kansas City Hay Dealers Association, 37 F.2d 83 (8th Cir. 1929).

Hopkins, B. R. (1998). *The Law of Tax-Exempt Organizations*. New York: John Wiley & Sons.

Income Tax Regulations, U.S.C.A. §§ 1.501(c)(3)-1(a)(1), 1.501(c)(3)-1(c)(1), 1.501(c)(3)-1(c)(3)-1(d)(1)(ii), 1.501(c)(4)-1(a)(2)(i), 1.501(c)(6)-1.

Internal Revenue Code, U.S.C.A. §§ 162(e), 170, 501(a)–(c)(25), 508(a), 509(a)(3), 527, 2055, 2522, 4911, 4912, 6033(e)(2)(A)(ii).

Kentucky Bar Association v. Commissioner, 78 T.C. 921 (1982).

National Muffler Dealers Association, Inc. v. United States, 440 U.S. 472 (1979).

Revenue Ruling 61-177, 1961-2 C.B. 117.

Revenue Ruling 76-366. 1976- 2 C.B. 144.

Revenue Ruling 71-504, 1971-2 C.B. 231.

Revenue Ruling 71-505, 1971-2 C.B. 232.

Revenue Ruling 71-506, 1971-2 C.B. 233.

Revenue Ruling 71-530, 1971-2 C.B. 237.

Revenue Ruling 73-567, 1973-2 C.B. 178.

Revenue Ruling 74-146, 1974-1 C.B. 129.

Revenue Ruling 75-384, 1975-2 C.B. 204.

Revenue Ruling 83-164, 1983-2 C.B. 95.

The Nationalist Movement v. Commissioner, 102 T.C. 558 (1994), *aff'd.* 37 F.2d 216 (5th Cir. 1994).

Virginia Professional Standards Review Foundation v. Blumenthal, 466 F. Supp. 1164 (D.D.C. 1979).

2

Establishing and Demonstrating the Value of a Credential

Michael S. Hamm
Michael Hamm & Associates, Rockville, Maryland

The process of establishing and demonstrating the value of a certification program is one of the most challenging aspects of the certification world. The proliferation of new credentials has resulted in a virtual "alphabet soup" of acronyms, which often confuse the public, employers, and practitioners. Growing interest in credentialing programs virtually guarantees that this trend will continue in the future.

I. Introduction

The proliferation of credentials has created a situation where the public and employers are usually skeptical about any new certification program until they find out enough about the credential to establish a confidence level that addresses the credibility issues. Practitioners are the easiest stakeholder group to reach, and, in many respects, they are the most critical stakeholders in the process. Employers (when they play a key role in the use of certified practitioners) tend to be more skeptical about certification. They typically are concerned with "bottom line" issues such as the tangible benefits that will occur in their organizations through the employment of certified individuals. The public is the hardest group to reach due to the magnitude of this audience and the fact that most individuals are not interested in certification programs unless the credential is related to a personal or business need. While the public education effort is typically a massive marketing challenge, this audience cannot be overlooked in this process.

Other stakeholder groups that need to be considered by credentialing bodies include government agencies (federal, state, and local). Regulatory bodies are showing increasing interest in certification programs, but these organization frequently know little about competency assessment issues or the fundamental concepts of good certification efforts. Also, government bodies are sometimes placed in an awkward situation of wanting to support good private credentialing efforts, but they are limited in their legal ability to recognize any specific private sector initiative.

Private certification initiatives do not usually meet all of the public protection interests of government agencies involved in the regulation of their disciplines. However, it is important to maintain constant communication with government stakeholders, and every attempt should be made to comply with as many of the needs of these groups as possible without jeopardizing the integrity of the certification effort or turning it into another form of regulation.

Related and affiliated associations are also potential stakeholders in certification efforts. Certification efforts supported or endorsed by all of the major associations involved in a discipline obviously enjoy a major credibility advantage from their inception, and it is easier to demonstrate the value of a certification program when all of the key players are "singing in harmony." Achieving unified support for certification is not easy in many fields, because offering certification is viewed as a strong competitive advantage in the association world. The organization that defines and measures competence in any field has a tremendous base of power in the discipline. This concept is also the basis for potential abuse when an association uses certification to achieve an objective not related primarily to measuring and identifying competency.

Certification organizations need to have a formal plan and strategy to establish and demonstrate the value of their credentials as well as to make certain that the key (as determined by the proposed credentialing body) stakeholders' needs are addressed in this process.

II. What Are the Issues that Need to Be Addressed in Establishing the Value of a Certification Program?

A. What Were the Motives for Developing the Credential in the First Place?

Certification programs are developed for a variety of reasons, and some motives tend to rapidly establish value with more of the stakeholders. For example, certification programs developed primarily to assist and protect the public are more easily accepted by consumer groups, government agencies, employer groups, and related associations. Public protection is an important motive that is hard to argue within most professions, but this goal is not always easy or possible to achieve through certification. Also, potential certificants may not be enthusiastic about seeking certification developed for this reason unless there are other more tangible benefits provided that will benefit the individual in a personal or business respect.

Public protection is a concept that is frequently cited as a motive for developing certification programs, but this motive sometimes demonstrates minimum support in terms of the structure, operation, and promotion of the certification organization. Other motives for developing certification programs include regulatory challenges, attempts to enhance the reputation of a discipline, competitive reasons, increasing revenues for associations, and the normal evolution of professions or disciplines. This last reason can be a combination of other motives that culminate in a decision that a profession or discipline needs to establish measurable competency standards at a particular point in its natural evolution.

Certification organizations need to analyze all of the reasons for developing the credential, and they need to identify the highest-priority motives to build an effective "case" for the credential. Ideally, *the certification program has been developed to address some need of each of the key stakeholders*. The importance of this concept cannot be overstated. Every certification organization should conduct some basic market research prior to initiating a credential. The leadership should participate in a strategic planning process to develop a credential that will demonstrate current and future value for the key stakeholders.

B. What Is the Reputation of the Organization that Provides the Credential?

The reputation of the association(s) or certification body plays a key role in the acceptance of a credential. If, for example, an association has a track record of strong advocacy and pursuing a path of supporting the narrow economic interests of its discipline, this type of organization will have a hard time convincing the public that a new certification program was developed to serve the public. On the other hand, an association that is identified with a strong public service mission and a history of responsible advocacy programs will have an easier time establishing the value of the credential. These reputation issues and other legal factors sometimes lead associations to develop certification programs in an administratively independent structure to avoid any confusion regarding the true mission of the certification effort.

The reputation of the organization providing the certification program is a double-edged sword in one respect. Sometimes a discipline will be more likely to embrace a certification developed and operated by its trade association simply because it has more faith and respect for this entity, even though the public and potential employers may be more comfortable with an independent certification organization with no connection to political positions or economic advocacy agendas. Organizations need to evaluate the strengths and weaknesses of their reputation as a provider of credentialing services from the perspective of each stakeholder. Certification programs will probably not be successful in changing the reputation of the organization providing the service if it is an established national association, but they can use a realistic assessment of this issue to best position the program to respond to strengths and weaknesses perceived by each stakeholder group.

C. What Information Does Market Research Tell You About the Potential Credentialing Needs of the Various Stakeholder Groups?

One of the most important steps in establishing and demonstrating the value of a credential is the collection of market research information on the potential certificants and other key stakeholders. Ideally, this process begins with a thorough and comprehensive feasibility study conducted prior to the initiation of the certification program. A feasibility study measures the potential interest in a field of participating in a certification program. Feasibility studies also examine topics such as attitudes toward certification, perceptions regarding the body of knowledge in a discipline, potential eligibility requirements, examination formats, employer perceptions, and administrative issues such as test fees. The most important question addressed by a feasibility study is the intent of the potential certificant audience to obtain the credential. Sometimes a discipline will support the concept or idea of a new certification program with few individuals actually committed to seeking the credential.

Ideally, the concept of certification has been discussed by the leadership and addressed in national meetings or educational programs to acquaint the potential audience with the key concepts and philosophies of certification. These preliminary educational efforts can help establish interest and commitment to a new certification effort. In addition to conducting a formal feasibility study, the leadership of the proposed certification body should be constantly talking to potential certificants and other stakeholders to measure their interests and needs in a credential. Some organizations use focus groups to explore interest in certification. A focus group utilizes a small target audience and a facilitator to explore particular issues in depth utilizing structured questions as well as having open-ended discussions to measure potential reactions or responses. Utilizing a focus group process permits an organization to explore in a detailed fashion the potential reactions to a certification program.

After a certification program is developed, the various audiences (stakeholders) should be surveyed periodically to determine whether the credential and the credentialing body are meeting their needs. Developing a system to provide continuous marketing data is an important component of any credentialing effort. There must be an ongoing mechanism to measure changes in the perceptions of the various stakeholders regarding the credential and its attributes.

Regardless of the research method used, any organization that is serious about establishing value for its credential must make some formal effort to identify the criteria that its stakeholder groups will utilize in arriving at their own value decisions. One must always remember that value is ultimately a perception of the customer (certificants and other stakeholders) rather than an attribute conferred by the leadership of the credentialing body. Listening and responding to stakeholders is a process that should take place prior to and throughout the life of the credentialing effort.

D. Does the Mission of the Credentialing Organization Adequately Address Value Enhancement?

The mission of the certification organization should be based upon a strategy that considers the unique needs of the potential discipline and the various participating stakeholder groups. This concept is important in establishing the value of the credential because mission statements usually drive governance and management decisions regarding program priorities and utilization of resources in the organization providing the credential. A strong mission statement will include a concept that the credential will be developed and operated in a fashion that provides an effective competency assessment process and increasing value for the certificants and other stakeholders. Most credentialing bodies would probably respond that this is one of their goals regardless of its inclusion in a mission statement, but it is still important to announce this philosophy to all of the stakeholders. Also, including a statement of this nature in an organization's mission statement implies that there is a consensus among the leadership regarding this goal.

Mission statements should specify the unique attributes and goals of the certification organization. This concept is even more important in fields with multiple credentialing organizations. Some of the goals in a mission statement can include the geographical scope of the credential. Will it be regional, national, or international? Certification programs with an international mission face a wide array of additional strategic and management challenges. The mission statement should also reflect the role the certification body intends to play in the discipline. Will the organization be one of several certification programs? Will it be the premier national/international program? Each of these positions creates a set of expectations in the community of stakeholders. A well-written mission statement can help educate the public and the discipline regarding the unique aspects of the organization's credentialing process.

If the certification body is part of a larger organization, such as a trade or professional association, the mission statement of the credentialing entity usually must conform to the overall mission of the parent organization. This concept does not usually create problems for the certification body, but sometimes the advocacy role of an association may conflict with the competency assessment role of the certification entity. To protect the credibility and value of the credential, sometimes credentialing bodies have to make unpopular policy decisions that may anger some members. This is a challenging aspect of the marketing philosophy which suggests that the customer's needs come first. These issues will surface in most credentialing efforts, and developing the proper responses calls for a strong leadership role in the governing body of the credentialing entity. Sometimes the membership service focus of an association conflicts with program integrity issues in certification. Examples of potential controversial areas include grandfathering, continuing competence rules, eligibility requirements, and examination scoring policies. These are among the many arguments for developing administratively independent certification bodies.

Credentialing governing bodies must maintain the integrity of the certification program at all times. Decisions on key policy questions should not be made based upon political considerations, advocacy philosophies of parent associations, economic interests of the discipline, or the financial needs of parent organizations. Addressing these challenges may be one of the most complex tasks for certification board members working under the umbrella of a national association. Mission statements are one of the most important policy matters for the governing body of any credential program. Accordingly, these statements must be reviewed periodically to determine whether the mission is still appropriate for the discipline. In some dynamic and rapidly changing fields, the mission statement of the certification body may require a thorough annual review to determine whether it is still appropriate. This process is of particular importance in technical, engineering, and healthcare disciplines. Each organization needs to establish some policy regarding a periodic formal review of its mission and goals.

III. Developing a Strategy to Establish and Demonstrate the Value of the Credential

After a certification body has collected and evaluated the appropriate market information from the key stakeholders, and the mission statement has demonstrated a high priority for demonstrating and assuring the value of the credential, a strategic and action plan should be developed to address the target areas that contribute to achieving this goal. Specific strategies will vary from one credentialing body to another, but the following areas should be considered in any planning effort designed to achieve the principles set for in its mission statement.

A. Enhancing the Performance and Reputation of the Credentialing Organization

The reputation of the credentialing organization will be tied to a certain extent to the perceptions of its parent organization(s) or founding groups. An administratively independent certification body can achieve more credibility and avoid any connection to controversial political agendas of parent associations. If the certification organization has to be maintained within an association, every attempt should be made to ensure that the credentialing board has the maximum amount of independence in determining the policies and principles of the certification program. Ideally, independence should extend to financial matters and staff support, but these areas usually involve even more complex management decisions and "trade-offs" from the parent association.

Regardless of the organization structure decided upon, every credentialing body will benefit from a governing board composed of the most respected leadership in the field or discipline. Individuals selected for slots on the governing body should be practitioners with the utmost integrity and dedication to the highest goals for the discipline. Sometimes these individuals are also board members for the association(s). This practice is acceptable and desirable to a certain extent, as long as the association board members do not compose a majority of the certification board or governing body. This perception of integrity and strict adherence to the mission of the credentialing effort is critical to the success and respect of the certification body.

Credentialing bodies can also seek external support and recognition of their certification activity. For example, the National Commission for Certifying Agencies (NCCA; NCCA, 1991) provides an accreditation program for national certification organizations. Achieving this accreditation is an excellent means of demonstrating to all of the stakeholders that the accreditation organization has met the highest standards of operation and structure for certification organizations. In addition to NCCA, there are umbrella groups in medicine and other professions that establish national standards for certification programs within their respective fields.

Even if a certification body does not choose to seek accreditation or recognition by an umbrella organization in the same field, the certification program can still decide to abide by the concepts espoused in publications such as the *Principles of Fairness: An Examining Guide for Credentialing Boards* (CLEAR, 1993). This publication, which was developed by the National Organization for Competency Assurance (NOCA) and the Council on Licensure Enforcement and Regulation (CLEAR) proposes acceptable testing procedures and practices for both certification and licensure programs. The Professional Examination Service (PES) *Guidelines for the Development, Use, and Evaluation of Licensure and Certification Programs* (PES, 1996) is another excellent publication proposing important principles for the development and operation of credentialing programs.

B. Improving the Management and Operation of the Certification Program

The management and operation of certification programs are important components of the reputation and value of the certification initiative. It is important to secure management leadership with the proper skills and background to manage a growing and dynamic credential. Some associations make the mistake of assuming that certification is like some other membership services that can be "tucked into the organization chart" by adding this assignment to the list of responsibilities for someone in the education or membership services departments. This practice tends to slow down the development of high-quality credentials, and it occasionally results in costly delays and mistakes from the normal learning process faced by anyone new to a field. Certification is a demanding activity, and full-time management is desirable and needed in most instances.

Growing certification programs also present a management challenge for logistics and staff support. Many certification programs suffer from minimal staffing. This situation is worst in rapidly growing programs. Inadequate staffing often results in frustrated applicants, missed opportunities, and poor perceptions of the certification program. Certification programs cannot provide world-class services with "bare bones" levels of staff support. The volunteer leadership needs to understand the trade-offs that occur when staffing levels are kept at unrealistically low levels to comply with budget limitations or other mandates from higher authorities in the parent organization.

Management for certification programs can be provided in several different formats. A free-standing certification program can secure its own senior management and staff support, or it can contract for these services from an association management or testing company. Certification programs housed within national associations usually rely upon the association for staff support. The certification governing body needs to ensure that the management and staff resources provided in any of these arrangements are sufficient to meet the needs of the organization, and to provide a level of service with which the board and certificants are satisfied.

C. Providing High-Quality Assessment Services

Since the assessment or examination process is one of the most important components of a good certification program, every effort should be made to ensure that the quality and performance of this aspect of the organization meets the highest standards in the industry. This goal can be achieved by utilizing the services of well-qualified psychometricians or testing companies. Credentialing organizations that want to ensure that their examination programs meet the highest national professional and legal standards should also consult the following publications for guidance on appropriate policies and standards:

- *Standards for Educational and Psychological Testing,* published by the American Educational Research Association, American Psychological Association, and National Council on Measurement in Education (AERA, APA, NCME, 1985)

- *Guidelines for Computer-Based Tests and Interpretations,* published by the American Psychological Association (APA, 1988)
- *Uniform Guidelines on Employee Selection Procedures,* published by the Equal Employment Opportunity Commission, Civil Service Commission, U.S. Department of Labor and U.S. Department of Justice (EEOC, 1978)

Assessment instruments should always be based upon well-designed role delineations or job analysis. Conducting a thorough role delineation usually involves a survey process that will solicit the input from many individuals in the discipline. Certification bodies should keep this fact in mind when defending the examination development process. The role delineation process is a means of involving many potential certificants in the development of the examination, and the end product can then be described as an assessment instrument developed through competencies suggested by the discipline itself rather than just the certification organization or a small committee.

The examination format selected should be suited to the needs of the discipline. Unfortunately, high-quality certification examinations tend to cost more than some credentialing bodies expect; as a result, there is a temptation to consider less costly methods of developing examinations. While everyone understands the needs of governing bodies to maximize the use of their resources, boards need to guard against the temptation to economize their operation by cutting corners on the assessment instrument.

The certification organization needs to constantly monitor all aspects of the examination process to ensure that the integrity of the assessment process is maintained and enhanced. This philosophy and practice need to be made known to the key stakeholders so there is no doubt in anyone's mind regarding the reputation of the assessment instrument.

Psychometric principles do present communication challenges for audiences unfamiliar with these concepts, but every certification body needs to plan an educational program to acquaint all of the key stakeholders with the core psychometric principles and practices of the examination process.

D. Developing a Comprehensive Marketing Strategy

Every certification organization needs a marketing plan. Marketing is not just advertising. It is a process of identifying the wants and needs of the stakeholders, and developing a systematic program to fill or meet them. Even in fields where the practitioners flood the organization with requests for application materials, it is important to develop a strategy to maintain and enhance this level of interest. No certification body should assume that marketing is unimportant because current candidate volume is sufficient or acceptable. Circumstances change rapidly in many fields; therefore, organizations should not pursue marketing only "when they have no alternative."

1. Developing a Profile of the Certificant and Applicant Population

One of the first steps in developing a marketing strategy is the development of a profile of the typical applicant and certificants. It is important to establish a database that will provide demographic information on this population. Data items that are pertinent to this profile include the following:

Age
Gender
Specialization within the discipline (if applicable)
Education level
Geographical information
Association/society memberships
Employment settings and related information
Any unique characteristics or attributes of the certificant pool in the discipline

This information will help a certification organization determine the best targets for promotional efforts. Also, developing a periodic profile of the current certificant population will help spot trends and measure the potential impact of promotional and communication programs.

Asking questions about the attributes of potential applicants and certificants quickly leads an evaluation of the adequacy of the database. Certification organizations should maintain information systems that can address marketing issues as well as all of the other management, financial, and operational requirements of the organization. Every credentialing body should prepare a detailed list of marketing information needs to evaluate the adequacy of its current and potential future information systems. A comprehensive database is also important for measuring the success of the credentialing body in achieving its goals. Governing bodies should consider these needs in working with their management staff to evaluate different software programs. It is also important to ensure that the certification program is properly using all of the marketing capabilities of its current software. Sometimes there are additional fields and analysis features in existing in current programs that have not been utilized to their maximum capability.

2. *Responding to Needs and Wants Identified Through Surveys, Focus Groups, and Conversations with Certificants and Applicants*

The marketing plan should address and respond to the information provided by the membership and other potential certificant categories. Examples of concerns addressed by this population frequently include the following topics:

a. What are the merits and value of the credential to applicants?   Certification organizations should utilize every possible opportunity to acquaint the pool of potential applicants about the value of the credential. There are many projects that can be undertaken to accomplish this goal. The following list represents some of the typical education and information efforts initiated by certification programs:

- Conduct salary surveys to determine the average salaries of certificants versus individuals in the field that do not hold the credential. Salary information is of interest to almost every individual in a discipline. Certification bodies should attempt to quantify the percentage differences of credential holders as a group. This fact is also important to note in promotional literature. In some fields, though, this data is of less value when the majority of the available jobs require the credential.
- Track employment trends and practices to find out the percentage of employers that seek certified applicants. Salary differentials for certified applicants should be analyzed and reported to potential applicants.
- Monitor federal, state, or local regulations that require or promote certification.
- Provide information to applicants regarding any accreditation or private quality assurance programs that specify certification requirements.
- Develop testimonials highlighting certified individuals who are leaders in the discipline. Leadership activities can include research, publications, association leadership, and other well-known advocates of the discipline.

Providing certificants and potential applicants with this type of information helps establish the value of the credential and helps build the impression that certified individuals are the best role models in the discipline.

b. Promoting the merits of the credential to employers and the public
Certificants are usually interested in expanding the publicity and awareness of the credential in their work settings and among the public. Certification bodies can assist in this process by developing a communication strategy to reach each of the key groups. Promotional materials should also be prepared for each certificant to announce the achievement of certification in their place of employment and community. Some certification organizations prepare model press releases and newsletter stories announcing certification recognition that can be modified for use in different employment settings. Each discipline has to examine all of the potential tactics for reaching this audience. In some respects, this is one of the most important activities that a credentialing body can undertake to increase the value and benefit of the credential. Employer and public recognition of a credential will create and sustain more interest in certification than almost any other aspect of the program.

c. Making the application and continuing competence policy as easy as possible Every certification organization should review all of its forms, policies, and procedures to make sure that they are as "user friendly" as possible. Organization have a natural tendency to develop an application and administrative process that meets the needs of the organization more than those of the customer. Examples of user-friendly application procedures include providing fax-on-demand application materials and providing application information on a web site. The key question to consider in this analysis is "What works best for our pool of applicants?" Certification organizations should provide as much information as possible to the applicant pool and make sure that the information is presented in a form and style that is easily understood.

d. Accessibility of test sites and examination options Certification bodies using a large network of national test sites can address the needs of most applicants. Smaller certification organizations utilizing limited test site options always have to consider the cost–benefit analysis of adding additional test site/test options. Computerized testing options are generating increasing interest in the certification world. Each discipline needs to consider how computerized testing would meet the potential needs of its field.

e. Payment options Most individuals would like to receive the maximum amount of benefit for a minimal expenditure. Certification bodies cannot address every need in this area, but they can develop payment procedures that make the process easier and less painful. Examples of desirable payment policies include:

- Offering discounts for association members
- Accepting major credit cards when possible
- Developing special payment provisions for unemployed practitioners
- Providing easy access (800 numbers) for questions regarding billing or other aspects of the application process
- Providing discounts for individuals who pay early for credentialing services

f. Providing special recognition for certificants   Most individuals are proud of achieving recognition by a national certification body. Certification organizations should consider every possible opportunity to give certificants recognition for this achievement. Examples of recognition procedures include:

- Certification cards
- Lapel pins displaying the logo of the certification program
- Plaques or certificates
- Press releases
- Special colored badges or ribbons at association meetings
- Highlighting the achievements of certified individuals in association publications
- Conducting special events (meetings, receptions) at gatherings of the discipline

Some organizations also assist certificants by helping them market themselves to employers, customers, and the public. This can be a very important value-added service of a credentialing body in some fields.

3. Developing a Communication Plan/Strategy as Part of the Marketing Effort

Many of the needs identified in the market research process can best be met through a coordinated communication strategy. Communication options are endless and these programs are only limited by the financial resources of the certification body. The overall communication strategy should address the information and educational needs of each of the key stakeholder groups.

a. Communication strategies for reaching potential applicants   The following strategies have been used to convey critical information regarding certification programs to applicants:

- Develop speeches and written articles for association leadership highlighting the benefits and advantages of certification.

- Write periodic stories in association newsletters describing various aspects of certification.
- Develop attractive and informative written brochures and promotional materials describing the certification program.
- Develop advertisements for certification for placement in key discipline publications and media sources.
- Develop a web site or a web page describing certification issues.
- Develop targeted promotional mail campaigns for specific groups of potential applicants.
- Involve regional, state, or local chapters of the association in the marketing and educational effort. These entities can be strong advocates for certification programs. Enlisting their active participation in a marketing effort is an excellent means of utilizing volunteer and staff resources outside of the certification body to extend the reach and network of the marketing effort.

Again, the key question to consider in deciding which strategies to utilize is "What works best for my discipline?"

4. Marketing and Public Relations Budgetary Concerns

Too many certification organizations fail to provide adequate funds for marketing and public relations activities. Many certification bodies allocate less than 5% of their total budgets to these projects. This practice is quite a contrast to most private businesses, which frequently plan to spend up to one third or more of their total budgets on marketing activities for new products or services.

Too many credentialing bodies have adopted a mind-set that applicants will flock to their doors because the benefits of certification are so obvious. Unfortunately, this attitude tends to persist in many certification bodies until a competitor arises. Then, marketing becomes a "crisis driven" initiative that attempts to address all of the classical marketing questions in a rushed manner or within an unrealistic time frame.

Volunteer leaders should demand that their organizations devote a reasonable amount of funds and staff support to marketing and public relations projects. In fact, this role should be part of the mission of a certification organization that is serious about communicating the value of the credential to its stakeholders.

5. Avoiding Potential Public Relations Misinformation and Abuses

Certification organizations need to guard against the potential to oversell the benefits and value of their credential. Sales- and marketing-oriented individuals may attempt to put the best "spin" on the promotional literature describing the credential. This tactic may seem harmless at first, but it can occasionally backfire when written materials describing the credential are cited in court cases or in other legal challenges of the certification.

This is a very sensitive issue. Certification organizations must guard against the temptation to imply that certified individuals routinely provide higher quality services than non-certified practitioners, unless the organization has some reputable research that can demonstrate this fact. Even under these circumstances, a claim of this nature could present potential future problems for the agency. Another potential "trouble area" is the provision of information to the public or potential consumer groups that implies that certification in itself is a guarantee of quality. Quality certification programs can help consumers in many respects by identifying a pool of well-qualified and competent practitioners based upon meeting the criteria established by the certification body. Also, promotional materials can discuss continuing competence requirements and discipline policies.

IV. Evaluating the Organization's Success in Adhering to Its Mission and Developing the Value of the Credential

There are several steps or methods that certification bodies can utilize to ensure that they are achieving the stated mission of the organization and enhancing the value of the credential. The following practices can be initiated by the volunteer leadership:

A. Establish a Formal Review Timetable to Evaluate the Performance of the Organization

Every organization needs to evaluate its performance and compliance with its stated goals at some frequency. Considering the rate of change taking place in most fields and disciplines, this should be an annual practice in most organizations. A thorough evaluation of mission performance and achievement should involve the participation of both the volunteer leadership and the management of the certification body. Sometimes utilizing the services of a neutral third-party facilitator can assist in this process and help ensure a more objective and unbiased evaluation.

Some organizations plan a formal review and potential update of their mission during a board retreat or a special board educational event that provides sufficient time to explore the wide range of issues that must be addressed. These types of meetings are also excellent settings to review new or current market research data, since the perceptions of the stakeholders are one of the most important aspects of this process.

Key questions that should be addressed in this process include the following:

- Does the volunteer and staff leadership believe that the objectives of the mission are being achieved in an acceptable fashion?
- What are the perceptions of the other key stakeholders on these issues?
- Does the current mission adequately address the importance of serving the needs of the key stakeholders?
- Does the program meet independently established measurement and ethical standards?
- Are the mission and plans of the certification body still appropriate for the discipline as of the date of this review?
- Is the governance and management structure still appropriate to achieve the current (and potentially new) mission of the organization?
- How will the results of this review be communicated to the stakeholders?

B. Use Achievement of Mission Objectives as a Key Component of Management and Staff Evaluations

Most organizations place a lot of emphasis on evaluating the performance of the CEO based upon achieving the stated mission and objectives of the organization. This is of particular importance in certification organizations. The governing body can elevate the importance of achieving mission objectives if it establishes a clear policy and practice of rewarding or penalizing management leadership for accomplishments in this area. Management should then in turn establish policies and procedures that hold staff accountable for meeting their components of the organization's mission. It is important that all parties in the process understand the importance and priority of achieving the organization's stated mission objectives. This concept has to become part of the philosophy and culture of the credentialing body.

C. Collect Information from Key Stakeholder Groups to Assess the Performance of the Credentialing Effort

This process is one of the most important aspects of completing the feedback loop in determining the success of meeting mission objectives. Every credentialing body must establish some basis for periodically evaluating the perception of stakeholder groups. This can be accomplished through formal market research projects, focus groups, telephone surveys, or other information-gathering procedures appropriate for the organization. Regardless of the method used, it is important that the information be collected in a scientific and unbiased fashion to ensure that the conclusions drawn are going to be as accurate as possible. Many organizations utilize the services of external evaluators to help ensure the accuracy of this information.

One area that should receive more attention in the certification research world is the question "What role does the achievement of certification play in the real performance of practitioners in the discipline?" Even though most people in the credentialing world believe that certified practitioners are better qualified and do provide better services for the public, there is little research documenting this critical assumption. If a credentialing body is serious about ensuring that value is established and created by the credential, there is no more important question to address in a research initiative. A definitive answer to this question can assist a credentialing body in building its case with all of the key stakeholders. Groups such as employers and government agencies are particularly interested in this type of information. Too many members of the public are skeptical about the real benefits of certification and there is a lack of sound research to defend most credentials.

D. Consider an Organizational Audit from an Unbiased External Evaluator

One method of examining an organization's performance in achieving its goals is to utilize the services of an external auditor to evaluate the organization and prepare a formal assessment report for the volunteer and staff leadership. Most credentialing bodies can benefit from utilizing this process at periodic intervals. The result of this type of assessment can form the basis for a board retreat or special educational board meeting to review the results. The board can stipulate specific areas that it would like examined, or it can ask an evaluator to analyze the total performance of the organization (top to bottom) utilizing direct observation, review of files, interviews, contacts with stakeholder representatives, and other audit techniques. It is important to note that undergoing an accreditation process will provide a third-party review of some of these issues, but a thorough performance audit geared around mission compliance can be achieved only by an in-depth on-site examination process.

V. Questions that Consumers or Employers Should Ask to Evaluate the Reputation of Certification Organizations and the Value of Their Credentials

Consumers and employers are constantly struggling with the issue of evaluating new certification organizations and their growing list of credentials offered. When a certification organization is accredited by organizations such NCCA, or if the organization is recognized by other large reputable entities, the evaluation process is simplified somewhat. Consumers and employers can take some degree of comfort in the fact that other individuals and peers in many cases have evaluated the organization and passed judgment that it meets some degree of acceptability. Unfortunately, most certification organizations do not seek any type of formal external recognition, so this leaves the evaluation process up to the interested individual or employer.

In these circumstances, the following list of questions might serve as a framework for conducting a formal evaluation of a certification program:

1. Who developed the certification program and why was it developed? Is the sponsoring organization a reputable not-for-profit entity and representative of the highest levels of expertise in the discipline? What factors led to the implementation of the certification program? (Note: In recent years certification programs have also grown in the private sector, especially in high-tech fields such as computers and electronics. Individuals investigating credentials in these settings have to address the reputation of the corporation and the integrity of its certification process, which is usually only a minor component of a large corporation's products or services.)

2. What is the reputation of the certification organization within the discipline, and do its staff and volunteer leadership adequately represent certificants and the field of interest?

3. Was the competency assessment instrument developed by a psychometrician (professional measurement/test expert) or a nationally recognized testing corporation? Examinations can be developed by anyone, but a valid and reli-

able examination requires a formal development process with the assistance of test experts.

4. How are the pass/fail cutoff scores established? Was an arbitrary passing score selected simply because it seemed reasonable, or was a systematic analysis of the examination conducted to determine an acceptable passing score through a nationally recognized cut score determination methodology?

5. Was a role delineation or job analysis conducted before the examination was developed? This is one of the most important building blocks of a credible certification program. A role delineation or job analysis helps ensure that examination questions are based upon knowledge, skills, and abilities identified for a particular discipline using the advice of a group of subject matter experts. The findings of these experts are often supplemented by surveys seeking validation from a larger external universe of practitioners.

6. Is the certification offered typically required by employers or government agencies? Does possession of the credential help certificants meet other regulatory requirements or licensure standards?

7. Do the benefits of seeking the credential justify the costs involved? Applicants should consider eligibility requirements, certification fees, annual maintenance fees, and continuing competency requirements. Obtaining and maintaining some credentials involve a virtual lifelong commitment to continuing professional development.

8. Is the credential offered "for life," or are there continuing competency/recertification requirements? Even though such requirements may seem to create a burden for employers, applicants, and certificants, their absence would detract from the credibility and reputation of a certification program.

9. Can anyone sit for the examination or, is it necessary to complete a reasonable set of educational or work experience requirements in order to be eligible to apply for the credential? Certification organizations have a delicate balancing act to perform in this regard. Minimal requirements sometimes detract from the credibility of the credential, while excessive requirements can be viewed as a potential barrier to practice and a potential factor limiting the number of individuals who may seek the credential.

10. Is the credential regional, national, or international in scope? Most employers and prospective applicants will want to seek credentials that have at least national recognition.

Asking these questions will help give potential applicants and employers a sound basis to judge the potential value of a credential. All individuals asking these questions should remember that even the best voluntary certification programs measure only an individual's knowledge, skills, and abilities at a particular point in time. Competence in any discipline is the result of many additional factors such as work setting, attitudes, and commitment to ongoing professional development. These aspects of competence are not easily measured in certification programs.

VI. Conclusions

Most credentialing bodies are committed to offering a service that will provide measurable and high-quality assessment benefits for the key stakeholders. Challenges arise in meeting this goal and measuring the success of the organization in achieving it. Working toward this goal is even more important in the 21st century due to the proliferation of credentialing bodies and the fact that credentialing programs differ considerably in their philosophy, structure, operation, and value to potential stakeholders. Organizations that are serious about providing high-quality credentialing services will have to back up these wishes with a strong commitment and adequate resources if they plan to establish and maintain a sound reputation in the credentialing world. Credentialing organizations will also need to educate the public and inform their other stakeholders about their success in meeting the stated mission objectives.

This process has never been easy, and the sheer growth in the number of credentialing efforts increases the challenge for the credentialing bodies in "high stakes" disciplines, where credibility issues are crucial to the success of the credential. The public is skeptical about many assessment programs, especially when they are developed and operated by the same organization that represent the economic and political interests of a field. This is a major challenge for the national associations that typically develop and operate many of the well-known certification programs.

There is no magic formula or "silver bullet" that can address all of these issues in one fell swoop. The process of establishing and demonstrating the value of any credential is long-term and involves a lot of analysis, hard work, and customer service. It is best facilitated when there is a serious and high-level commitment to these objectives by the volunteers and staff of the credentialing body.

In the final analysis, the real value of any credentialing program will be established by the perceptions of the key stakeholders. These perceptions will determine the ultimate success or failure of any credentialing effort, regardless of the philosophies, tactics, or other attributes of the credentialing organization.

References

American Educational Research Association, American Psychological Association, and National Council on Measurement in Education. (1985). *Standards for educational and psychological Testing.* Washington, DC: American Psychological Association.

American Psychological Association, Division of Industrial-Organization Psychology. (1988). *Guidelines for computer based tests and interpretations.* Washington, DC : Author.

Council on Licensure, Enforcement and Regulation, and National Organization for Competency Assurance. (1993). *Principles of fairness: An examining guide for credentialing boards.* Lexington, KY: Author.

Equal Employment Opportunity Commission, Civil Service Commission, U.S. Department of Labor and U.S. Department of Justice. (1978, August 25). *Uniform Guidelines on Employee Selection Procedures.* Fed. Reg., 43 (166), 38290–38315.

National Commission for Certifying Agencies. (1991). *NCCA Guidelines for Certification Approval.* Washington, DC: Author.

Professional Examination Service (1996). *Guidelines for the Development, Use, and Evaluation of Licensure and Certification Programs.* New York: Author.

3

The Governance Structure of Credentialing Programs

Susan Dorn

Dorn & Klamp, P.C., Washington, D.C.

> *The art of progress is to preserve order amid change and preserve change amid order.*
>
> —A. N. Whitehead

Certification is a powerful force in shaping educational policies, licensure requirements, and workforce expectations. Selecting the right governance structure can help balance the competing needs of certificants and those relying on certification to identify competent practitioners.

The goals of the credentialing program should be to offer standards by which (1) the workforce is managed, (2) the accreditation process can establish baseline measures, and (3) professionals can be held accountable. While self-regulation has long been utilized to meet these goals (as well as avoid excessive government regulation and scrutiny) (Jacobs, 1992), the governing board structure of credentialing bodies often fails to offer public accountability or openness in decision making. According to the Pew Health Professions Commission, private, voluntary credentialing

---

The interpretation of NCCA Standards contained herein are those of the author, and no official endorsement of the NCCA is implied or intended.

boards are more likely to promote economic self-interest than ensure public protection (Finocchio, Dower, McMahon, & Gragnola, 1995). Many perceive that self-regulation ultimately fails to protect the public from incompetent practitioners.

I. Introduction

In this chapter, I will explore how, through carefully crafting an appropriate governance structure, certification bodies may forge greater public accountability while continuing to accurately identify, assess, and uphold valid measures of practitioner competence. In preparation for writing this chapter, I conducted a survey of existing credentialing organizations to find out more about governance structures currently in use and organizations' perceptions of how well these structures function. The survey instrument covered a broad range of topics ranging from the tax-exempt status of the organization, whether certification is conducted by a free-standing agency or as a component of a membership association, the number of board members, term limits, the existence of public representative board members, and the nominations process. The survey instrument is included in this chapter (see Appendix). One hundred certification organizations listed in the Certification and Accreditation Programs Directory (CAPD) in health-related fields were chosen (Pare, 1996).

The choice of targeted respondent was made somewhat randomly. I targeted health-related certification programs because of my personal familiarity with the variety of organizational structures offered and because many current reform efforts are focused on health care regulatory bodies. I tried to reach a representative sampling of programs listed in the following CAPD occupational chapters: health-diagnosing practitioners, health-assessment and -treating occupations, and health technologists and technicians. Because the CAPD lists programs by the credential conferred, effort was made to send only one survey to an organization that confers multiple credentials, on the theory that the governing structure of related credentialing bodies would be similar.

There were 61 respondents. Although the survey represents only a small cross-section of the over 1600 credentialing organizations in the United States, it provides some insight into the governance issues facing credentialing organizations.

Finally, whenever one is reviewing the field of credentialing, it is important to acknowledge the empirical contributions made by the National Commission for Certifying Agencies (NCCA), the accrediting arm of the National Organization for

Competency Assurance (NOCA). NCCA exists to "regulate the regulators" and is one the few accrediting bodies that is entirely independent of the profession from which the credentialing program is drawn. NCCA has set out principles by which it believes a sound credentialing program should be governed; these principles are embodied in NCCA's Standards for Accreditation of National Certification Organizations (NCCA, 1991). NCCA evaluates the processes (as opposed to content expertise) of credentialing programs and grants its approval to those programs that meet its Standards. This chapter therefore analyzes the various components of good governance in relation to the relevant NCCA Standard.

II. What Makes a "Good" Governing Board for a Credentialing Body?

In general, the ingredients for good governance of a credentialing program are obvious. Certainly, a strong governing board needs to be the right size. The board must be receptive to concerns of the credentialed profession while responsive to the public. In addition, the governing board needs to cultivate innovative ways to address new and continuing issues of defining, assessing, and enforcing measures of competence while sustaining its institutional history. Finally, the board members themselves need to be motivated individuals drawn from diverse backgrounds with technical expertise in the profession, who are capable of working together.

But specifically, how is this mix achieved? Are there measurements that can be employed to guarantee success? Although the broad parameters of good governance are obvious, it is just as clear that there is no one recipe capable of meeting the governance challenges of every credentialing program. This chapter focuses on the factors that I believe foster a strong governance structure and discusses forces affecting each credentialing program, including the unique status of the stakeholders of the affected profession.

III. Should the Governing Body Be Separate from or Affiliated with Professional Membership Societies?

A threshold question in setting up a governance structure is whether the credentialing program should be a separate legal corporation or a component of another organization (usually a sponsoring professional society).

Provided that autonomy in standard setting and in the disciplinary mechanism is secure, and the revenues of credentialing are maintained by that component responsible for the program, it is possible that a credentialing program will not suffer unduly from a close association with a professional society, despite what may be seen by some as a conflict of mission. However, it is much simpler conceptually to maintain a separate organization. The decisive factor for many organizations is the unique array of liability issues faced by certification and other standard-setting programs that may put the assets of professional societies at risk unless the certification activity is divested.[1] Such liability may arise when certification is negligently granted or maintained (Restatement [Second] of Torts §§ 311, 324A, 551, 552). Further, credentialing programs that create barriers to the practice of a profession may violate federal antitrust laws, including Sections 1 and 2 of the Sherman Anti-Trust Act (15 U.S.C. §§ 1–2) and the Federal Trade Commission Act (15 U.S.C. § 45).

Separate incorporation is one method of protecting the assets of the professional association from possible disputes involving certification. However, if the certification board fails to maintain a truly separate existence (for instance, by sharing the same board members with a related professional society, failing to maintain separate bank accounts and/or employees, using integrated facilities, and/or a failing to observe corporate procedures), the shield of corporate separateness may be vulnerable to attack. If the credentialing program does not have a true separate legal presence from the professional society, a person injured by the certification corporation

---

[1]Further, especially for professional societies recognized as tax-exempt organizations under Internal Revenue Code Section 501(c)(3), there is the concern that the IRS generally does not consider certification to be a proper exempt activity of 501(c)(3) organizations. The IRS generally views certification as a permissible exempt activity to be carried out by 501(c)(6) organizations. While an individual society may wish to dispute the reasoning of the IRS, a more conservative course of action for 501(c)(3) societies that have established credentialing programs is simply to incorporate the certification activity *separately*. It is not impossible for an autonomous credentialing program to be recognized by the IRS as a 501(c)(3) organization. Certification may be a permissible activity for 501(c)(3) organizations where it serves to lessen a governmental burden (such as professional licensure), or if the organization can otherwise demonstrate that it meets the charitable goal of protecting larger public concerns rather than professional interests. Typically, this is the case in which board composition reflects representatives drawn, for the most part, from outside the credentialed profession. See Chapter 1 for further discussion regarding the possibility of 501(c)(3) recognition of credentialing programs.

may be allowed to use the doctrine of "piercing the corporate veil" to obtain access to the society's assets in satisfaction of any claim against the certification board.

Some credentialing programs and professional societies begin as one operation and later separate from each other. For instance, the ACNM Certification Council (ACC) is a fully independent corporation as of 1991; previously, it was a component of the American College of Nurse-Midwives (ACNM). Despite full autonomy in standard setting while a part of ACNM, ACC believed that independent incorporation would counter a public perception of a conflict of interest.

Finally, NCCA's Standards demand administrative independence by requiring the certification program to be "independent in decision making" (NCCA, 1991).

Four-fifths of the survey respondents identified themselves as a fully separate legal entity. However, most continue to have some liaison with other organizations related to the profession. This relationship is typically achieved through a formal process of board selection in which the professional society nominates or appoints a portion of the certification board.

In this chapter, it is assumed that the "governing body" or "certification board" of the credentialing program is the board of directors of a separate corporation. Nevertheless, the same balancing that weighs into the choice of board structure and selection of board members applies equally to the selection process employed in selecting the committee structure and members of a certification committee or council members integrated within a professional society.

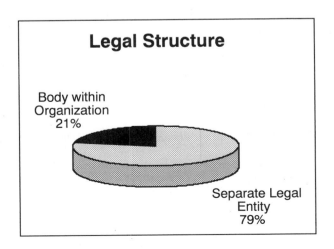

Legal Structure

Body within Organization
21%

Separate Legal Entity
79%

IV. Choosing the Process of Selection

A. The Right to Select Board Members Defines a Stakeholder

The right to select the members of a board of directors defines those who have not only a stake, but a voice, in the development and enforcement of standards of the profession. It is important for boards—particularly boards of credentialing programs—to be accessible and accountable to all affected constituents (Finocchio et al., 1995). Thus it is crucial to choose a selection process that will be receptive to professionals' concerns as well as responsive to the greater public affected by the certified profession. Taking into account professional and public concerns through adequate board representation ensures that each constituency maintains a stake in the evolution of the profession.

One of the few legal filings required of nonprofit corporations is a public declaration (in the articles of incorporation) of whether the organization has members who are entitled to vote. This initial self-identification will guide all future consideration of organizational mission by defining to whom the board shall answer. Nearly all states require corporations to identify whether they have members.[2] Some states, such as Texas and Delaware, require nonprofits to have members. However, credentialing programs may easily circumvent the need for meaningful "members" by defining board members to be members of the corporation. So, initially, the Board must decide: shall we have members? And, if so, who shall the members be? What duties should they have?

B. The Board Must Be Receptive to Concerns of the Certified Profession

As a rule, credentialing programs have been founded by professional membership associations wanting to establish reliable indicators of competence not established through licensure. Professional societies often make a capital outlay, seldom recov-

---

[2]The Revised Model Nonprofit Corporation Act adopted by The Subcommittee on the Model Nonprofit Corporation Law of the Business Law Section American Bar Association, Summer 1987. Prentice Hall Law & Business 1988 Section 1.40(21) defines a "member" of a corporation to be, "without regard to what a person is called in the articles or bylaws," "any person or persons . . . who on more than one occasion, pursuant to a provision of a corporation's articles or bylaws have the right to vote for the election of a director or directors."

ered, in financing an initial survey of the profession (or even a role delineation study), which serves as the foundation of the subsequently developed certification examination. Then, when the credentialing program begins to grow and becomes self-sufficient, it will inevitably demand greater autonomy from the professional society in making its operational decisions. At the same time, the professional society will invariably become concerned that the certification body is too far removed from the experience of the average practitioner to be able to adopt appropriate standards and policies.

Choosing the appropriate selection process can help maintain professionals' stake in their standard-setting organizations. There are a number of ways to accomplish this. The certification governing board may be chosen by certificants. The governance structure can also incorporate certificant input by direct appointment from professional membership associations or other sponsoring organizations. Alternatively, credentialing programs can rely on a nominations process that assiduously courts certificant input.

Is membership in the context of a certifying organization desirable? Member-certificants can offer a pool from which to draw expertise and enthusiasm. A membership-based organization also provides a forum for interaction between the credentialing organization and the certificants that extends beyond certification, continuing education, and recertification. However, when membership is conferred by a corporation, the governance and mission of the organization is defined in part by the legal rights of the members. The extent of membership rights will vary by state law, and may include the right to vote on any bylaws amendment that (1) materially and adversely affects member rights, (2) increases or decreases the number of members, (3) reclassifies or cancels membership, or (4) authorizes a new class of members, removes member-appointed directors, or fills the vacancy caused by removal of a member-appointed director (as is true with California nonprofit corporation law) These rights are powerful tools and may give professionals too great a voice in shaping credentialing policies.

Some organizations define their certificants as members and bestow on the certificant-members the right to choose board members. (NCCA criteria provide this selection as a permissible option, as is discussed later.) Seven of the 61 respondents in our survey permitted certificants to select directly at least some members of the board. Only two of the respondents allowed certificants to select all members of the governing body. Although one of the advantages of professional certification is the establishment of a national (or international) credential (two-fifths of the survey respondents identified their credential as *international*), the very creation of such an expansive professional community consisting of diverse, dispersed, separated, and isolated individuals may make it difficult to identify leadership with solid governance skill and vision as well as expertise in articulating technical professional standards.

Organizations that decide not to give certificants the right to select the board may still give certificants the ability to participate in a nomination process. Over a third of the survey respondents indicated making efforts to solicit nominations from their certificants. Bringing certificants into the nominations process gives an organization the ability to reach beyond the chance acquaintance of sitting board members and the ability to identify new individuals with expertise and enthusiasm. The most flexible governance structure will avoid conferring voting power on certificants, while nurturing a nominations process that solicits input from both certificants and the professional communities from which certificants are drawn. Assuming that the credentialing program has no members, how should board members be chosen? Should they be chosen by the sitting board and thus "self-perpetuate"? There are arguments that can be made against adopting a self-perpetuating board, as well as many that can be made in its favor. I will examine each in turn.

1. NOCA/NCCA Considerations Opposing a "Self-Perpetuating" Board

NCCA Standards require a governing body to include individuals from the discipline being certified. According to NCCA Standards, the board members who "represent the certified discipline" should be selected by either (1) the certificants or (2) a related or relevant membership organization (NCCA, 1991). There must be a formal procedure for the selection of members and the selection may not be subject to approval by any other individual or organization. This NCCA standard is designed to prohibit the board from selecting a majority of its successors. (In addition, certification boards are required by NCCA Standards to have at least one voting public member.)

NCCA's attempt to prohibit self-perpetuating boards revolves around a number of concerns. One is that boards that choose their own replacements will inevitably limit their selection to the reelection of current members or to persons known to support the current standards and norms of the organization. The concern is that self-perpetuating boards, by virtue of the ever self-narrowing pool upon which they are likely to draw, are less likely to embrace revised eligibility polices or alternatives in education or technology, thereby inhibiting the effectiveness of the credentialing program.

Another concern is simply an argument for "fairness" of representation. Limiting the current board's participation in the election process may help ensure representative board composition and gives access to certificant members. These interests are focused around the notion that a certification board should be accessible to the certified profession.

2. In Defense of the Self-Perpetuating Board Model

The countervailing argument, which would promote at least some self-perpetuation (rather than selection by certificant election), is supported by the reality that it is difficult to identify volunteers who have a sufficiently outstanding background (knowledge and experience) as well as a verifiable resources (especially time) to lend recognition to the organization and to attend to the business of the organization. The number of persons suitable to board service in many programs, especially smaller professions, is limited. Current board members are more likely to be well informed about those persons capable of serving the organization and are in a better position to weigh the respective strengths and weaknesses of potential board members than are certificants as a whole.

Assuming that the board members respect their fiduciary duty as board members and do not resist input from and about the profession, the ability of the board to perpetuate itself can greatly benefit the organization. Board members who are also members of the profession have the knowledge and experience to identify professionals who are well respected within the community. Self-perpetuation gives board members the opportunity to use their resources to select those people who will be an asset to the organization and who will add to the prestige of the overall profession.

In addition, prohibiting board members from choosing their successors could actually harm the organization. Organizations may become extended beyond the scope of their mission because of the inclusion of consumers or public members. The stable board, chosen by the previous sitting board, will retain the confidence in its previous decisions necessary to consider embracing revised standards, education requirements, and new technology.[3]

---

[3]There may be a downside to establishing a board composed only of a rarified group of certificants. In a study of physician self-regulation, it was found that inclusion of a disproportionate set of medical educators established guidelines of practice that, while ideal, were too stringent for even the most diligent clinician to consistently achieve. *See Govern-*

3. The Nominations Process and Scrutiny of Candidates for Board Service

One resolution to the question of board member selection is to empower a Nominating Committee to select the slate of board member candidates. The Nominating Committee can be one of an organization's most important committees, but it is often one of the least understood and underutilized. The Nominating Committee can determine the composition of the board, which is especially critical in the first few years. Early policies are crucial for determining the direction of a credentialing program.

All interested stakeholders shall be encouraged to make recommendations to the nominating committee. It is also useful to extend an invitation to the related professional society to make an appointment to the nominating committee. Extending this appointment power cultivates a continuing, active relationship with the professional society. (Appointments made by the society should not be current officers of the society and preferably would not be current directors of the society either.) The certification board should appoint the remaining members of the nominating committee. The nominating committee should have representation from the board, but should also include non-board members.

Particularly in programs with a small pool of possible candidates (certainly in credentialing programs with fewer than 2000 certificants), the nominating committee should identify only one individual as a candidate for each open position. Contested elections for most smaller organizations will only create losing candidates, who later refuse to stand for election at another time. Most organizations cannot lose prospective board members so easily. As long as election of this limited slate is then voted on by certificants, NCCA Standards seem to permit this process.

Finally, the nominating committee should be charged to complete a thorough investigation of possible candidates. It needs to ensure that persons chosen as candidates maintain current knowledge of emerging technologies and developments in the

---

ment Policy Toward Medical Accreditation and Certification: Antitrust Laws and Other Procompetitive Strategies, Philip C. Kissam, 1983:1 *Wisc. L. Rev. 1*, 22–23. However, such an effect is equally as likely to be achieved by a democratic election process as by a self-perpetuating process. Educators are far more likely to be active in a credentialing program and are more likely to nominate candidates and to vote than are other subsets of professionals. A board can guard against the undue influence of a readily-identified subset by establishing limits to that group's participation on the board (e.g., permit no more than one director who is a tenured faculty member to serve on the board).

field, can recognize any deficiencies in the examination instrument, and are able to adapt the examination instrument accordingly. The currency of board members with respect to emerging technology and professional practice relates to making the certification board accountable to the public. The credentialing program has a duty to the public to make sure that its certificants' level of knowledge is not obsolete.

4. Preemptive Recognition of Conflict of Interest

Being responsive to the concerns of the profession is not limited merely to addressing the profession's needs with regard to credentialing standards and new technologies. Responsiveness to the profession also entails creating safeguards that will protect the organization from board leadership that may have conflicts of interest. Conflicts of interest may endanger the integrity of the credentialing program and may be detrimental to the reputation of the credentialed professionals.

State law varies to some degree on the question of what constitutes a conflict of interest. As a result, an organization should determine whether serving on a certification board and a related professional society's board creates an impermissible conflict of interest. It is good practice to require board members to disclose any and all business, financial, and organizational interests and affiliations they (or persons close to them) have that could be construed as related to the profession or related to the interests of the certification organization. It is also advisable to prohibit the officers, and possibly a percentage of the directors, of the related professional society from serving on the certification board. This also guards against the confusion that may arise in the community external to the profession. Without such a prohibition, there may arise, especially early on, immediate and real conflicts for those individuals who are serving on both boards. Any person serving as a liaison should, if voting on two related boards, be asked to sign a conflict of interest statement, in part so that the individual understands the obligations of dual service. A Conflict of Interests Statement should include the process for board review of a potential conflict. Generally, state law allows the board to choose whether to permit the individual to continue the action in question.

One way to avoid conflicts is to require board member candidates to sign a statement of fiduciary responsibility prior to the commencement of their service on the certification board. Along with an agreement to keep all matters confidential, the statement of fiduciary responsibility should include specific provisions about what types of transactions or affiliations produce inherent or potential conflicts of interest. Some examples are business transactions between the board member and the credentialing program, use of the credentialing program's name to promote the board member's personal, for-profit ventures, and board member-sponsored review courses for the credentialing program's examination. By requiring board member candidates to agree to comply with the standards set forth in the statement of fiduciary responsibility, the credentialing program and the certificants create a basis for addressing board member misconduct.

In addition to the statement of fiduciary responsibility, candidates for the board should also be asked to name any business, financial, and organizational interests or affiliations that relate to the certified profession or the credentialing program. Board member candidates, particularly those who have not served on other boards, may not be aware that certain affiliations pose an actual or apparent conflict. For instance, it may not be immediately clear to candidates that family relationships with other directors on the board, or family relationships with members of other credentialing programs' boards, or with officers in a sponsoring organization of the credentialing program, create a potential conflict of interest. However, the credentialing program has a duty to its mission, its certificants, and the public to discover latent conflicts before allowing the board member to begin serving. Including a form for candidates to the board to list their affiliations along with the statement of fiduciary responsibility allows the credentialing program to make its own determination of whether any actual, apparent, or potential conflicts exist.

C. Responsive to the Public and Other Stakeholders Affected by the Certified Profession

Credentialing programs, especially in rapidly evolving fields such as health care, have been criticized for not keeping up with advances in professional knowledge and technology (Finocchio et al., 1995). One reason may be the lack of involvement by a greater community of interests—especially notable is the lack of employer, payor, or the general public in the governance of boards that set those standards (Finocchio et al., 1995). This absence focuses credentialing programs on the needs of the profession and those already credentialed within the profession, rather than the broader needs of society. There has been increasing pressure to put public protection and service above institutional and limited constituent advancement by gathering input from all interested parties into decision and policy making (Finocchio et al., 1995).

It is important to have a selection process that is responsive to those who are directly and indirectly affected by the credentialed profession. One way to demonstrate a commitment by the credentialing program to the public is to include a public representative on the board. Historically, public members were appointed to professional licensing and certification boards to combat criticism that those boards were trying to limit access to the profession or to raise prices.[4] The inclusion of a public member was meant to provide a voice to address concerns specifically related to these consumer issues. Including a public member was also meant to provide boards with the opportunity to hear other perspectives that could help the organizations self-evaluate and evolve.

1. NCCA Standards Require a Public Member

Credentialing programs seeking NCCA approval are required to have at least one voting public member on the governing body to represent the interests of consumers and protect the interests of the public at large. These representatives may represent a variety of groups including consumers, the general public, employers, or regulators. A credentialing program that certifies more than one discipline is required to have a representation of each group on the governing body. To meet the NCCA Standards, NOCA's interpretive Guidelines for Certification Accreditation: (1) strongly suggest that the public member not be a member of the credentialed profession, an employee of the profession, or an employee of the certifying organization and (2) require that public member appointees and their spouses may not derive a significant amount of their income from the profession or certifying organization.

NCCA also requires public member applicants to sign a Public Member Declaration (NCCA, 1991) to demonstrate their autonomy from the credentialed profession. Among the questions in NCCA's declaration is whether the applicant or the applicant's family is a member of the relevant profession, whether the applicant is an employee of any credentialing organization, and whether more than five percent of the applicant's total income was derived from the profession. The declaration helps assure that the public representative will be working in the interests of the consumer and minimize the danger that the focus of the public representative will be the same as the other members of the board.

---

[4]The Citizen Advocacy Center (CAC) provides training, research, technical support, and networking opportunities for public member on healthcare regulatory boards and governing bodies. The report is based on a December 1994 workshop that CAC held to address the desire for public representation and the reality of disappointing past experiences of public participation (CAC, 1995).

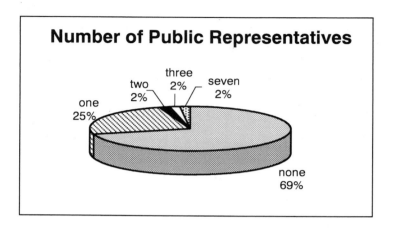

Number of Public Representatives

one 25%

two 2%

three 2%

seven 2%

none 69%

Certification boards often have been reluctant to include public members, concerned that public members lack the technical abilities to participate in setting standards for the profession. Not surprisingly, the survey demonstrated that only a very small percentage of certification boards include a public representative. Of the 61 organizations surveyed, only 18 had a public representative on their boards. Of those boards containing at least one public representative, the highest ratio of public representatives was 7 out of 15 board members. Even with the participating public representatives, the results have not been universally beneficial to consumers or credentialing organizations. One problem has been in defining the role and responsibilities public members should take. One board in the survey noted that the public advisor on the board was most useful in offering assistance in strategic planning only.

Antitrust law offers an additional reason to consider selecting a consumer representative or an independent expert as a board member. Certification boards can be vulnerable to antitrust claims to the extent that failing candidates or professionals ineligible due to seemingly restrictive educational criteria may claim that standards have been established to hinder competition. Organizational standards that are drafted by competitors or parties motivated to limit competition or harm consumers are likely to be considered suspect by the courts (Gerla, 1994) A way to avoid the appearance of impropriety is for organizations to include noncompetitors such as independent experts in their standard-drafting process. Courts may look even more favorably upon a standard-setting process when there is adequate consumer representation involved in the board. In at least one case, *Consolidated Metal Products,*

Inc. v. American Petroleum Institute (1988), the court seemingly supported this theory, reasoning that the defendant was not engaged in anticompetitive activities since the defendant's standard-setting committee did not include members who were also the plaintiff's competitors.

Credentialing programs that do not formally reserve a governance position for at least one person external to the certified profession are not current with modern thinking. All state medical licensing boards have at least one voting nonphysician board member.[5] As with other board members, care must be taken to select an appropriate individual and to support the individual in his or her role as public member.

V. Choosing an Effective Board

How does a board make sure that it will be effective in carrying out the goals of the credentialing program? At a minimum, the board should consist of a workable number of individuals. Too large a group limits the ability of responsive decision making; too small a group creates the appearance, if not reality, of undue influence. In addition, there should be some form of term limits on the length of an individual's consecutive service on the board. Finally, both professional and public board members should be carefully recruited to reflect the diversity of the affected community, with advance understanding and accepting of the demands of service, and should be trained by the board to be effective in performing their roles.

A. A Workable Number of Members

In determining the number of members who will sit on the board, the credentialing program must account for several concerns. First, the law of the state in which the program is incorporated will require a certain minimum number of board members

---

[5] As mentioned in conversation by Dr. Barbara S. Schneidman, Associate Vice President of the American Board of Medical Specialties (ABMS). It is notable that only one ABMS board, the American Board of Pediatrics (which happened to be a survey respondent), has had a public representative. Its current public representative is an attorney with a background in child advocacy issues. Dr. Schneidman commented that 15 of the ABMS boards give oral examinations, which public members are not able to administer. She further noted that because ABMS boards do not adopt sanctionable standards of conduct, there is no role for public members in disciplinary matters.

(typically three to five) and may set an upper limit to the number of board members. State law will typically also require that the bylaws either provide a "fixed" number or minimum and maximum range of number of board members.

Having determined the allowable range of board size within state law requirements, it is necessary to consider the optimal board size for each program. Boards that are too large are difficult to manage in that holding meetings, even by conference call, will require extensive scheduling efforts. Further, it will be difficult to efficiently and thoroughly discuss issues and reach a resolution. Power may become concentrated in the few board members who become the "leaders" of the board. However, a board that is too small will not allow for an adequate inflow of new and innovative ideas. The program may stagnate.

Among the survey respondents, the most common board size was 6 to 10 members. I suggest, however, that the ideal board would contain 10 to 15 members, with a smaller executive committee (usually consisting of the officers and one additional board member). The executive committee should be empowered to address more immediate issues facing the board. This configuration allows for a greater diversity of input, with the executive committee as a tool to focus recommendations, research suggestions, and handle more routine, less strategic issues that will arise. The full board is then granted greater time to deliberate policy matters and establish strategic direction.

B. Term Limits

Term limits are a tool that may be used, particularly in rapidly evolving fields, to bring fresh ideas to the board. Term limits prevent the same board members from continuing to govern for an indefinite period, thereby permitting the interjection of new insights and strategies for consideration by the board. Judicious use of term limits can be an effective method of keeping the board aware of new developments in the field.

The drawback to term limits is that they may prevent the most knowledgeable, dedicated, and experienced board members from continuing to serve the credentialing program. This would have a detrimental effect on the program and could lead to ineffective leadership by less experienced board members. The key is to balance these two effects, considering the field in which the credentialing program operates, the pool of eligible board candidates' general background, and other relevant factors. Of the 61 survey respondents, 49 utilized term limits. The most common limit on consecutive years of service was 6 years. When in doubt, it is best not to employ term limits, particularly during the initial creation of the program, when it is crucial to maintain consistent goals, a steady vision of the purposes the program should serve, and the process by which this will be accomplished.

C. Cultivation of Leadership

Volunteers are needed not only on the board, but also on committees to perform other certification functions. Important committees to certification board operation are the examination committee, liaison committees with professional associations, disciplinary committees, and application and recertification application review and audit committees. Committees are useful to groom volunteers for future board service by acquainting individuals with the often intricate eligibility standards of certification. Observation of an individual's participation in committee work can assist the board in determining whether the individual can be a meaningful contributor in the work of the board and the certifying organization. An article in the *Harvard Business Review* urged nonprofits to engage potential trustees as members of a task force or a committee so that everyone can become better acquainted—a mutual tryout. Rather than extend an invitation to join the board based chiefly on a prospect's track record, it is preferable to arrange a conversation to explore the fit between the individual and the institution and its board. "Some . . . for instance, are intolerant of the convoluted decision-making processes and dispersed powers characteristic of most nonprofits. Those individuals, however successful, are unlikely to be effective trustees. Board members should love the organization for what it is as well as for what they hope to make it" (Taylor, Chait, & Thomas, 1996, p. 44).

D. Diversity

Diversity of board members can affect the appearance of public accountability both within the profession and externally. This is particularly true if there is a perception that the credentialing organization is trying to limit access to the profession. Credentialing boards and their nominating committees should define diversity with regard to gender, race, profession, age, geography, and education. The NOCA Standards address diversity only to the extent that elimination of bias is discussed. However, in addition to building a public reputation for inclusion, it may additionally assist an organization, should it be necessary, when building a defense from a claim that the examination instrument is biased, to be able to show that there was diversity in the governing body.

E. Willingness to Serve

Perhaps a greater challenge rests in identifying those individuals willing to make the commitment to serve as a board member. This is particularly true where the board includes a public member. Membership on any board is time consuming. Some certification boards use a "willingness to serve" form and summarize the time commitment necessary for active, involved board service.

Steven Bryant, Executive Director of the National Board for Respiratory Care (NBRC), stated that NBRC alerts prospective board nominees that board member service requires a minimum commitment of 15–20 days per year. The American Society of Clinical Pathologists utilizes a several-page form for all nominees to complete and on which to summarize their curriculum vitae. The form notifies candidates prior to nomination of their obligation as board members, as follows:

> All Board Members must fulfill their assigned obligations and responsibilities by attending Board meetings and carrying out all assigned tasks on a timely basis. In addition to two regular Board meetings, all Board members may also be expected to attend ¾ day of the Research & Development committee meetings held in conjunction with the Spring and Fall Board meetings. This requires a total time commitment of approximately five days, 1 and ¾ days in the Spring and Fall. Further, many Board members serve as examination committee liaisons or hold other committee appointments which may require significant additional time.

For those certification boards planning to include a public representative, there is the added consideration of how to choose a selection process that will yield effective participation by all members. In the past, when public representatives were chosen by a governor or from lists supplied by interested organizations, the technical nature of the discussion and the specialized subject matter tended to alienate rather than engage the public member. Public members often either stopped attending board meetings altogether or let their votes become co-opted by other board members whose opinion the public representative trusted. Even those public representatives who were able to engage themselves with the work of the board may not have reached beyond their own social strata into the issues of the broader consumer pool (CAC, 1995). In any case, the inclusion of a public member often did not ultimately improve responsiveness to the general public.

The first challenge is to identify criteria for choosing such public representatives. There are basic qualifications desirable for any public representative, including experience as an advocate, familiarity with the organization's work, ties to consumer groups, and general board member consensus-building and group dynamics skills (CAC, 1995). But credentialing organizations, unlike arts organizations or service organizations, must additionally address whether the public representative should possess some expertise about the professional field or whether the crucial characteristic of public members should instead be their ability to represent the general public effectively as advocates. Some might argue that public members cannot function effectively as part of the board if they cannot understand technical discussions related to credentialing. However, it would seem that the public member only needs to possess technical expertise if such expertise is necessary to serve effectively the public interest. It is important for public representatives to be aware of new developments in the field in order to participate in any discussion about whether the testing instrument needs to be updated, but ultimately a public member is still able to recognize whether something is in the public interest even if that member is not fully versed in the intricacies of the profession.

F. Training and Orientation

A good orientation to board policies and procedures as well as organizational mission and board member responsibility is also essential. One way to offer board member orientation is through providing an orientation manual or handbook. Another tool is a mentoring program that pairs a new board member with an experienced member. Such a program provides another way to foster fellowship and to engage newcomers faster. On one board, the pair are seated together for the first year so that the mentor can quietly explain the history of issues before the board, answer questions, decipher the board's unwritten rules, and debrief the new trustee after meetings. A more careful approach to the selection of trustees, combined with a mentoring program, can help a board form the constellation it needs to work at peak effectiveness (Taylor et al., 1996).

It is critical that some kind of orientation be provided. At a minimum, new members should review the mission and history of the organization, and its governing documents and credentialing standards. Each board member should be provided with names, addresses, and access information for all board members and key staff persons. Effective orientation will equip the new board member to participate productively on the board.

VI. Conclusion

[G]overning boards are among the least innovative, least flexible elements of many nonprofits. . . . A sympathetic explanation for the reluctance of most boards to experiment with substantial governance reforms would be the trustees' desire to do no harm. A less charitable explanation would be the trustees' desire to do no work. (Taylor et al., 1996, pp. 36, 46)

The work of a credentialing program and its leadership can be substantially reduced by adopting a governance structure appropriate to its mission. The exact parameters of this structure will be dictated by the professional field regulated by the program and the effect of the program's work on public stakeholders. It is crucial to the success of a credentialing program to resolve these matters in the initial stages of formation in order to promote the long-term fulfillment of its mission.

References

Citizen Advocacy Center. (1995). Public Representation on Health Care Regulatory, Governing, and Oversight Bodies: Strategies for Success 3. Washington, DC: Author.

Consolidated Metal Products, Inc. v. American Petroleum Institute, 846 F.2d 284 (5th Cir. 1988).

Finocchio, L., J., Dower, C. M., McMahon, T., Gragnola, C. M., & the Taskforce on Health Care Workforce Regulation. (1995). *Reforming health care workforce regulation: Policy considerations for the 21st century.* San Francisco, CA: Pew Health Professions Commission.

Gerla, H. S. (1994). *Federal antitrust law and trade and professional association standards and certification,* 19 U. *Dayton L. Rev. 471.*

Jacobs, J. A. (1992). *Certification and accreditation law handbook 25.* Washington, D.C: American Society of Association Executives.

National Commission for Certifying Agencies. (1991). *NCCA Guidelines for Certification Approval.* Washington, D.C.: Author.

Pare, M. E. (Ed.). (1996). *Certification and accreditation programs directory*: A descriptive guide to national voluntary certification and accreditation programs for professionals and institutions. Detroit, MI: Gale Research.

Taylor, B., Chait, R. P., & Thomas, P. H. The new work of the nonprofit board. *Harvard Business Review, 100,* 36–46.

Appendix
Questionnaire on the Governance Structure of Credentialing Organizations

Unless you grant permission, information acquired through this survey will remain confidential; results will be reported for the entire set of respondents and not on an individual basis.

Check to waive confidentiality of information.   ☐
Check to receive a copy of the tabulated results.   ☐

I. Organization Profile
1. In what area does your organization offer certification? (Check the one that is most appropriate.)
   ☐ Art & Culture
   ☐ Health
   ☐ Human Service
   ☐ Other (Please specify):_____

2. What is the scope of your certification program? ☐ National ☐ International

3. Is your organization a nonprofit organization? ☐ Yes   ☐ No

4. If so, how is it classified by the IRS?
   ☐ 501(c)(6)
   ☐ 501(c)(3)
   ☐ Other (Please specify): _____

II. Board Composition and Structure
5. Is your certifying program conducted by:
   ☐ your board of directors?
   ☐ a separate body in the organization?

6. How many people serve on the governing board of the certification program?
   ☐ 3–5   ☐ 5–10   ☐ 11–15
   ☐ 16–20   ☐ >20

7. Of the current members of the certification governing board, how many have served on the board for:
   0–3 years? _____
   4–7 years? _____
   8–10 years? _____
   More than 10 years?_____

8. Are any salaried staff to the certification program also voting members of the certification governing board?
   ☐ Yes   ☐ No

9. If so how many? _____

10. How are the certification governing board members selected?
    ___% Selected by current board members
    ___% Elected by organization's members (including non-certificants)
    ___% Elected by organization's certificants
    ___% Selected by the board of a separate membership society
    ___% Elected by the members of separate membership society
    ___% Selected by a government agency.
    ___% Other: _____

11. How many public representatives are on your board? _____

12. Is every public representative entitled to vote on the board?
    ☐ Yes   ☐ No

13. If not, what is the rationale? _____
    _____

14. If you have public representatives on your board, how are they selected?
    ☐ Selected by current board members
    ☐ Elected by organization's members
    ☐ Elected by organization's certificants
    ☐ Appointed by a separate membership society
    ☐ Appointed by a government agency.
    ☐ Other:_____

15. Is your certification program accredited by another organization?
☐ Yes ☐ No

16. If yes, which one(s)? _____

III. Board Policies

17. Does your organization have in writing a conflict-of-interest policy for the board and staff?
☐ Yes ☐ No

18. Does your organization currently have in writing a list of responsibilities for board members?
☐ Yes ☐ No

19. Do board members serve terms for a designated number of years?
☐ Yes ☐ No

20. If yes, how many years in each term?
_____ years

21. Is there a limit on the number of terms or consecutive years someone can serve on the board?
☐ Yes ☐ No

22. If yes, please provide the maximum number of either or both:
Terms? _____ Consecutive years? _____

23. How many persons serve on the nominating committee? _____

24. Please identify any that serve on the nominating committee:
☐ President/Chair
☐ Present/Chair-Elect
☐ Past President/Chair

25. How are nominating committee members chosen?
☐ Appointed by Board
☐ Appointed by current Chair/President
☐ Other (please describe): _____

26. How are nominations solicited? (Check all that apply.)
    ☐ From board discussion
    ☐ From certificants
    ☐ From related membership organizations
    ☐ From other organizations
    ☐ From consumer/patient constituencies
    ☐ Other (please describe): _____

27. How many candidates are nominated for each vacant position? _____

28. Are candidates required to sign a "willingness to serve" form before being nominated?
    ☐ Yes   ☐ No

IV. Board Restructuring
29. When did your organization most recently review its certification governing board structure? _____ [date]

30. Please describe any changes implemented as a result of that review.
    _____
    _____
    _____

Organization's Name:

_____

Respondent's Name:

_____

Respondent's Title:

_____

4

Missions of Organizations Involved in Certification

The Mission of the Board of Pharmaceutical Specialties

Richard J. Bertin

Board of Pharmaceutical Specialties, Washington, D.C.

The Board of Pharmaceutical Specialties (BPS) is an organizational component of the American Pharmaceutical Association, which is incorporated as a 501(c)(6) nonprofit corporation. BPS was established in 1976 in response to growing interest and need within the pharmacy community to recognize specialty practice. Pharmacy was rather unusual among the large health professions in coming so late to this point in its evolution. Prior to the 1970s, pharmacy as a profession was relatively undifferentiated at the practice level, with the vast majority of pharmacists involved principally in drug distribution in community and institutional settings. It was the emergence of highly complex therapies, as well as the pharmacist's formal clinical role as a member of the healthcare team, that led to the formation of the BPS and recognition of nuclear pharmacy as the first specialty in pharmacy. Since that time, BPS has recognized four additional specialties at the advanced practice level.

The current BPS mission statement was revised as the result of a strategic planning meeting held in 1997. However, the agency's principal role as the specialty credentialing body serving the pharmacy profession has remained constant since its inception.

I. BPS Mission Statement

The mission of the Board of Pharmaceutical Specialties is to improve public health through recognition and promotion of specialized training, knowledge, and skills in pharmacy by certification of pharmacist specialists.

The Board will accomplish this mission by:

- Providing leadership for the profession of pharmacy in the discussion, evolution, direction, and recognition of specialties in pharmacy;
- Establishing the standards for identification and recognition of specialties in consultation with the profession;
- Establishing standards of training, knowledge, and skills as the basis for certification of individuals;
- Developing and administering objective and valid means to evaluate the knowledge and skills of pharmacist specialists;
- Evaluating areas of specialization for their value and viability; and
- Communicating the value of specialization and specialty certification in pharmacy.

To date, BPS has recognized five specialties in pharmacy and has certified nearly 3000 pharmacists in one or more of those specialties. The specialties include the following:

1. *Nuclear Pharmacy* (recognized in 1978). Specialists seek to improve and promote the public's health through the safe and effective use of radioactive drugs for diagnosis and therapy.
2. *Nutrition Support Pharmacy* (recognized in 1988). Specialists promote the maintenance and/or restoration of optimal nutritional status, designing and modifying treatment according to the needs of the patient.
3. *Oncology Pharmacy* (recognized in 1996). Specialists address the pharmaceutical care of patients with cancer.
4. *Pharmacotherapy* (recognized in 1988). Specialists are responsible for ensuring the safe, appropriate, and economical use of drugs in patient care and

frequently serve as a primary source of drug information for other health care professionals.

5. *Psychiatric Pharmacy* (recognized in 1992). Specialists address the pharmaceutical care of patients with psychiatric disorders.

II. The BPS Specialty Recognition and Certification Process

BPS recognized each of the aforementioned specialties after profession-wide review and discussion of a petition submitted by an interested group on behalf of pharmacists practicing in the proposed area of specialty. The nine-member Board, composed of six pharmacists, two nonpharmacist health professionals, and one public member, evaluates petitions for specialty recognition against seven criteria that differentiate a new specialty from nonspecialty practice and existing specialties.

Once a specialty is approved, a Specialty Council is appointed to direct the development and implementation of the specialty recognition process, within established BPS policies. A Specialty Council, composed of six pharmacists from the specialty area and three pharmacists from outside that area, develops standards, eligibility criteria, specialty examinations, and recertification requirements with the assistance of a testing consultant.

Although all candidates for BPS specialty certification must be graduates of approved pharmacy programs and hold a current, active license to practice pharmacy, each specialty also has its own unique eligibility criteria in terms of years of specialized training and/or experience. The goal of the eligibility criteria is to help ensure that an examination candidate has attained an appropriate level of formal training and concentrated, focused practice experience, prior to sitting for the examination. In specialties where residencies exist, completion of a residency may substitute for all or part of the practice experience requirement.

BPS examinations, which are administered annually at multiple sites across the United States and other countries, consist of 200 multiple-choice questions. Test specifications are developed as the result of a formal task analysis. The entire BPS examination development, administration, and scoring process follows policies and procedures established to ensure psychometric soundnes and legal defensibility. Passing points are determined for each BPS specialty examination using criterion-referenced methodology.

Each BPS certificant must recertify every seven years. Currently, approved professional development programs are available as an alternative to sitting for a 100-

item recertification examination in the nuclear pharmacy and pharmacotherapy specialties. In addition, the use of such programs has been endorsed in principle by BPS for the nutrition support and psychiatric pharmacy specialties, but no programs have yet applied for approval.

BPS continually evaluates and updates its certification and recertification processes. Every five years, a specialty's role delineation study is repeated, and examination specifications modified accordingly. In an effort to keep its item banks well stocked with appropriate items, new item solicitations and item development workshops are held annually for most specialties. Separate item bank maintenance meetings are held as needed. Because the specific material tested in each of the specialty examinations changes frequently with the introduction of new therapies, maintaining currency of its examinations is a constant challenge for BPS and its Specialty Councils.

III. Added Qualifications

In addition to offering certification in its five specialties, BPS has implemented a program to recognize focused practice areas within those specialties. The term *added qualifications* is used to denote the demonstration of an enhanced level of training and experience within one segment of a specialty practice area recognized by BPS. The added qualifications designation may be granted to a BPS-certified pharmacist specialist who can document an established level of focused training and experience in the area (e.g., Infectious Diseases within the Pharmacotherapy specialty or Geriatrics within the Psychiatric Pharmacy specialty). Candidates for added qualifications submit a structured portfolio, which is assessed by the Specialty Council in accordance with published standards.

IV. Communication: A Primary BPS Objective

Throughout the certification process—from initial inquiry, through score notification, to recertification and added qualifications—BPS attempts to make its contacts with candidates and certificants as informative and user friendly as possible. A new database has been created to maintain applicant and certificant files for quick access and response. Triennial newsletters are supplemented with frequent news releases and a recently established website (www.bpsweb.org). All of these mechanisms facilitate communication with BPS's primary constituencies.

Education is a critical aspect of the BPS mission. Since specialty recognition is a relatively recent development in pharmacy and fewer than 2% of licensed pharmacists have attained this credential, many pharmacists and their employers are not aware of BPS and its certification activities. The Board has launched a major informational campaign to acquaint practicing pharmacists, pharmacy school faculty, and pharmacy students about specialization. At the same time, an effort has been made to begin educating employers, payers, other health professionals, and the public about the existence of specialties in pharmacy. Much of this education is being accomplished through exhibits and presentations at professional meetings and academic settings, as well as informational articles and mailings. BPS has recently begun to identify particularly innovative or successful specialty practices that can be used as models in its educational materials.

One of BPS's long-term challenges has been to help the pharmacy profession understand the difference between various credentials available to pharmacists. Most pharmacists are familiar with licensure as the mandatory process whereby a regulatory body determines that an individual has the required education and skill to practice a profession safely at the entry level. Less clear has been the distinction between licensure, certification and certificate programs. BPS has adopted the well-accepted definition of certification as a voluntary process, usually established by a professional, nongovernmental agency, that evaluates an individual's training, experience, knowledge, and skill at a level beyond that required for licensure. A certificate program is a formally organized educational or training program that typically awards a certificate of completion to those who meet its requirements. Many certificate programs currently available to pharmacists do not incorporate any formal assessment of knowledge and skill, yet participants and sometimes even providers of these programs refer to those who have completed them as "certified." The American Council on Pharmaceutical Education (ACPE) has developed specific standards for certificate programs which will clearly differentiate them from other academic or continuing education programs.

V. Why Do Pharmacists Seek Additional Credentials?

There appear to be several interrelated motivations for pharmacists to seek credentials beyond those required for basic level practice. A significant motivator is simply the sense of personal and professional accomplishment that the credential represents.

Most pharmacists want to advance their knowledge and skills in order to provide optimal care for their patients. Setting and attaining a personal goal of successfully completing a residency or earning specialty certification is often easier when there is a tangible end point. When that end point is visible to and appreciated by others, a second powerful motivator comes into play. Recognition of professional accomplishment by one's peers and superiors is important in today's hierarchical health systems. As just one example, pharmacists who work closely with physicians often note that residency training and specialty board certification are expected in the medical profession. Pharmacists who share this bond with their medical colleagues are usually accorded additional collegial respect and credibility.

A third motivator, and one that seems to be growing in impact, is that of monetary reward. In almost all employment relationships, credentials perceived to have value for an employer or payer are rewarded—by preferential hiring or job retention (in times of business downturns), promotion, or salary and bonus payment. A survey of journal advertisements for pharmacists indicates that many require or prefer credentials beyond basic entry-level degree and pharmacy licensure. A number of local and national employers, including several federal agencies, have career and salary ladders that incorporate specific credentials, including residency training, specialty board certification, or completion of certificate training programs of particular interest to the employer. Recently, some payers have expressed interest in providing compensation for certain cognitive services to pharmacists who are credentialed to provide those services. Pharmacists, particularly those in community settings, have long sought a compensation mechanism that is not tied to product dispensing. Meaningful credentials that can facilitate such compensation will certainly be well received by many in the pharmacy profession.

VI. Documentation of the Value of Specialty Certification in Pharmacy

A high priority for BPS is collaboration on research projects to document the value of pharmacist specialists in current and future health care programs. Potential measures of this value may include documented improvement in patient outcome, more appropriate use of therapeutic agents, or lower cost for equal or better treatment results. Qualitative measures, including personal, employer, and patient satisfaction, will also be studied as pharmacy seeks to demonstrate the value of its specialists.

Professional and societal recognition of the value of specialty certification in pharmacy has already been demonstrated in several ways. National recognition has come from the federal Department of Defense, Public Health Service, and Department of Veterans Affairs in the form of bonus pay for BPS-certified pharmacist specialists. A growing number of healthcare organizations, universities, and other employers provide additional compensation, hiring preferences, or career advancement for BPS certificants. BPS expects this to increase as the number of certificants grows and its educational and research efforts continue.

VII. Intraprofessional Involvement

One of the real strengths of BPS over the years has been its ability to work closely with several major pharmacy organizations in the development of specialties. The sponsors of petitions for recognized specialties include the American College of Clinical Pharmacy, the American Pharmaceutical Association, the American Society of Health-Systems Pharmacists, and the American Society for Parenteral and Enteral Nutrition. In addition, BPS maintains excellent working relationships with the American Association of Colleges of Pharmacy, the American Council on Pharmaceutical Education, and several other national organizations representing pharmacists in various practice settings.

In late 1998, seven national pharmacy organizations collaborated to establish a Council on Credentialing in Pharmacy. The role of this body includes providing leadership, coordination and oversight of the various postlicensure credentialing programs in pharmacy. It will also have a major role in the establishment of standards for such programs and the provision of information about the credentialing process to individuals within and outside the pharmacy profession. BPS will provide the administrative expertise and support for this body, and will therefore be actively involved in its future direction and activities.

VIII. The Future

The mission of the BPS provides a mandate for strong leadership and advocacy of specialty practice in pharmacy. For more than 20 years, the Board and its Specialty Councils have served as the profession's single agency for the recognition of specialties and the certification of advanced practice specialty practitioners. The Board's Strategic Plan calls for proactive support of emerging specialties, as well as working with the rest of the profession to ensure coordination of pharmacy's credentialing efforts. All of these challenges and responsibilities point to a full and bright future for BPS.

Recommended Reading

Bertin, R. J., (1997). Added qualifications: A new dimension in pharmacy specialty certification. *The Annals of Pharmacotherapy, 31* (12), 1532–1534.

Directions for specialization in pharmacy practice. (1991). *Proceedings of an invitational conference sponsored by the American Association of Colleges of Pharmacy, the American College of Clinical Pharmacy, the American Pharmaceutical Association, and the American Society of Hospital Pharmacists.* Bethesda, MD: American Society of Hospital Pharmacists.

Final report: APhA Task Force on Specialties in Pharmacy. (1974). *Journal of the American Pharmaceutical Association, NS14* (11), 618–622.

Gebhart, F. (1992). What Board Certification Can Mean to Pharmacists. *Hospital Pharmacist Report. 6* (2), 14.

Maddox, R. R. (1990). Specialization and pharmacy's future. *DCIP, The Annals of Pharmacotherapy, 24* (6), 637–639.

McArtor, J. P., & Rascati, K. L. (1996). Benefits of specialization for pharmacy specialists. *Journal of the American Pharmaceutical Association, NS36* (2), 128–134.

Meade, V. (1991). Specialization in pharmacy. *American Pharmacy, NS31* (1), 24–29.

Ukens, C. (1998). Credentialing: Is pharmacy on the right track? *Drug Topics. 142* (14), 48–56.

The Mission of the AACN Certification Corporation

Melissa Biel

AACN Certification Corporation, Aliso Viejo, California

In 1975, the American Association of Critical-Care Nurses (AACN) established the AACN Certification Corporation as a separate 501(c)(6) corporation to develop the CCRN Certification Program. The purpose of the CCRN Certification Program was to promote high standards of critical care nursing practice. The mission of the newly incorporated AACN Certification Corporation was "to certify and promote critical care nursing practice that optimally contributes to desired patient outcomes" (Biel, 1997, p. 7).

The AACN Certification Corporation's certification program had several goals. First and foremost was the establishment of a body of knowledge necessary for critical care nursing practice. This common body of knowledge was to be tested through a written examination. Granting the CCRN credential to nurses who had successfully completed the certification program would recognize professional accomplishment. Ultimately, promotion of the continued professional development of critical care nurses could occur (Niebuhr, 1993).

The healthcare environment has been characterized as increasingly complex and uncertain. Emery and Trist (1965) noted how this "turbulent" environment increases an organization's "area of relevant uncertainty" (p. 26). Critical care nurses and the nursing practice itself were affected as hospitals increasingly transferred patients out of critical care units (and discharged them home) much sooner and reduced nursing staffing. With trust in the healthcare system eroding and critical care nurses facing a hostile environment, the AACN Certification Corporation became aware of the need to review its mission for relevancy.

In 1995, 20 years after the framing of its original mission, the AACN Certification Corporation Board of Directors and the management team at the National Office met to examine the organization's mission statement. The group utilized a nonprofit organization assessment tool developed by Peter Drucker. The tool, which was structured as a workbook, asked a series of five questions. The first series related to the mission of the organization and focused on the nature of our business. It included the results being sought, the setting of priorities, and the organizational strengths and weaknesses. Additionally, the questions forced the group to rethink the extent to which the current mission reflected the organizational goals, competencies, and customer needs (Drucker, 1993).

All participants were asked to answer the questions ahead of time, and the answers were then synthesized for presentation and discussion. When asked, "What is our reason for being?" the group responded by noting that certification should lead to better patient outcomes, promote a level of competence, move clinical practice forward, and provide leadership in critical care nursing (AACN Certification Corporation memo, 1995). During the course of the meeting, the group came to an agreement that the current mission statement needed to be refined and expanded to include the needs of all professionals offering critical care services. It also needed to focus on the continuum of care and emphasize meeting patient and family needs. The new mission statement thus needed to accommodate several concepts. It had to be able to influence those who work inside and outside the hospital while remaining relevant and congruent to the current healthcare environment. Furthermore, it had to broaden our scope of potential certificants, assure consumers the highest quality of care and accountability for their care, and recognize practitioners who have achieved a high level of clinical excellence.

There were risks involved in developing a new mission statement, however. AACN Certification Corporation was well known and respected in the field of nursing certification. We had established our reputation for certifying critical care nurses, and now we were discussing the possibility of not even referring to critical care nurses in our mission statement. Other problems that were raised included the possibility of diluting our identity and disenfranchising current and future certificants. There was the realization that potential new markets might not value our certification programs, as we had not established a track record with anyone other than critical care nurses. In spite of these concerns, the Board of Directors felt that the best opportunity for success was for the organization to reframe its mission.

The new mission that emerged is "to be a leader in providing comprehensive credentialing programs that contribute to the desired health outcomes for individuals" (Biel, 1997). This new mission statement reflects our position as a leader in nursing certification. It also broadens our scope from critical care nursing alone to any program that contributes to desired patient outcomes.

The mission statement has guided our activities over the past three years. Whereas our original mission would have restricted our activities, the new mission has directed us as we have undertaken several new initiatives. These new initiatives include a partnership arrangement with another nursing certification organization to provide a certification program for acute care nurse practitioners, the development of a clinical nurse specialist program for advanced practice nurses in acute and critical care, and the exploration of a partnership with a regulatory body to develop a set of services to assist nurses working with unlicensed personnel. In addition, we have updated and refined our successful adult, neonatal, and pediatric CCRN certification programs.

The Board of Directors approved the new mission statement on November 1, 1995. By focusing the credentialing effort on the needs of the patient, the new mission statement encompasses a broader range of AACN Certification Corporation activities. AACN Certification Corporation is well positioned to address future needs with its broad-based mission statement.

References

AACN Certification Corporation. (1995). Drucker workbook summary. Internal memo. October 30, 1995.

Biel, M. (1997). *Reconceptualizing certified practice: Envisioning critical care practice of the future*. Aliso Viejo, CA: AACN Certification Corporation.

Drucker, P. F. (1993). *The five most important questions you will ever ask about your nonprofit Organization: Participant's workbook*. San Francisco, CA: Jossey-Bass Publishers.

Emery, F. E., & and Trist, E. L. (1965). The causal texture of organizational environments. *Human Relations 18* (1): 21–32.

Niebuhr, B.. (1993). Credentialing of critical care nurses. *Clinical Issues in Critical Care Nursing, 4* (November) (4): 611–616.

The Mission of the National Commission for the Certification of Crane Operators

Graham J. Brent

National Commission for the Certification of Crane Operators, Fairfax, Virginia

The National Commission for the Certification of Crane Operators (CCO) was established as an independent, not-for-profit 501(c)(6) organization in January 1995. Its mission was first to establish, and then to administer, a nationwide program for the certification of crane operators. Its activities were to center around three specific areas: (1) validating the knowledge and proficiency required of crane operators, (2) developing and administering examinations to test the knowledge and proficiency of operators, and (3) granting designations to those operators meeting the criteria for crane operator certification.

CCO had its origins in discussions on workplace safety (particularly construction) initiated in the late 1980s by an ad hoc industry group representing the principal users and manufacturers of cranes in a variety of industries. In response to what they considered to be an unacceptable level of workplace accidents, this industry group determined that worker skills needed to be improved. It was thought that an independent national program of operator certification could motivate employers to meet an existing federal mandate to provide structured, professional training for their crane operators.

Crane safety had been an issue of growing concern to both private and public sector organizations for more than a decade. Construction firms, steel erectors, crane rental companies, crane manufacturers, utilities, petrochemical companies, pulp and paper enterprises, nuclear energy companies, labor unions, and government agencies had long recognized the need for performance standards in safe crane operation, as well as for an effective method of measuring the skills and knowledge of crane operators.

In 1987, this group brought their concerns to the Specialized Carriers and Rigging Association (SC&RA), an organization representing more than 1000 companies engaged in lifting and specialized transportation work. Two years later, a well-publicized crane accident in San Francisco involving multiple fatalities brought into sharp focus the dangers to employees and the general public of untrained, uncertified crane personnel. SC&RA subsequently spearheaded an effort to further the aims of this group by establishing an industry forum and providing initial funding for a crane operator certification project. CCO was formed in January 1995 and offered its first written examinations in April 1996.

Key components of the CCO certification program are that it is

- National in scope,
- Operated by the private sector,
- Independent of labor relations policies,
- Tailored to different types of cranes,
- Designed so certificants must be recertified every five years, and
- Tested in three parts: medical, written, and practical ("hands-on").

Through written and practical examinations, the CCO program addresses four main types of mobile cranes for which "specialty" exams have been developed:

- Lattice boom crawler crane
- Lattice boom truck crane
- Telescopic boom crane up to 17.5 tons
- Telescopic boom crane over 17.5 tons

In order to be certified, candidates must pass the written core exam and one specialty exam, including the corresponding practical exam for that specialty. They must also meet CCO's medical requirements.

The content of the written and practical exams has been determined through professional job analysis and verified through industry surveys and pilot programs. One of the many challenges of the program has been to provide the flexibility of test administration demanded by the construction industry, while retaining its integrity. In particular, employers requested that they be able to evaluate their own employees on the skills portion of the program, a process provided for by the ANSI/ASME B30.5 mobile crane standard. Consequently, much of the two-year work of CCO's Practical Exam Task Force went towards designing a system of test site set-up and candidate evaluation that would remove, as far as possible, all opportunity for subjectivity by the practical examiner. Intensive, three-day practical examiner workshops prepare eligible individuals for this role.

The validity of the practical exam also rests on its ability to test skills required of crane operators in real-world conditions. The four tasks developed increase progressively in the skills tested, with demerits being incurred by the candidate though performance errors and/or exceeding time limits. The exam has met with consistently positive response since its implementation in January 1999.

CCO's work continues through five committees:

1. *Written Examination Management Committee*, responsible for monitoring and participating in the development of certification exams, suggesting revisions for testing procedures, and overseeing the testing company contracted to provide development and administrative services for the written exams.
2. *Practical Examination Management Committee*, responsible for monitoring and participating in the development of certification exams, suggesting revisions for testing procedures, and overseeing the testing company contracted to provide development and administrative services for the practical exams.
3. *Certification Committee*, responsible for developing and administering the minimum standards set by CCO for certification and recertification.
4. *Review Committee*, responsible for establishing conduct standards in such areas as ethics, policy and procedures for disciplinary action, and implementation of the standards.
5. *Appeals Committee*, responsible for creating policies and procedures for hearing appeals and decisions of the Certification Committee.

The five committees report to the 25-member Commission, whose decisions are ratified by a 9-member Board of Directors representing a broad array of industry interests. Given the importance of effective instruction in improving worker knowledge and skill, CCO also works with many providers of training in the scheduling of test administrations, while being careful not to jeopardize its independent status as a third-party provider of certification services.

Since the implementation of the program, the work of CCO has been officially recognized in five major ways:

1. The awarding, in April 1998, of a five-year accreditation by the National Commission for Certifying Agencies (NCCA) as meeting its standards for examination development and administration.

2. Recognition by the Occupational Safety and Health Administration (OSHA) that the CCO program meets its requirements for crane operator proficiency. A Voluntary Agreement between CCO and OSHA, signed in a formal ceremony at the Department of Labor, Washington, DC, by representatives of the two organizations in February 1999, also provides significant benefits for those employers whose crane operators are certified through the CCO program.

3. Election of CCO to the Decision Council of the Construction Industry Coalition, established to develop construction industry standards under the auspices of the National Skill Standards Board (NSSB).

4. Adoption of CCO crane operator proficiency criteria by several states and cities, and active consideration by other jurisdictions that currently have, or are considering implementing, a requirement for crane operator licensing.

5. Incorporation of CCO certification as a requirement in employers' conditions of hire. Firms requiring or recommending CCO certification of their employees and those of their subcontractors include several Fortune 500 companies.

Operators certified through CCO possess the fundamental knowledge and skills necessary for crane operation and knowledge as assessed by a professionally constructed and validated examination and recognized as such by NCCA. By requiring CCO certification of all operators on their sites, employers stand to reduce their risk of accidents as well as the accompanying financial and personnel loss. Moreover, with the signing of the Agreement with OSHA, employers can be confident that CCO certification meets the requirements of OSHA's standards for crane operator competency.

Clearly, there is much to be gained from ensuring that only qualified personnel operate cranes. The CCO program is already helping to save lives; protect life, limb and property; and generally make the work site a safer place. Participation in the CCO program is truly a win–win situation—for users of cranes, for providers of crane services, for the crane operator, and for the general public.

In the first three years of test administrations, CCO tested more than 7000 crane operators, through 220 test administrations, in 37 states, a significant step towards its goal of improving workplace and public safety in all industries that use cranes. As a result, a new, clear awareness of and consensus on the need for credentialing of crane operators has been created.

The formation of CCO is the result of the single-minded dedication of a large number of professionals, representing diverse industry interests. The time and energy spent, as well as the financial support, has been enormous, indicating the importance placed on improvement in the safe operation of cranes by those involved. Regardless of industry, or how cranes are used, the benefits to be realized through crane operator certification apply to all those who work with or around cranes.

The Mission of the Pharmacy Technician Certification Board

Melissa M. Murer

Pharmacy Technician Certification Board, Washington, D.C.

The Pharmacy Technician Certification Board (PTCB) is a 501(c)(6) corporation that was established in January 1995 through a year-long effort by the founding organizations—the American Pharmaceutical Association (APhA), the American Society of Health-System Pharmacists (ASHP), the Illinois Council of Health-System Pharmacists (ICHP), and the Michigan Pharmacists Association (MPA)—to create one consolidated voluntary national certification program for pharmacy technicians. PTCB is the national credentialing organization for pharmacy technicians.

PTCB develops and administers a certification program including the Pharmacy Technician Certification Examination and recertification process. The PTCB certification program is psychometrically sound and legally defensible based on current and valid standards that provide reliable indicators of knowledge of the work of pharmacy technicians. PTCB is responsible for the development and implementation of policies related to national certification for pharmacy technicians. The PTCB certification process applies to all practice settings. The PTCB mission is to certify pharmacy technicians to enable them to work more effectively with pharmacists to improve patient care.

Since its founding in 1995, PTCB has reached several milestones that support its mission:

- Certified over 48,000 pharmacy technicians through the national Pharmacy Technician Certification Examination and certification transfer process. The overall passing rate is 82%.
- Developed a valid and reliable national exam that applies to all practice settings. Practice settings represented include community (independent), community (chain), hospital, home health care, long-term care, mail service facility, managed health care, pharmaceutical industry, and the military.
- Administered the national exam at 120 sites nationwide three times per year.
- Tested overseas to reach U.S. pharmacy technicians serving overseas in the military.
- Created a recertification program to help Certified Pharmacy Technicians (CPhTs) maintain a high level of knowledge and skills. CPhTs must earn at least 20 contact hours of continuing education in pharmacy-related topics, with at least one hour of credit in pharmacy law within the two-year recertification period.
- Promoted the value of PTCB certification to PTCB stakeholders: pharmacy technicians, pharmacists, major employers of pharmacy technicians, regulatory bodies, national and state pharmacy organizations, and the public. Major employers of pharmacy technicians are embracing the PTCB certification program. This leadership by employers such as Walgreen, Kmart, Owen Healthcare, and Schnucks not only encourages pharmacy technicians to take the PTCB examination but also offers salary and reimbursement incentives to successful candidates.
- Established an Innovations in Pharmaceutical Care Awards Program, working with Baxter Healthcare Corporation for leadership in improving patient care.
- Secured representation from all 50 states as PTCB State Marketing Partners. The PTCB program has been a catalyst for many state organizations to work together more closely.
- Launched an interactive Web site: www.ptcb.org.
- Planned to host an Employer Forum for PTCB stakeholders.

I. Pharmacy Technician Certification Examination

The national voluntary Pharmacy Technician Certification Examination is developed by the PTCB Certification Council, a group of subject-matter experts (pharmacists, pharmacy technicians, and technician educators) drawn from various practice settings (including community and institutional practice), geographical areas, and diverse backgrounds. A Pharmacy Technician Resource Panel provides additional expertise on the work of pharmacy technicians. The PTCB Board of Governors also appointed a State Advisory Panel in the formative years of the program. The State Advisory Panel, consisting of representatives from state pharmacist groups, advises the PTCB Board of Governors on matters relating to the policies, procedures, and communications of the national voluntary certification program for pharmacy technicians.

The Pharmacy Technician Certification Examination is administered at 120 sites nationwide, three times per year. PTCB Examination dates for 2000 are March 25, July 22, and November 18. All examinations are developed under the guidelines of the National Commission for Certifying Agencies, the American Psychological Association, and the U.S. Equal Employment Opportunity Commission.

II. Revocation of Certification

The certification of an individual may be revoked by PTCB for any of the following reasons:

- Documented material deficiency in the current knowledge base necessary to achieve pharmacy technician certification
- Documented gross negligence or intentional misconduct in the performance of services as a pharmacy technician
- Conviction of a felony or a crime involving moral turpitude (including the illegal sale, distribution, or use of controlled substances and other prescription drugs)
- Irregularity in taking, cheating on, or failing to abide by the rules regarding confidentiality of the Pharmacy Technician Certification Examination (including post-examination conduct)
- Failure to cooperate with PTCB during the investigation of another Certified Pharmacy Technician
- Making false or misleading statements in connection with certification or re-certification

III. Recertification

To maintain a high level of knowledge and skills, renewal of PTCB certification is required every two years. PTCB launched its recertification program with a renewal mailing to the group of Certified Pharmacy Technicians who passed the first examination or completed the transfer process in July of 1995. Since that time, renewal notices have been sent to all those who were certified in the first two years of the program.

To recertify, PTCB requires that the CPhT earn 20 contact hours of pharmacy-related continuing education during each two-year certification period; at least one contact hour must be in the areas of pharmacy law. Acceptable continuing education must be earned in pharmacy-related topics.

Recertification presents an opportunity for personal and professional growth. Continuing education, carefully selected to fit the individual's needs, is the way to enhance knowledge and skills in the rapidly changing world of the pharmacy technician. Adapting to the needs of pharmacy technicians, the PTCB will establish a reinstatement policy and consolidated recertification dates in the year 2000.

IV. Current Status of Pharmacy Technicians

Pharmacy technicians work in community pharmacies, health-system pharmacies, long-term care facilities, mail service facilities, and home care organizations. Since July 1995, PTCB has certified over 48,000 pharmacy technicians through the Pharmacy Technician Certification Examination and certification transfer process. The APhA/ASHP white paper on pharmacy technicians notes that there are over 150,000 technicians nationwide, and current estimates are 200,000+.

V. Advancing Pharmaceutical Care

Certification of pharmacy technicians will help pharmacists in their efforts to implement pharmaceutical care. Certified pharmacy technicians now have the opportunity to demonstrate that they have mastered the knowledge needed for success in their occupation. The pharmacy employer, pharmacist, technician, and patient all benefit from the team relationship. The better qualified the technician, the higher the quality of care this team may bring to the patient, and the greater value it brings to the pharmacy.

VI. State Marketing Partners

The PTCB program has been a catalyst for many state organizations to work together more closely. All 50 states are currently represented as PTCB state marketing partners. This representation includes 34 joint agreements with state affiliates of the APhA and the ASHP. There are also unilateral agreements with APhA or ASHP affiliates independently promoting the PTCB certification process. State Marketing Partners promote the examination and offer review courses, technician training programs, and continuing education programs.

VII. Communication Vehicles

PTCB uses several vehicles to communicate with key stakeholder groups. As well as issuing candidate handbooks that are carefully designed to provide information about the program and facilitate the application process, PTCB provides fact sheets to help address candidate questions. PTCB has established a web site, www.ptcb.org, to provide information to potential candidates and serve as an important resource on pharmacy technician issues. In addition, PTCB places advertisements for the certification examination in national and state pharmaceutical publications.

PTCB has hosted media briefings and issues frequent news releases to a mailing list of over 450 stakeholders. Furthermore, PTCB exhibits at national and state pharmacy association meetings. Lastly, PTCB has published articles in the pharmaceutical press that detail the mission of the certification program as well as its implications for employers, pharmacists, technicians, and patients.

VIII. Data Collection

PTCB has established a data collection process to gather demographic information for a national Certified Pharmacy Technician Databank and to document the value of certification for pharmacy technicians. Data are collected in three main ways: through a survey that is administered to candidates prior to each examination session, through a questionnaire of individuals completing the recertification process, and through surveys of PTCB committee members.

The data collected relate to the areas and settings in which pharmacy technicians work, the education and training of technicians, the reasons candidates seek certification, and the benefits or outcomes of certification. Data are used to review and refine PTCB policies and procedures, and for PTCB presentations, articles, and the web site.

The PTCB has recently made a substantial investment in its data warehousing abilities by developing and implementing a new certification database. Implemented in July 1999, the new database has substantially increased the ability of the PTCB to store and use data to provide workplace solutions to employers of pharmacy technicians.

IX. Transfer Process

The PTCB national program recognized pharmacy technicians who have already been certified through the previous Illinois or Michigan certification examinations. This was done through a process of certification transfer, which involved documentation of current certification through the Illinois or Michigan programs, completion of an application form, and payment of a certification transfer fee. The transfer process concluded in December 1996.

X. Task Analysis

PTCB recently completed the development of a new task analysis for pharmacy technicians. PTCB contracted with Professional Examination Service to provide the necessary psychometric expertise for this project.

A special task force, composed of experienced pharmacists, certified pharmacy technicians, and technician educators, and representing the diversity of pharmacy practice in terms of demographics and practice settings, was selected to conduct this significant, year-long project. Additional volunteers from these same categories and with the same regard for demographic diversity were selected for interviews and survey panels.

The task force completed the review and revision of the existing role delineation of pharmacy technicians. The results of the study will be used as the basis for the blueprints for future Pharmacy Technician Certification Examinations. The immediate goal of this important undertaking by PTCB is to ensure that the certification examination is a valid, accurate, and up-to-date measurement of the job that pharmacy technicians do today. As pharmacists devote more time to pharmaceutical care, they are turning increasingly to pharmacy technicians to help them with functions that do not require the judgment of a licensed pharmacist.

XI. National Accounts

Striving to improve pharmacy practice, PTCB is constantly looking for new ways to benefit technicians, major employers, pharmacists, and their patients. PTCB is building and strengthening relationships with the military, major employers of hospital technicians and large chain pharmacy groups.

PTCB announced that Walgreen, with over 2500 pharmacies nationwide, is developing training programs and materials to assist its pharmacy technicians who are preparing for the PTCB certification examination. This landmark initiative not only encourages technicians to take the examination but also offers salary and reimbursement incentives to successful candidates. Other groups supporting the PTCB certification process are Kmart, Kings Soopers, and Schnucks.

XII. The Future for Pharmacy Technicians

The CPhT credential aims to benefit employers, pharmacy technicians, and patients by allowing pharmacists to spend more time counseling patients and providing other elements of pharmaceutical care.

PTCB will continue to commit its resources to the recognition of pharmacy technicians in all sectors of practice who have demonstrated their mastery of the knowledge required to assist pharmacists. This mission will serve to benefit all aspects of the pharmacy profession as the healthcare industry continues to evolve through the next century.

For more information on the Pharmacy Technician Certification Board, contact PTCB at (202) 429-7576 or visit its Web site at www.ptcb.org. Also available on the web site is the APhA/ASHP *White Paper on Pharmacy Technicians*, which is an excellent resource for information and recommendations of pharmacy practitioner organizations on the functions, training, and regulation of technicians.

The Mission of the National Board for Certification in Occupational Therapy

Edna Q. Wooldridge

National Board for Certification in Occupational Therapy, Gaithersburg, Maryland

The National Board for Certification in Occupational Therapy (NBCOT) is a 501(c)(6) nonprofit corporation. Above all else, the mission of NBCOT is to serve the public interest. NBCOT provides a world-class standard for certification of occupational therapy practitioners. It does this by developing, administering, and continually reviewing certification processes based on current and valid standards that provide reliable indicators of competence for the practice of occupational therapy.

I. NBCOT's Principles

In pursuit of our mission and in all we do, the members of the board, committees and the staff of the National Board for Certification in Occupational Therapy will be guided by the following principles:

• We will ensure fairness, accuracy, validity and integrity in the development and administration of the certification program.

- We will build public confidence in the quality and credibility of the occupational therapy community.
- We will engage in research that clarifies the full range of professional activities and validates the competencies essential for every occupational therapy practitioner.
- We will endeavor to anticipate changes in the delivery of health care services in all sites (including hospitals, schools, industry and communities) and the new competencies needed in occupational therapy.
- We will ensure that our credentialing meets the highest standards of measurement and competency assessment as defined by experts in that field.
- We will support the safe, proficient, competent practice of occupational therapy and the willingness and capacity of the practitioner to improve. We see the certification process as a lifelong tool for the development of occupational therapy practitioners.
- We will be ever mindful of the prudent use of resources and cost-effective principles of good management in administering the certification process. Toward this end, we will support efforts to improve the regulatory process, supporting actions that recognize competency rather than adherence to established mechanisms.
- We will involve the public in continuous review of the competence, practice and contributions of occupational therapy practitioners.
- We will protect the health and welfare of the public by, for example, removing or restricting certification of any practitioner who demonstrates an inability or failure to safely, proficiently or competently practice occupational therapy.
- We will support the development of board members and staff by recognizing the diversity of their contributions, assessing their needs, and providing support for their professional growth.

II. Board of Directors Composition and Public Protection

NBCOT's Board of Directors is composed of three categories of directors: (1) at least four "public" Directors, (2) at least three Occupational Therapist Registered OTR® Directors, and (3) at least two Certified Occupational Therapy Assistant COTA® Directors. Further, no fewer than one-third of the Directors are public Directors. Consistent with its mission to protect the public, the board benefits from the perspective of those who sit on its board to represent the perspective of the practitioner and the profession as well as the public.

III. NBCOT Programs that Support Its Mission

NBCOT has in place several programs that support and are guided by its mission. The following programs reflect the activities of a full-service certification board whose mission is to serve the public interest: the Certification Examination Program, Internationally Educated Candidate Screening, Certification Verification, Certification Renewal, Qualifications Review, Disciplinary Action, and Research. Among the public beneficiaries are those who receive care from occupational therapy practitioners, the communities and the organizations within which and with whom these practitioners work, the families of those who receive occupational therapy services, those studying to become future professionals in occupational therapy, and those official agencies that regulate the practice of occupational therapy.

The NBCOT certificate reflects the value of each of these programs, assuring the public that certified individuals have met appropriate standards which affirm the possession of knowledge and skills required to practice occupational therapy competently, safely, and proficiently, and that the public is protected from practitioners who are unethical, incompetent, or impaired. The certification process extends over the individual's professional life.

IV. The Certification Examination Program

Passing the NBCOT's certification examinations for Certified Occupational Therapy Assistant COTA® (COTA) or Occupational Therapist Registered OTR® (OTR) is the gateway to entry to the profession as a certified occupational therapy practitioner. In order to be admitted to the examination, candidates must have completed all of the NBCOT required academic and fieldwork preparation in occupational therapy. They then must pass the appropriate level certification examination in order to be certified. These examinations have been developed by NBCOT's Certification Examination Development Committee (CEDC) with the assistance of a testing service and in conformance with the standards established by the National Council on Measurement in

Education, the American Psychological Association, and the U.S. Equal Employment Opportunity Commission.

The CEDC is a group of COTA and OTR content experts representing a wide variety of work environments, geographical areas, and practice settings. It is charged to develop certification examinations that are objective measures of the knowledge and skills required for entry-level practice in occupational therapy. Trained examination item writers also possess content expertise in occupational therapy. Each of the items included on the examinations has been subjected to rigorous review and validated by the Committee as appropriate to the assessment of entry-level knowledge and skill and validated that the language, content, and terminology are appropriate for all segments of the candidate population. The item banks for the COTA and OTR examinations are separately reviewed and maintained.

NBCOT has always relied upon its practice analyses to provide the foundation for the development of the certification examinations. Content validation of the certification examinations is supported by the data collected in these studies. In preparation for the update of its certification examinations, NBCOT conducted the National Study of Occupational Therapy Practice, which concluded in 1997. The findings of this national study provide content validation for examinations to be administered beginning in the year 2000. These undertakings are compliant with the professionally recognized standards for the development of examinations in the professions and ensure the content validity of these measures, having identified the appropriate content domains. Relying on the study as the foundation for examination development also ensures that the NBCOT examinations assess current knowledge and skills necessary for protection of the public and required for competent and safe practice of occupational therapy. The examination specifications are based on a template that describes the occupational therapy process; it is not organized around diagnostic groups or practice settings, which allows the examination items to remain current in times of rapidly changing practice.

V. Internationally Educated Candidate Screening

The International Department of the NBCOT prescreens candidates educated outside of the United States to determine their eligibility to take the certification examination for OTR. Consistent with the NBCOT mission, this eligibility screening evaluates the candidate's education, supervised experience, and English language proficiency in order to ensure that internationally educated candidates possess professional qualifications comparable to those of therapists educated in the United States.

VI. Qualifications Review

All applicants for initial certification, certification renewal, and examination pre-screening for the internationally educated are required to provide information and documentation relating to any illegal, unethical, and/or incompetent behaviors as a part of the certification application process. To affirm standards of professional conduct in the practice of occupational therapy and serve the public interest, NBCOT has adopted procedures for screening for these behaviors. It evaluates whether these acknowledged behaviors impact the individual's ability to provide safe, proficient, and competent practice in occupational therapy and meet ethical and professional standards prior to entering the profession and continually thereafter.

The Qualifications Review process is initiated in response to a candidate's providing information or documentation that suggests felony-related behavior, misrepresentation of eligibility to examine, and/or illegal, unethical, or incompetent behaviors. NBCOT's Qualifications Review Committee reviews the information and documentation to determine whether further investigation is necessary. The Committee may conclude that (1) no further action is needed, (2) the matter should be referred to the Disciplinary Action Committee for formal investigation as it may directly impact the safe, proficient, and/or competent practice of occupational therapy, or (3) stay the review pending the receipt of further information.

VII. Disciplinary Action Program

The central purpose of the Disciplinary Action Program is protection of the public from occupational therapy practitioners who are incompetent, unethical, or impaired. While the majority of occupational therapy practitioners reflect positively on the profession, there are a few who do not meet these standards. This program offers a mechanism by which such individuals can be identified and investigated and, as appropriate, disciplined.

NBCOT has a process by which it receives complaints from individuals who believe they have information about NBCOT-certified individuals or certification candidates who may be incompetent, unethical, or impaired. It has clearly stated Grounds for Discipline in order that there be parameters identified where violations could result in discipline, which can range from reprimand to removal of certification. The findings of discipline-related investigations are reviewed by the NBCOT's Disciplinary Action Committee. Where action is taken, the results of these investigations are posted on a regular basis, with the exception of a "reprimand," to NBCOT's Web site (www.nbcot.org) and are reported to employers and regulatory entities upon request. When verifying the certification status of an individual, if there has been any disciplinary action taken, it is reported.

Keeping ever-mindful of its mission, whose focus is public protection, NBCOT has as its Chair of the Disciplinary Action Committee a public member of its Board of Directors.

VIII. Certification Verification

If NBCOT is to provide its public protection function, it must be able to identify to the public those practitioners who have met its standards for certification in occupational therapy. To that end, persons certified by NBCOT receive a certificate confirming that the standard has been met. For the past several years, there has been an increased interest in verifying that individuals possess the credentials appropriate for competent and safe practice and that they have not been subject to discipline resulting from findings of incompetence, unethical behavior, or impairment. On a daily basis, it provides this service to regulatory entities, third-party payers, and employers.

IX. Certification Renewal

Recognizing that the need for competent practice continues throughout one's professional life, the NBCOT in 1996 launched its certification renewal program (for certification to be renewed beginning in 1997). In today's dynamic healthcare environment, the public wants to be confident that a healthcare professional continues to meet professional standards of competent practice on an ongoing basis and that the practitioner continues to embrace professional ethical standards. So, many years after completing occupational therapy education and fieldwork and passing the certification examination, the NBCOT certificate indicates that it is still appropriate for the practitioner to be delivering occupational therapy services.

With the renewal program, the NBCOT screens for illegal or incompetent behavior among those who continue to hold its certificate beyond entry level. The kinds of inquiries made on the renewal application with respect to illegal and incompetent behaviors are comparable to those made by state regulatory entities and those that NBCOT makes of its entry-level candidates who have just completed occupational therapy education. Where questionable behavior is identified, the NBCOT investigates to determine whether there has been a violation of the safe, proficient, or competent practice of occupational therapy.

Upon announcing its certification renewal program, NBCOT indicated that the program would have two phases. Phase I, which began in 1996 for 1997 renewals and will continue until 2002, monitors certificants through information collected on the NBCOT screening questionnaire. Phase II is to be a more comprehensive assessment of continued competency. NBCOT is currently engaged in considering models for evaluating continued competency and has sponsored the independent National Commission on Continued Competency in Occupational Therapy. The Commission was an independent body composed of a wide range of stakeholders, and it provided a vehicle by which the occupational therapy profession could engage in discussion on continued competency. The Commission forwarded its recommendations to NBCOT to inform further consideration of the conceptualization of Phase II. NBCOT will share the results of the Commission's recommendations with a broad constituency representing the profession, regulators, third-party payers, and employers. NBCOT seeks the participation of the profession in making recommendations to the Board regarding continued competency.

X. Research

NBCOT has as a board-level standing committee, its Research Advisory Committee (RAC), which is composed of both professional and public directors of the board. RAC's functions include (1) identifying relevant research issues, (2) advising the board regarding research priorities, (3) recommending strategies for accomplishing research objectives, (4) overseeing of the board's research activities, (5) reviewing requests for access to NBCOT data for research purposes, and (6) reviewing and transmitting research products to the Board of Directors.

The most recent research initiative for which RAC has had oversight responsibility is the board's National Study of Occupational Therapy Practice, a practice analysis conducted between 1995 and 1997. The 27-month study examined the practices within the profession of occupational therapy, describing the roles of both the OTR and the COTA. The study outcomes included a description of the tasks performed by occupational therapy practitioners and a description of the knowledge and skills needed in occupational therapy practice, in particular at entry-level. This practice analysis forms the foundation upon which the board develops, maintains, and defends the content validity of its certification examinations for OTR and COTA. The results guide the development of the examinations into the 21st century.

As a part of its ongoing research efforts, the board has collected data on the profession as part of its certification renewal program. The data collected by the certification renewal application provide practice-related information from certified practitioners, which help track trends in the profession and inform the development and currency of the certification examinations.

NBCOT, with each administration of its examinations, continues to collect data on candidate examination performance and school performance. The data on school performance are shared with the Accreditation Council for Occupational Therapy Education. This information is useful in the ongoing evaluation of the certification examination program.

Since the board's inception, every effort has been taken to maintain the credibility and integrity of all of its programs. Serving the public continues to be the board's major focus.

The Mission of the American Society of Association Executives

Gary A. LaBranche

American Society of Association Executives, Washington, D.C.

The American Society of Association Executives (ASAE), a 501(c)(6) non-profit corporation, is the world's leading membership organization for the association management profession. Founded in 1920 as the American Trade Association Executives, today ASAE has more than 24,000 individual members, who manage over 12,000 leading trade, professional, and philanthropic associations, which in turn serve more than 287 million people and companies worldwide. ASAE also represents companies that offer products and services to the association community.

Members of ASAE have access to a wide variety of programs, services, and benefits. Annually, ASAE offers more than 40 educational programs, ranging from small seminars to an annual convention for more than 5500 people, plus online education. *Association Management*, a monthly four-color magazine, features articles that cover the spectrum of issues of interest to association executives. More than 200 books and publications are offered through the ASAE bookstore. Thirteen special interest sections provide in-depth information and networking opportunities. ASAE's Web site, www.asaenet.org, provides easy access to these and other resources, including the ASAE-ASSIST database, which features more than 5000 abstracts and other resources of interest to association executives.

All of these programs and services are directed at association executives—professionals who manage the day-to-day operations of associations. The association community plays an important and unique role in society, and the role of association executives is one of great diversity and complexity.

I. Associations in America

With roots in ancient civilizations and ties to Old World guilds, associations have evolved to occupy a unique place in America. The Puritan influence, America's geographic expanse, and a societal culture of independence and individualism have fostered a vibrant association community.

Associations exist to satisfy the needs and concerns of their members. Trade associations promote and advocate business growth, encourage ethical practices, set industry standards, conduct research, and provide economic and industry information. Professional societies strive to advance the bodies of knowledge of their field, provide networking opportunities, communicate developments and changes in practice, provide educational opportunities, monitor legislative actions affecting the profession, and often offer a certification process.

Nine out of 10 adult Americans belong to one association, and—1 out of 4 belong to four or more associations, according to a 1998 study by the American Association of Retired Persons.

A 1998 study by ASAE found that America's trade, professional and philanthropic associations allocate one of every four dollars they spend to member education and training and public information activities. The survey also found that Americans active in the 8000-plus organizations devote more than 173 million volunteer hours each year—time valued at more than $2 billion—to charitable and community service projects.

The research quantifies the economic contributions ASAE member associations provide nationally. Among the key findings:

- Associations' annual budgets now exceed $21 billion, which translates into billions of dollars more in indirect benefits to the U.S. economy.
- Associations employ 260,000 people full time and another 35,000 part time.
- Although largely tax-exempt entities, associations still pay more than $1.1 billion annually in local, state, and federal taxes.

- Associations spend over $3.6 billion per year to deliver educational programs to their members.
- Associations spend $1.7 billion annually on public and consumer information activities.
- ASAE member associations are the source of health insurance for more than 8 million Americans, while close to 1 million people participating in retirement savings programs offered through associations.

Associations undertake a wide range of activities and serve a critical role in society. To succeed in this environment, association executives must possess a broad spectrum of knowledge, including such areas as financial and administration, legal issues, human resources, publications, meeting planning, and volunteer management. Serving association executives is the focus of ASAE's mission.

II. Mission of ASAE

The mission of ASAE is to promote and support excellence and professionalism among association executives, and to work diligently to increase the effectiveness, image, and impact of associations to better serve their members and society.

ASAE's Strategic Plan envisions a future in which association executives will:

- Be effective executives with a commitment to excellence.
- Demonstrate a balance between visionary thinking and short-term action.
- Effectively implement programs and activities of strategic importance to their organizations.
- Maintain the highest standard of personal conduct.
- Contribute to the enrichment of society.
- Be socially responsible and embrace openness and diversity within their organizations.

A key focus of the ASAE Strategic Plan is to "advance association management as a recognized discipline in the study of management." Support for ASAE's certification effort, the Certified Association Executive Program, is a key objective in achieving this part of the Strategic Plan and in achieving the envisioned vision future for association executives.

III. ASAE Certification Program

ASAE established what is now known as the Certified Association Executive (CAE) program in 1960. The CAE program is designed to elevate professional standards, enhance individual performance, and designate those who demonstrate knowledge essential to the practice of association management.

The CAE examination is an objective examination of knowledge and experience. The CAE examination is based on a statistically validated, role-delineation study of the body of knowledge common to the successful practice of association management. Questions are written by qualified peers who hold the CAE designation and are tied to the exam content outline. The pass/fail score is based on a standard of individual performance against a predetermined standard.

Successful candidates maintain their designation by demonstrating that they have participated in at least 50 hours of continuing profession education over a three-year period.

Participation in the CAE program is voluntary. Association executives are not required to be certified or licensed to practice association management.

Since the program was founded in 1960, nearly 3000 people have earned the CAE designation. Today, more than 2400 CAEs are in active practice in association management. Twenty-one percent of eligible association executives within ASAE's membership are CAEs. To be eligible to take the CAE examination, candidates must meet the following minimum requirements:

- Show experience of at least three years full-time employment as an association chief executive officer or five years full-time employment in some other association management capacity
- Be currently employed full-time with a trade association, professional society, or philanthropic organization
- Demonstrate evidence of a commitment to continuing professional education and development
- Agree to pledge in writing to adhere to the ASAE Code of Standards of Conduct and have no felony convictions

IV. Code of Standards of Conduct

A Code of Standards of Conduct for members of ASAE, first adopted in 1922, is designed to promote and maintain the highest standards of association service and personal conduct among its members. Adherence to these standards is expected from ASAE members and serves to assure public confidence in the integrity and service of association executives. CAE candidates are required to pledge, in writing, to adhere to these standards:

As a member of the American Society of Association Executives, I pledge myself to:

• Maintain the highest standard of personal conduct.
• Actively promote and encourage the highest level of ethics within the industry or profession my association represents.
• Maintain loyalty to the association that employs me, and pursue its objectives in ways that are consistent with the public interest.
• Recognize and discharge my responsibility and that of my association to uphold all laws and regulations relating to my association's policies and activities.
• Strive for excellence in all aspects of management of my association.
• Use only legal and ethical means in all association activities.
• Serve all members of my association impartially, provide no special privilege to any individual member, and accept no personal compensation from a member except with full disclosure and with the knowledge and consent of my association's governing board.
• Maintain the confidentiality of privileged information entrusted or known to me by virtue of my office.
• Refuse to engage in, or countenance, activities for personal gain at the expense of my association or its industry or profession.
• Refuse to engage in, or countenance, discrimination on the basis of race, sex, age, religion, national origin, sexual orientation, or disability.
• Always communicate association internal and external statements in a truthful and accurate manner by assuring that there is integrity in the data and information used by my association.
• Cooperate in every reasonable and proper way with other association executives, and work with them in the advancement of the profession of association management.

• Use every opportunity to improve public understanding of the role of associations.

IV. Advancing America

Along with continuing education, knowledge exchange, and networking, ASAE's voluntary certification program is designed to assist in achieving ASAE's mission of promoting excellence in the professional practice of association management. By enhancing the ability of association executives to practice association management, ASAE strives to enhance the effectiveness and impact of associations. This is the larger goal achieved as a result of ASAE's efforts in certification and other areas: to help associations advance America.

5

The Mission of Stakeholder Organizations in Certification

The Mission of the National Organization for Competency Assurance and the National Commission for Certifying Agencies

Larry Allan Early

Northeastern Ohio Universities College of Medicine, Rootstown, Ohio

This chapter provides a detailed description and the current structure of the National Organization for Competency Assurance (NOCA) including the role of the National Commission for Certifying Agencies (NCCA), previously known as the National Commission for Health Certifying Agencies (NCHCA). Voluntary credentialing organizations can be perceived as stakeholders in credentialing activities. Each stakeholder organization has its own needs in relation to credentialing activities. NOCA, itself a stakeholder in the credentialing community, helps meet the needs of other stakeholders.

I. History of NOCA and NCCA

A. NOCA

NOCA is a membership organization for individuals and organizations interested in the field of competency assurance, and through NCCA—its accrediting arm—provides a set of standards against which voluntary certification programs can measure themselves. For more than 25 years, NOCA has advocated the responsible use of a voluntary certification program in lieu of a governmental licensing process for practice in many occupations, professions, and trades. NOCA has provided a focal point and a healthy forum for the discussion of issues about voluntary certification. As an advocate for voluntary certification, NOCA has evolved to encompass a wide range of communities that depend on certification programs. Throughout the history of NOCA, the participants in its various educational conferences have advanced the state of the art of certification processes by way of workshops and seminars to learn more about the many issues facing a responsible and credible certification program from developing stages to full maturity. Through these initiatives, NOCA has become a leading voice for many of the stakeholders in the credentialing community.

The Institute of Public Administration (IPA) in March of 1974 issued The Feasibility Study of a Voluntary National Certification System for Allied Health Personnel (unpublished proceedings). This study concluded that a certification system, national in scope and based on voluntary collaboration of certifying bodies, was feasible. However, governmental involvement beyond creation of a compatible policy environment and operational recognition of the value of certification would not be needed to sustain the system. In January 1975, a conference was held with representatives of the federal government and 26 organizations that participated in the IPA study. This resulted in the initiative in 1977 to found NCHCA, the forerunner to NOCA.

NCHCA was to appeal to health-related organizations, particularly the allied health organizations that offer certification programs to their constituents. The proposed NCHCA was to develop specific criteria and standards to determine membership status in the organization. The intent was to evaluate applications by certifying agencies in order to provide a comprehensive system of review that recognized high standards of certification programs. Applicant organizations represented professions and occupations that would provide healthcare services to the public. With the momentum of credentialing via certification rather than licensure, NCHCA was expected to fulfill a role of monitoring and evaluating the certification program standards of many health-related organizations that previously sought recognition via state and/or federal licensure legislation.

In 1987, NCHCA was renamed NOCA, which then opened its membership base by reorganizing itself into a membership and resource organization for all parties interested in certification via nongovernmental credentialing. NOCA's mission was intended to reflect broader (beyond health related) interests in certification. NOCA has become the leader is establishing standards for credentialing via certification. Through its annual conference, regional workshops and seminars, and publications, NOCA serves its membership as a clearinghouse for information on the latest trends and issues of concern to practitioners and organizations focusing on certification, and oftentimes licensure.

B. NCCA

NCCA measures voluntary certification organizations against its standards and accredits those organizations that meet all of those standards. Initially, NCCA was created in 1989 by NOCA as a commission to establish national voluntary standards for and recognize compliance with these standards by agencies certifying individuals in a wide range of professions and occupations.

The Federal government provided the initial financial investment needed to bring NCHCA into existence as a voluntary national organization. NCHCA served as a platform for the development of standards of excellence in private certification. NCCA continues to support and extend the original NCHCA mission that now includes a wider range of professions and occupations.

Accreditation standards were established and maintained for many years by NCHCA. These guiding principles are trusted, recognized, and understood by a diversity of stakeholders in competency assurance.

II. Mission Statement and Functions

A. NOCA

Over the years, NOCA has carefully crafted a set of mission and vision statements that guide the organization. NOCA promotes excellence in competency assurance for practitioners in all occupations and professions. According to its vision statement, NOCA will be the international leader in advancing the theory and practice of competency assurance through education, research, and the promulgation of standards in the public interest.

NOCA's functions include:

- Developing standards and accrediting organizations that meet them through the NCCA
- Evaluating methods for assuring competency
- Disseminating findings of competency assurance research
- Helping employers make informed hiring decisions
- Establishing standards, recommending policies, and defining roles for certifying organizations
- Assisting consumers to make informed decisions about qualified providers

NOCA has continued to develop an ever-broadening membership base. Organizations and individuals can become NOCA members based on a logical menu of categories, with each category offering appropriate benefits.

Member benefits include discounted registration for the annual conference, workshops and seminars; subscriptions to *NOCA News*; NOCA's member directory; discounts on NOCA publications; NCCA application fee wavier for NOCA member organizations; and updates on the important issues in certification, licensure, testing, and competency assurance that are regularly communicated to NOCA members.

NOCA is registered as a 501(c)(3) organization with the Internal Revenue Service (IRS). As noted in Chapter 1, NOCA is organized for tax-exempt purposes as are many other professional societies and associations. The accrediting function (NCCA) is an entity within NOCA, with a separate management structure so that independent decisions will be made in the best interests of their respective constituencies. It is clear that the mission of NOCA and NCCA emphasizes education and standard-setting objectives that benefit a broad and diverse constituency. As is true of many associations that offer certification programs, there is not a separate IRS status for NCCA. Hopkins (Chapter 1) uses the term *bifurcation* to describe how in such organizations there is at least a perception of greater objectivity when a certification is under an entity separate from the membership association. This model is widely observed in the nonprofit organizations throughout the United States. The activities and functions of NOCA and the NCCA are not readily available nor efficiently functioning in any other organization specifically directed at voluntary certification programs. To this end, NOCA and the NCCA work hard to meet the needs of members and accredited organizations as well as all the other stakeholders, which depend on and seek meaningful certification within an occupation, profession, or trade. Furthermore, NOCA and the NCCA meet the definition of an organization with educational purposes as defined in Chapter 7.

NOCA provides all the benefits and services normally found within any other organization that conducts business as a professional society or an association. In this unique case, the society or community is that of certification and certifiers. NOCA provides a valuable resource for certification programs with workshops, annual meetings and educational conferences, seminars, publications, and networking opportunities. NOCA keeps its members informed on certification issues, cooperates with other organizations interested in certification issues such as the Council on Licensure, Enforcement and Regulation (CLEAR) and the Center for Quality Assurance in International Education (CQAIE) by joint sponsorship of conferences, workshops, and publications.

B. NCCA

The NCCA helps to ensure the health, welfare, and safety of the public through the accreditation of a variety of certification programs/organizations that assess professional competence. The NCCA uses a peer review process to establish accreditation standards, evaluate compliance with these standards, recognize organizations/programs that demonstrate compliance, and serve as a resource on quality certification. According to its vision statement, NCCA will be an administratively independent resource recognized as the authority on accreditation standards for professional certification organizations/programs. Based on sound principles, NCCA standards will be optimal and comprehensive criteria for organizational process and performance. The standards will be broadly recognized, objective, and current benchmarks for certifying bodies to achieve and by which they operate.

NCCA has developed a set of standards that are used in the process of accrediting voluntary certification agencies. NCCA maintains information on best practices for certifying programs including issues about testing and psychometrics, examination administration and how to work with candidates, and all the other aspects of developing and maintaining a responsible certifying program. NCCA establishes standards for its accreditation program based on the best practices and recognized standards in the testing and credentialing communities.

NCCA emphasizes the concept of competency assurance in the certification and examination process. The initial demonstration of competence can be determined by use of several methods of testing and evaluation that results in a certification and/or a credential. NCCA, having identified the essential components of a national certification program, determines if certification organizations meet established standards based on those essential components. Organizations may apply and be accredited by the NCCA if they demonstrate compliance with each accreditation standard.

III. Standards for Accreditation of National Certification Organizations

The Standards for Accreditation of National Certification Organizations are available from the NOCA Web site (http://www.noca.org) or by contacting the National Office (202-857-1165). The Standards include guidelines for how a certification organization is structured and spells out the responsibilities of the governing body of the certification organization. According to the NCCA Standards, it is essential that the governing body of a certification organization include public membership and input. The certifying organization must have the resources and capability of conducting meaningful certification activities now and into the foreseeable future and must have conducted at least two national administrations in order to be ready to apply to NCCA. Other standards include the appropriate and responsible use of testing technology and all the tasks incumbent on a testing organization to provide a valid, reliable, fair, and responsible program (NOCA, 1991). NCCA Standards are based on a foundation that an entity conducting a certification program or programs that evaluates the competence of practitioners has a responsibility to individuals seeking and holding certification; the employers of those individuals, the agencies and customers that pay for or require the services of the practitioners; and the public. The competent practitioner performs work accurately and in the best interest of the consumer, makes correct judgements, and interacts with other professionals and customers effectively. Competence must be demonstrated and maintained throughout the individual's practicing life.

The NCCA Standards were developed for voluntary certification organizations. The Standards "represent a compilation of the relevant research, guidelines, and essential principles available from government, testing and licensure organizations, as well as important knowledge and experience from a wide variety of certifying organizations who administer voluntary certification programs" (Maronde, 1996, p. x). These are nationally recognized principles utilized by a variety of certification organizations for many programs in diverse professions and occupations. Accreditation by NCCA indicates that the certification organization has been evaluated and found to meet all of its established standards. To earn accreditation by NCCA, the certification organization and its program(s) must meet the Standards and provide evidence of compliance through the documentation requested in the application. NCCA monitors continuing compliance with the standards through the entire accreditation period. To be eligible for accreditation, a certification program must have completed at least two national examination administrations.

All certification organizations are expected to review the Uniform Guidelines On Employee Selection Procedures (1978), developed by the Equal Employment Opportunity Commission; Joint Technical Standards for Educational and Psychological Tests (1985), developed jointly by the American Educational Research Association, the American Psychological Association, and the National Council on Measurement in Education; and Principles of Fairness: An Examining Guide for Credentialing Boards (1993), developed by the Council on Licensure, Enforcement, and Regulation, and NOCA. These publications will assist certification organizations to assure that their certification examinations comply with principles that may be referred to in case of legal challenges of examinations.

The Standards have existed since 1977 and have been the subject of periodic review. In the mid-1980s, a thorough review was conducted. Since then, the world of certification has broadened with new ideas and programs about certification that partially may be the result of the strength and success of NOCA and NCCA. It appears that state regulatory agencies are working more closely with voluntary certification bodies. Many individual state legislatures do not provide adequate funding to maintain an appropriate program for developing a licensing examination process, nor are the state lawmakers motivated to pass additional laws that, in the final analysis, are usually less about consumer protection than about self-serving interests using the mechanism of law to avoid self-regulation. In the next decade, certification and voluntary credentialing from within the community of an occupation, profession, trade, skill, expertise, special training, and the new technologies and specializations may create a very different climate for emerging certification programs.

NOCA and NCCA are committed to several important ideals of consumer protection including requiring consumer representation on the Board of Directors of all the NCCA-accredited programs, periodic recertification, and disciplinary procedures for certificants who are brought to the attention of the certifying agency for malpractice or malfeasance. NCCA standards are written in a manner to allow the community to open its practices to their respective consumers, ensure the continued competence of those it certifies, and take care of its own problems as they arise with certificants. It is NCCA's intent that the accredited agencies provide fair processes in accordance with common law and consistent with the accreditation standards. In these activities, NCCA and NOCA speak well for credentialing via a nongovernmental process.

NOCA and NCCA have embarked on the Zero-Based Standards Review Study to consider how best to meet the needs of credentialing and competency assurance in the voluntary certification community (Smith, 1999). At the heart of this review is the assurance that the NCCA Standards continue to reflect best practice and the high level of achievement recognized by NCCA in view of contemporary technology, organizations, and needs of all domestic as well as international stakeholders. The NCCA Standards will continue to maintain a high level of quality as well as provide inclusiveness to all those who aspire to the recognition offered by the NCCA application and accreditation process. Consistent with previous efforts at reviewing and revisiting the NCHCA/NCCA standards throughout its history, experts in certification policy and psychometrics and representatives from NOCA membership and NCCA-accredited organizations and public representation will provide input and energy to the process of the Review. As required, any proposed revisions to the Standards will require ratification and positive affirmation by vote of two-thirds of the NCCA-accredited agencies.

IV. Advancing the Mission of NOCA and NCCA

The Standards provide a common language for certification endeavors. Any entity considering developing a certification program can look to the Standards as a road map to developing a high-quality program by incorporating the best practices for the planning and delivery of its certifying activities. By using the Standards, certifying programs are able to justify their efforts whenever there may be a question about how or why they have chosen to embark on a particular course of action. Conversely, if a particular NCCA standard were not met, the certifying entity would have to explain and justify not accepting the standard.

It is a fundamental component in developing a sense of community to have similar experiences, common practices, shared interests, and common language with formal and informal opportunities to share these experiences with others. The process of preparing applications and meeting standards across a variety of occupations and professions provides a common experience for many organizations. NOCA and NCCA activities are aimed at developing and nurturing this sense of community among the many who are engaged in certification. This process creates awareness among the stakeholders in credentialing that the various organizations are interested in promoting the best of practices and that there exists a forum organized to continue the development of their missions in certification. Within any community, the opportunity exists to stand united on important issues and to raise the level of practice through the continual development of new ideas.

The organizations represented at NOCA conferences and meetings send the leaders of their respective communities, thus providing others the opportunities to share and exchange ideas with the most active and best thinkers the certification organizations have to offer. It is very rewarding to participate in the interchange of experiences and ideas from the most visible individuals from the various communities represented at NOCA meetings, workshops, and seminars. These meetings also provide opportunities for the further development of leadership skills by providing opportunities to hold elected positions in NOCA and NCCA. This, in turn, provides NOCA and NCCA with one of the richest pools of talent available to lead the efforts in the certification community.

References

American Educational Research Association, American Psychological Association, and National Council on Measurement in Education. (1985). *Standards for educational and psychological testing.* Washington, DC: American Psychological Association.

Council on Licensure, Enforcement, and Regulation (CLEAR) & National Organization for Competency Assurance, (NOCA). (1993). *Principles of fairness: An examination guide for credentialing boards.* , Lexington, KY: CLEAR & NOCA.

Equal Employment Opportunity Commission, Civil Service Commission, Department of Labor, and Department of Justice. (1978, August 25). Uniform guidelines on employee selection procedures. *Federal Register, 43* (166), pp. 38290–38315.

Maronde, J. (1996). Introduction to the standards for accreditation of national certification organizations. In Browning, A., Bugbee, A., & Mullins, M. (Eds.), *Certification: A NOCA handbook.* Washington, DC: National Organization for Competency Assurance.

NCCA guidelines for certification approval: Executive summary. (1991, January). Washington, DC: National Organization for Competency Assurance.

Smith, I. L. (1999). Questions and answers about NOCA/NCCA's zero-based standards review study. *NOCA News.* Washington, DC. National Organization for Competency Assurance, p. 4.

TWO: The Licensure Mission

6

Legal Issues in Licensure Policy

Dale J. Atkinson
Atkinson & Atkinson, Evanston, Illinois

The power of the state to provide for the general welfare of its people authorizes it to prescribe all such regulations as in its judgment will secure or tend to secure them against the consequences of ignorance and incapacity, as well as of deception and fraud. As one means to this end it has been the practice of different states, from time immemorial, to exact in many pursuits a certain degree of skill and learning upon which the community may confidently rely; their possession being generally ascertained on an examination of parties by competent persons, or inferred from a certificate to them in the form of a diploma or license from an institution established for instruction on the subjects, scientific and otherwise, with which such pursuits have to deal. The nature and extent of the qualifications required must depend primarily upon the judgment of the state as to their necessity. If they are appropriate to the calling or profession, and attainable by reasonable study or application, no objection to their validity can be raised because of their stringency or difficulty. It is only when they have no relation to such calling or profession, or are unattainable by such reasonable study and application, that they can operate to deprive one of his right to pursue a lawful vocation. (*Dent v. State of West Virginia*, 1889)

I. Introduction

The entire premise of a licensure requirement is a legislative determination of the necessity to legally regulate a recognized profession for the primary purpose of public protection. In order for a profession to be "legally" regulated, legislation must be enacted that designates the profession and creates an administrative body (referred to as a board) to act as the regulator. Generally, such enabling legislation is referenced as a practice act, enacted to establish: (1) the criteria for licensure eligibility, (2) the authority of the governing body (board), (3) the grounds for disciplinary actions, and (4) the standards for licensure removal or limitation, licensure renewal, continuing competence, and continuing education.

Although numerous variations of hierarchy exist relative to these governing bodies, this chapter will use the term "board" to describe the legislatively created body charged with carrying out the mandates of the practice act. Certain boards are entirely autonomous, operating on independent budgets and revenue receipts, while other boards operate under an umbrella of a governing department that may regulate numerous professions. This hierarchy affects facets of regulation such as the ability to control revenue, budgets, and expenditures, and to determine the fate of applicants for licensure, licensees, and others implicated by the practice act. The legal implications of regulation depend on the hierarchy within a particular jurisdiction and change along the autonomous board–umbrella board continuum.

II. Definitions

Before embarking on the legal aspects of licensure policy, it is worthwhile to define various terms used throughout this chapter.

- *License:* A property right bestowed on an applicant by a regulatory board based on statutorily set criteria designed to assess and determine minimum competence to safely practice the particular profession. (It is assumed that one must possess such a license to lawfully practice the profession.)
- *Certification:* Private sector recognition of specialized skills of an individual based on set criteria established by the credentialing body. Private sector credentialing bodies are not accountable to the general public and can be created virtually by any person(s) or private entity(ies) or entities that chooses to establish such a body.
- *Registration:* The listing of individuals with a board or boards for the purpose of tracking or establishing a recordkeeping log of practitioners. Generally, few if any criteria exist for qualifying to register, and registration may or may not be a prerequisite to practice. In some jurisdictions, registration is synonymous with licensure, creating much confusion among regulators.

In this chapter, registration, as defined, will not be addressed. Discussion of the overall regulatory process will be confined to credentialing.

III. Public Protection

The very reason for the existence of a democratic government is to act or legislate on behalf of the people in a manner designed to best protect the public good. Thus, legislation is enacted and regulatory boards are created and empowered to function in a manner to protect the public. Public protection forms the foundation on which regulatory boards exist; without this goal, no form of governmental regulation is necessary, and legislation should not be promulgated. From a legal perspective, public protection must be emphasized as the primary reason for the existence of a board.

Conversely, private sector certification programs are established to provide a professional with an additional form of recognition which distinguishes this individual from others within the profession. Assuming a regulated profession in which licensure by a board is a prerequisite to practice, certification does not enhance nor create additional legal "rights" for the professional or obligations necessary for the professional to practice.

A major reason certification programs exist is to enhance the economic opportunities of the individual professional and provide benefits to the individual practitioner—not the public. Any public protection element to certification programs is incidental. As a result, the legal issues, parameters, and protections recognized by the judiciary through the interpretation of state and federal constitutions, statutes, and regulations as applied to private sector certifying entities are generally much less stringent than those applied to state and federal agencies. Courts are reluctant to interfere with the decision making of a private sector group involved in the certification process. Judicial decisions have determined that the denial or removal of certification is not an impediment to practice and, thus, not subject to heightened legal scrutiny and constitutional protections (*NCAA v. Tarkanian*, 1988; *San Juan v. American Board of Psychiatry and Neurology,* 1984).

Licensure, on the other hand, is a public process, legislatively created and a prerequisite to practice. Because a license is bestowed on an applicant by a public body—a board—the legal protections placed on the process are heightened and subject to rigid constitutional, statutory, and regulatory scrutiny (*Greenlee v. Board of Medicine of District of Columbia*, 1983). These substantive and procedural "due process" rights are strictly enforced by the judiciary based on legislative authority granted to a board including the right to: (1) deny an individual the right to enter the practice and (2) remove one's existing licensure rights and thus prohibit the right to practice in the profession.

When analyzing a board, its makeup, its purpose and how it fulfills its statutorily imposed duties and responsibilities, public protection must always be of primary consideration. Public protection is the impetus behind practice acts, which result in the heightened judicial scrutiny described above.

IV. Accountability

One simple step in assessing the legal implications of a credentialing system is to ask the question "To whom is the credentialing body accountable?" Boards, which are statutorily created to protect the public, are by definition accountable to the public. These boards are created by legislatures, duly elected and empowered to act on behalf of the people who make up their constituency. In contrast, certification entities are accountable to an entirely different population. Certification entities are internally accountable and are free to establish criteria determined to advance the interests of the certificate holder. Private sector certification has no primary public accountability, and as a result, the legal oversight of the certification process is far less stringent, based on the right conferred and the resulting legal analysis. Without public accountability, private sector programs are free to establish criteria and enforce programs free from the substantive due process requirements imposed on public sector licensure programs (*NCAA v. Tarkanian*, 1988).

V. Regulatory Boards

A. Mission

Regulatory boards are created and empowered through legislative action, the results of which are referred to as a *practice act*. These practice acts are adopted pursuant to the police powers reserved to the states by the 10th Amendment of the United States Constitution, by which states may regulate professions in the interest of protecting the public health, safety, and welfare.

In adopting a practice act, the legislature must determine that public protection is the most compelling reason for regulating the particular profession. In the interest of creating effective legislation, it is recommended that certain declarations and statement of purpose be incorporated into the practice act at the outset.

For example:

Section ___. Legislative Declaration

The practice of _____ in the state of _____ is declared a professional practice affecting the public health, safety, and welfare and is subject to regulation and control in the public interest. It is further declared to be a matter of public interest and concern that the practice of _____, as defined in the Act, merit and receive the confidence of the public and that only qualified persons be permitted to engage in the practice of _____ in this state. This Act shall be liberally construed to carry out these objectives and purposes.

Section ___. Statement of Purpose

It is the purpose of this Act to promote, preserve, and protect the public health, safety, and welfare by and through the effective control and regulation of the practice of _____; the licensure of _____, the license, control, and regulation of persons, in or out of this state, who practice _____ within this state.[1]

---

[1]This language constitutes the Legislative Declaration and Statement of Purpose of the Model Act of the National Association of Boards of Pharmacy (NABP) and the American Association of State Social Work Boards (AASSWB).

The legislative declaration and statement of purpose set forth the mission of a regulatory board. They also clearly define the legislative intent to create a system to regulate the profession in the interest of public protection. These provisions not only establish the mission of the board, but also help shape judicial interpretation through an analysis of this important language that can be cited to support board decisions in the event of a legal challenge. Unfortunately, a legislative declaration and statement of purpose are often conspicuously absent from practice acts.

B. Parameters of a Practice Act

While it is not the intent of this chapter to provide a detailed analysis of a model practice act and specific suggested language, a regulatory board and its mission cannot be discussed without an overview of a typical practice act. By its very nature, a practice act is enacted to prevent entry into the profession of any individual who does not possess and cannot substantiate qualifications. Thus, legislation of this type is intended to discriminate between qualified and unqualified persons based on criteria set forth in the act. These criteria or qualifications for licensure must be specified in detail to assure an effective practice act.

It must also be emphasized that the criteria or qualifications set forth to determine licensure eligibility are premised on minimum competence. A legislative determination must be made to set forth the threshold level of safe practice, not the heightened, specialized threshold of an advanced certification program. Practice acts address minimum competence to determine licensure eligibility. While certain advanced standing may be granted by the public sector in the form of an advanced license, this chapter addresses minimum competence.

The act should also specifically define the practice in order to establish what activities can be performed only by those licensed professionals and what activities fall within the regulatory scope of the board. It is essential that the practice be carefully defined, taking into consideration overlapping scopes of practice among related professions, effect of technological advancements, and location of the practitioner and recipient of services.

Practice acts must also contain language that grants the board broad authority to act in order to carry out its mission of regulation for public protection. This authority is necessary to provide the board with the ability to efficiently and effectively carry out its purpose. As part of its authority, the board must be granted the power to promulgate regulations necessary to provide specifics and expertise in refining the broad language contained in the enabling legislation.

Regulatory boards must also be provided with the authority to discipline licensees found to have engaged in wrongdoing or to have violated the practice act. The specific grounds for discipline should be enumerated in the act with certain "catch all" grounds to provide flexibility to the board in the event of unusual circumstances, which may confront boards from time to time.

As part of the authority to discipline, boards must be provided with the authority to summarily suspend the license of a practitioner. Summary suspension is the authority to summarily remove the license of a professional whose actions are so egregious as to render the practitioner an immediate threat to the public. A formal hearing must follow the suspension within a short period of time, usually 30 days. Summary suspensions can be invoked only under limited circumstances such as where there is imminent harm or imminent potential harm to the public.

Practice acts should also provide the board with the authority over unlicensed individuals who improperly engage in the practice. Under these circumstances, boards should be empowered to exercise disciplinary actions such as the issuance of cease-and-desist orders, fines, and assessment of costs (including attorneys' fees) against such unlicensed individuals. While practice of most professions without a license violates the criminal statutes of many jurisdictions, reliance on the already overburdened criminal justice system is not enough. The authority to initiate administrative action is essential under these circumstances if the board is to effectively carry out its purpose and substantiate its primary reason for existence—public protection.

Additionally, boards should be granted the authority to set standards of practice and adopt a code of ethics. A board may set the standards of practice through the promulgation of regulations to guide practitioners as to the expectations of practice. Standards of practice help the professional determine appropriate conduct and standards of care for continued licensure and the avoidance of disciplinary action. Delineated standards of practice also provide guidance to the current and future board members, who must interpret the act and regulations when deciding matters of licensure and discipline. Similarly, an adopted code of ethics provides guidance and definition to practitioners and board members as to accepted ethical behavior relative to the practice.

Furthermore, boards should be empowered to approve the required school(s) or program(s) recognized as a prerequisite to licensure. Customary to entry into a profession is graduation from an accredited school or program within the field. Approval of the school or program should be vested in the board, which is free to recognize those schools approved by the accrediting body within the profession. This two-step recognition process is essential to avoid improper delegation of authority from the legislature or board to an outside accrediting body. Delegation issues are discussed below.

C. Legal Principles

The policies and missions of a regulatory board are dictated by legal principles governing an analysis of legislative actions. Based on the enabling legislation, boards are empowered to carry out the intent of the legislation. Numerous legal principles thereafter guide the board in undertaking its mission.

1. Due Process

The 5th and 14th Amendments to the U.S. Constitution and similar sections of the state constitutions provide legal protections to applicants and licensees related to the licensure process. Individuals are entitled to "due process of law" before a board can take adverse action against one's license. These protections secure individuals against any arbitrary deprivation of rights relating to life, liberty, or property through governmental action. Due process protections are interpreted by the judiciary to exclude everything that is arbitrary and capricious in legislation affecting these rights of individuals. Notions of due process involve, simply stated, fairness. However, due process analysis also provides the basis for legal scrutiny of board activities and is incorporated into literally thousands of judicial opinions (*Greenlee v. Board of Medicine of District of Columbia*, 1983).

Specifically, due process issues are relevant to the application for licensure and disciplinary processes of a licensee undertaken by a board. Applicants for licensure must be afforded, at a minimum, procedural due process. Procedural due process involves an individual's right to reasonable notice and a right to be heard (*Brody v. Barasch*, 1990). Because an individual, upon application to the board, has yet to be conferred a license (property right), the due process requirements may be somewhat lessened. Should there be a denial of the application, procedural due process would likely call for an appeal avenue.

However, once a license is bestowed upon an applicant by the board, the license holder maintains a property right in the credential (*Aylward v. State Bd. of Chiropractic Examiners*, 1948). Before a board may suspend, remove, or limit that license for disciplinary reasons or render a fine, the licensee must be afforded substantive due process rights (*Greenlee v. Board of Medicine of District of Columbia,* 1983). Substantive due process rights afford the accused license holder the right to the following (*Gibson v. Barryhill,* 1973):

1. Notice of the proceedings with enough specificity to inform the licensee of the alleged wrongdoing
2. The right to defend
3. The right to participate in the proceedings including the right to present evidence, call witnesses, and confront and cross-examine witnesses
4. The right to be represented by counsel
5. The right to be heard before a fair and impartial tribunal
6. The right to an appeal.

These substantive due process rights are constitutionally mandated and specifically protect individuals against the deprivation of property rights without due process of law. These mandates provide the licensee with the necessary protections in the event of a legal challenge on a property right. Failure to adhere to these fundamental rights will likely result in judicial reversal of board's actions in the event of an appeal.

2. Vagueness

One legal theory used by licensees to challenge the practice act or a portion thereof is the "void for vagueness" argument. A statute violates the due process clauses of the United States or state constitutions on the basis of vagueness only if its terms are so ill defined that the ultimate decision as to its meaning rests on the opinions and whims of the trier of fact rather than any objective criteria or facts (*Snyderman v. Silverman,* 1998). While mathematical certainty is not required, a statute's terms must be explicit enough to serve as a guide to those who must comply with it.

The fact that a statute is susceptible to interpretation or misinterpretation does not render it unconstitutional. Nor does the fact that hypothetical situations could call into question some terms of the statute necessarily render it unconstitutional. Consequently, the verbiage used by the legislature, which necessarily sets policy for the regulatory board, must be carefully crafted, taking into consideration case law that addresses vagueness issues. Terms with commonly understood meanings such as "gross," "willful," "good moral character," "moral turpitude," and the like have been upheld as capable of meaningful understanding by professionals and are contained in many practice acts (*Abrahamson v. Illinois Dept. of Professional Regulation,* 1990; *Snyderman v. Silverman,* 1998).

3. Delegation

An additional legal theory of importance when analyzing policy of a regulatory board is the principle of delegation. The authority to enact laws is a sovereign power vested in the legislature and cannot be delegated to an administrative body or board. The legislature determines what the law should be, but the authority to execute the law may be delegated by the legislature to the regulatory board (*Douglas v. Noble,* 1923; *Gumbhir v. Kansas State Bd. of Pharmacy,* 1990). Legislatures must provide sufficient standards to guide the administrative body in the exercise of its functions. Absolute criteria, however, whereby every detail necessary in the enforcement of the law is anticipated need not be articulated by the legislature. Generally, the constitution merely requires that intelligible standards be set to guide the board empowered to enforce the law (*Douglas v. Noble,* 1923; *Snyderman v. Silverman,* 1998).

It has been held that to constitute a proper delegation of legislative authority from the legislature to a board, there must be three factors identified within the statute:

1. The persons or activities potentially subject to regulation
2. The harm sought to be prevented
3. The general means available to the administrator to permit the identified harm.

Practice acts that identify these three criteria will likely be lawful in delegating authority to the board to enforce these mandates.

Upon enactment of the practice act, the board defines the specific parameters of practice with more certainty through the adoption of regulations. Appropriately delegated authority granted from the legislature empowers the board to adopt regulations identifying these parameters. However, like the legislature, the board cannot delegate this authority to an outside entity, particularly a private entity, as that would constitute an improper delegation of authority (*Garces v. Dept. of Registration and Education,* 1969). For a board to avoid this peril, it should adopt those standards set forth from time to time by the private entity (on which the board is relying) as the standards of the board. This subtle distinction will avoid the argument of improper delegation by ensuring that the board is the decision maker, not the private entity.

For example, many professional education programs or schools are accredited by an independent, private entity whose mission is solely to assess educational achievements based on certain criteria. In social work, the accrediting body recognized by the United States Department of Education is the Council on Social Work

Education. To avoid an allegation of an improper delegation of authority, it is recommended that the practice act provide, as one criterion for licensure eligibility, graduation from a school or program "approved by the board," rather than "accredited by the Council on Social Work Education." Thereafter the board should formally adopt those standards set from time to time by the Council on Social Work Education and formally recognize the specific schools and programs, rather than recognizing "those schools and programs accredited by the Council on Social Work Education." From a legal perspective, this distinction will differentiate between an appropriate reliance on an outside private entity and an impermissible delegation of authority.

Regulatory boards must undertake their statutorily imposed duties with these legal principles in mind. The mission of a board is dictated by statutorily imposed mandates set by the legislature in the practice act. Such legislation, in and of itself, is premised on the needs of the general public. Public protection is the overriding consideration of all regulatory boards and constitutes the board's primary mission.

VI. Associations of Regulatory Boards

The regulatory board may also belong to an association of regulatory boards. Associations of regulatory boards have been incorporated in numerous professions. Membership in these associations consists of each of the individual state boards charged with regulating the profession. Generally, these associations do not provide for membership of an individual professional. Examples of these associations include the following:

> American Association of State Social Work Boards
> American Association of Veterinary State Boards
> Association of State and Provincial Psychology Boards
> Federation of State Medical Boards
> International Association of Boards of Examiners in Optometry
> International Association of Boards of Pharmacy
> National Council of State Boards of Nursing

It is critical to emphasize that the membership in these associations consists only of regulatory boards. Therefore, the mission statements and other objectives undertaken by these associations must be congruent with the mission statements and objectives of its membership, the regulatory boards.

A. Mission

Like regulatory boards themselves, an association of regulatory boards should adopt a mission statement in order to identify its general objective and purpose for existence. The mission statement identifies the goals and objectives of the association and, accordingly, identifies its membership by limiting eligibility to those whose activities fall within the mission statement.

The association must undertake an analysis of its intended membership in setting forth its mission statement. Associations whose membership consists of regulatory boards or public entities whose primary mission is public protection must maintain a consistent position with such membership.

First and foremost, it is recommended that the association adopt the protection of the public health, safety, and welfare as its primary purpose statement. Thereafter, additional objectives and criteria can be set forth outlining in general the goals to be achieved. An example of a mission statement is set forth below.[2]

The purpose of the Association is to aid state Boards in the protection of the public health and welfare by:

1. Facilitating communication and providing a forum for exchange of information and ideas among member boards concerning legal regulation of_____.
2. Encouraging and aiding collaborative efforts among member boards in developing compatible standards and cooperative procedures for the legal regulation of_____for the goal of simplifying and standardizing the licensing process.
3. Representing the opinions of the Association in serving to protect the public in those matters relating to the rendering of_____services through interaction with other_____organizations, legislative, judicial, regulatory, or executive governmental bodies in with other groups or associations whose areas of interest may coincide with those of member boards.
4. Providing assistance to member boards and for filling statutory, public, and ethical obligations in legal regulation enforcement.
5. Engaging in and encouraging research on matters related to legal regulation.

---

[2]From the Purpose and Mission Statement of the American Association of State Social Work Boards, a not-for-profit association recognized as exempt from taxation as a 501(c)(3) organization.

The mission statement and objectives of the association may be generally stated, while specific programs and other activities undertaken will specifically address the needs of its membership. As long as these activities fall within its stated purpose, the association will continue its operations and not legally jeopardize the ability of member boards to participate in the organization.

Associations of regulatory boards whose membership consists of public entities must maintain appropriate goals and objectives as their mission. Of first concern is the membership. Individual regulatory boards, as noted above, are statutorily created and can undertake activities only within the objectives set forth in the enabling legislation, the practice act. Regulatory boards that undertake activities outside these objectives are subject to legal scrutiny by the judiciary.

The consequences of legal scrutiny will likely result in invalidating these particular board activities as acts outside the scope of legal authority, referred to by the courts as *ultra vires* acts. On a larger scale, the board may endanger its own existence by questioning why it was legislatively created and empowered. Activities that are undertaken by the board that are outside the scope of its authority may lead to the legislative termination or disbanding of the board through the sunsetting process or otherwise. Without the board, public protection is threatened through the loss of the regulation of the profession.

Consistent with its mission statement, an association should limit its membership to the boards themselves. As such, the constitution and or bylaws of the association will limit its membership to *boards*, which may be defined as:

> The governmental agency empowered to credential and regulate the practice of_____in any of the states of United States of America, the District of Columbia, territories and insular possessions of United States of America, individual provinces of Canada and comparable entities.[3]

With an appropriately drafted clause, the association will limit its membership to regulatory boards and ensure that its policies and programs are set by public entities whose primary purpose is public protection.

Thereafter, "member boards," which make up the membership of the association, will be limited to boards as defined above. These member boards will comprise the delegate assembly and set the policies under which the association will operate. Based on the limited objectives and goals of the regulatory boards, the membership

---

[3]See footnote 2.

of the association will limit its policies and objectives to undertakings consistent with the boards' statutory responsibilities.

Associations of regulatory boards initiate and implement programs designed to assist and facilitate the public protection element of the regulatory boards. By providing expertise in various areas where boards may be lacking, the corroboration with similar state boards, as well as the strength in numbers, the association can provide enormous benefits to its membership. Associations of regulatory boards generally hold at least one annual delegate assembly whereby future policy is set forth and elections of leadership can take place. Associations may also hold educational assemblies to educate their membership on regulatory aspects impacting member boards. Examples of programs undertaken by associations include an examination program, disciplinary data bank, model legislation, compilation of statutes and regulations concerning the profession, practitioner data banks, licensure transfer clearinghouse, general publications, and board member training.

B. Examination Program

One of the most important services an association can provide for use by its member boards is a uniform examination program. The development of a psychometrically sound examination program is an expensive and time-consuming procedure. The independent development of examinations by individual member boards does not lend itself to uniform recognition of examination results from one jurisdiction to another. State-specific exams are also generally more vulnerable to attack based on the lack of resources and expertise available to a regulatory board.

While this chapter does not address exam development, it is worthy to note that associations undertake stringent procedures as part of the examination development process to ensure the validity and defensibility of its exam program. These procedures include a job analysis, exam blueprint development including content areas identified through the job analysis, item development, pretesting of items, psychometric analysis, and the establishment of a cut score to differentiate between successful and unsuccessful completion.

Because examinations are developed nationally yet administered locally, all member boards have a basis for relying on examination results in making licensure decisions. This uniformity provides public protection safeguards while providing practitioners with the ability to transfer exam scores from one state to another. Also, based on its relationship to the job analysis, as well as the established cut score, member boards are able to rely on examination results as an indicator of minimum competence to safely practice the profession irrespective of where the examination was administered.

Because of issues related to expertise as well as the volume of examinations administered, the association can economically provide examination services to its member boards. Regulatory boards are under strict fiscal constraints which would likely prohibit an independent development of a state-specific examination, even if such were desirable.

C. Disciplinary Data Bank

An association of regulatory boards also compiles a disciplinary data bank which maintains records relating to final adverse actions administratively taken against licensees. The information contained in the disciplinary data banks is public and contains enough data to inform additional member boards or other interested entities or individuals of the final adverse administrative action against a licensee. The primary purpose for maintaining a disciplinary data bank is to provide member boards with a one-source reference for checking the licensure status of an individual applying for licensure within their state. Through a simple process, a member board may query the data bank to determine whether the candidate for licensure has been disciplined in any other jurisdiction. Without a national disciplinary data bank maintained by the association, regulatory boards would have to query all other regulatory boards to determine whether any adverse actions exist.

D. Model Legislation

An additional service provided by the association to its member boards is the development of a model practice act to which member boards may refer when drafting or modifying the statutes and regulations within their jurisdictions. Model legislation generally fosters standards at the state level that are relatively uniform from jurisdiction to jurisdiction. Member boards are free to use any or all portions of the model act as it may relate to regulation of the profession within their state.

Associations may also develop model regulations, a code of conduct, a code of ethics, guidelines, and/or administrative procedures to assist member boards in carrying out their statutory duties to protect the public.

E. Compilation of Statutes and Regulations

An additional service provided by the association may be a compilation of the statutes and regulations of all member boards within the profession. Access to the compilations provides member boards with a source of information to compare the laws and regulations for improving the statutes regulating the profession within their jurisdictions. Associations provide these compilations as both hard copy and electronically.

F. Practitioner Date Banks

Associations of regulatory boards also compile data banks maintaining important information on all practitioners within the United States. Such data may include licensure information, licensure status, examination results, additional credentials, educational background, experience, or supervision. These manpower studies serve an important function by providing all member boards with access to relevant information necessary to determine licensure eligibility issues that promote public protection.

G. Licensure Transfer Clearinghouse

Based on the disciplinary data banks and practitioner data banks referenced above, the association may also maintain a licensure transfer clearinghouse whereby practitioners may request all relevant information necessary to reciprocate or endorse a license from one jurisdiction to another. The association, on behalf of its member boards and the practitioners themselves, can act as a conduit of data between member boards to facilitate information exchange and board determinations of licensure eligibility.

H. General Publications

Associations of regulatory boards routinely provide general publications to their membership as well as others in the form of licensure requirement compilations, candidate handbooks, study guides, board reference materials, training materials, sample forms, and many other forms of publications. Generally, these publications are provided free of charge to the membership and at nominal costs to others.

I. Board Member Training

Associations also provide training sessions to individuals who are newly appointed to serve on their state boards. These board member training sessions provide the necessary background to such individuals to familiarize them with state board activities in general including the impact of legal issues and relevant statutory applications such as the Americans with Disabilities Act. New board members are also provided with information regarding the association in order to take full advantage of access to materials and information. Training is also provided to board administrators.

It is through these programs that an association of regulatory boards provides much needed expertise, resources, and access to valuable information to its member boards. By accessing this information, regulatory boards are better equipped to regulate the profession pursuant to the practice act. In conjunction with one another, the association and its membership can meet the primary purpose and mission of regulation for the benefit of public protection.

VII. Tax Status of the Association

Of critical importance to the existence of an association of regulatory boards is its tax status or classification recognized by the Internal Revenue Service. To legally justify its existence and allow regulatory boards to participate as members, an association of regulatory boards must be a nonprofit organization as recognized under state law where incorporated. This nonprofit status provides benefits to the association at the state level and may also provide a mechanism for recognition of the association by the Internal Revenue Service as exempt from federal taxation. Additional potential benefits from a tax standpoint include exemption from state sales tax, certain retirement plan opportunities for employees, deductibility of contributed funds, and exemptions from real estate taxes. As these benefits are often vital to the maintenance of a membership consisting of regulatory boards, the association should seek status as an organization recognized as exempt from taxation by the Internal Revenue Service under section 501(c)(3) of the Internal Revenue Code (26 U.S.C.A § 501 (c)(3)).

A. 501(c)(3) Status

Section 501(c) of the Internal Revenue Code exempts from federal taxation certain organizations categorized by the Internal Revenue Service. Specifically, Section 501(c)(3) reads as follows:

> Corporations, and any community chest, fund, or foundation, organized and operated exclusively for religious, charitable, scientific, testing for public safety, literary, or educational purposes, or to foster national or international

amateur sports competition (but only if no part of its activities involve the provision of athletic facilities or equipment), or for the prevention of cruelty to children or animals, no part of the net earnings of which inures to the benefit of any private shareholder or individual, no substantial part of the activities of which is carrying on propaganda, or otherwise attempting , to influence legislation (except as otherwise provided in subsection h.), and which does not participate in, or intervene in (including the publishing or distributing of statements), any political campaign on behalf of or in opposition to any candidate for public office.

For purposes of analyzing the mission of an association of regulatory boards, it is important to focus on the terminology of section 501(c)(3), specifically references to "charitable" purposes. Judicial precedent concludes that activities undertaken by associations of regulatory boards are charitable as defined under section 501(c)(3) (*Virginia Professional Standards Review Foundation v. Blumenthal*, 1979). These opinions support the fact that organizations that provide a community benefit may be regarded as engaging in charitable activities. As stated by one court:

> Charitable or educational activities will almost invariably promote the esteem of members of organizations that engage in such activities. Presumably, individuals involved with such well-recognized charitable activities such as the United Way, the American Cancer Society, or various church-related activities, gain esteem in the eyes of the community, and it may well be that some of them participate more because of the prestige or esteem they derive from the activity than because they're motivated to assist unfortunates. Yet the charitable nature of such activities is not seriously in question merely because of that intangible benefit. (*Virginia Professional Standards Review Foundation v. Blumenthal*, 1979)

Case law also supports the fact that organizations established in response to duly enacted legislation, and that provide services to meet the needs set forth in such laws, constitute charitable activities (*Virginia Professional Standards Review Foundation v. Blumenthal*, 1979). In short, such organizations obviate or minimize the need for governmental intervention or expenditure of resources in the respective area of concern. As recognized by the judiciary, such activities "lessen burdens" on government and are, thus, deemed charitable (*Virginia Professional Standards Review Foundation v. Blumenthal*, 1979).

The activities undertaken by associations of regulatory boards fill a void in the licensure process by providing services and/or products not otherwise easily obtainable by the member boards. Associations with examination programs provide a psychometrically sound, defensible examination to their member boards to assist such boards in determining minimum competence for licensure eligibility of applicants. Individual member boards do not have the expertise nor financial wherewithal to independently prepare a defensible examination program. Also, the uniformity of examinations among states provides an assessment mechanism to regulatory boards for determining licensure eligibility through licensure transfer, referred to as *endorsement* or *reciprocity*.

While the programs provided by these associations of regulatory boards may also incidentally benefit individual practitioners, such benefits are ancillary to the mission and purpose of the association. These ancillary benefits do not provide a legal basis to render the association ineligible for 501(c)(3) status (*Virginia Professional Standards Review Foundation v. Blumenthal*, 1979). Of course, should the association modify its mission or provide services that primarily affect the individual practitioner or the economics of the profession, such activities may adversely impact its 501(c)(3) classification.

B. 501(c)(6) Status

Section 501(c)(6) of the internal revenue code exempts from taxation the following (26 U.S.C.A § 501(c)(6):

> business leagues, chambers of commerce, real estate boards, boards of trade, or professional football leagues (whether or not administering a pension fund for football players), not organized for-profit in no part of the net earnings of which inures to the benefit of any private shareholder or individual.

Perhaps due to strict scrutiny by the IRS, certain associations of regulatory boards maintain a tax status classification as a 501(c)(6) organization. The application process for a 501(c)(6) organization is simplified and is not as closely examined as the application process for 501(c)(3) status. However, maintaining classification as a 501(c)(6) entity may jeopardize the very existence of an association of regulatory boards.

As discussed above, associations of regulatory boards maintain as their membership only statutorily created boards that are empowered to carry out the mandates of the legislatively adopted practice act. The activities of the individual boards are limited to those powers granted by the legislatures. These limitations provide a check-and-balance from a legal perspective as well as maintaining the mission of public protection for which all such legislation exists.

Because of these severe limitations placed on the activities that may be undertaken by a board, participation in an association of regulatory boards will also be subject to such limitations. Organizations classified as exempt from taxation under 501(c)(6) of the Internal Revenue Code are free to undertake activities that individual member boards could not undertake based on their status as a governmental agency. Based on this potential to deviate from the public protection element as the primary purpose, and irrespective of whether the association provides limitations in its mission, regulatory boards would likely be prohibited from membership in section 501(c)(6) entities based on a legal analysis.

This conclusion is based on the fact that a 501(c)(6) entity may, under its tax classification, undertake activities that would clearly violate the authority granted to a regulatory board in its enabling legislation. These activities include lobbying efforts and other programs primarily designed to impact the economics of the profession. While the bylaws may not currently allow for the development of such programs, there is no legal prohibition from modifying the mission if the membership should so dictate. This fact alone provides a legal justification for ineligibility of regulatory boards in any 501(c)(6) organization.

Primarily, the membership of section 501(c)(6) organizations consists of individual professionals or practitioners. Consequently, the fundamental goal of such organizations is to enhance and promote the economic benefits of the professional, an activity that cannot otherwise be undertaken by regulatory boards. Examples of certain section 501(c)(6) organizations include the American Medical Association, the American Dental Association, and the American Bar Association. While an incidental consideration, public protection does not comprise a primary purpose of 501(c)(6) organizations.

The mission statement, makeup of membership, as well as the tax status recognition of associations of regulatory boards are vital to the continued existence of these organizations. It can, therefore, be argued that regulatory boards are legally prohibited from membership in any association other than those classified as 501(c)(3) by the IRS.

VIII. Conclusion

The mission and goals of both regulatory boards and associations of regulatory boards encompass public protection as their primary purpose. Through a cooperative effort of regulatory boards from differing jurisdictions, associations can be incorporated which provide benefits to the member boards. By joining forces, individual state regulatory boards can, through the association, accumulate resources and valuable information to assist in fulfilling their statutory mandates. The association must maintain its mission and goals consistent with the mandates of its membership. Overall, the association provides a uniform perspective on regulation, including access to relevant information, while maintaining the rights of each individual state to locally regulate under the police powers granted by the United States Constitution. This freedom allows each state to legislate in a manner that takes into consideration the nuances of their individual jurisdictions. However, the access to information and programs via the association provides valuable services to regulatory boards that would otherwise not be available. This access to information and flexibility to accept or modify programs also coincides with the legal concepts of delegation and allows for each jurisdiction to customize participation to the extent deemed necessary and appropriate. Associations of regulatory boards are encouraged to continue to develop services and programs to assist member boards in furthering public protection interests while legally regulating the professions.

References

Abrahamson v Illinois Dept. of Professional Regulation, 606 N.E.2d 1111 (1990).
Aylward v. State Bd. of Chiropractic Examiners, 192 P.2d 929 (1948).
Brody v. Barasch, 582 A.2d 132 (1990).
Dent v. State of West Virginia, 129 U.S. 114, 9 S.Ct. 231 (1889).
Douglas v. Noble, 261 U.S. 165 (1923).
Gibson v. Barryhill, 411 U.S. 564 (1973).
Greenlee v. Board of Medicine of District of Columbia, 813 F. Supp. 48 (1983).
Gumbhir v. Kansas State Bd. of Pharmacy, 618 P.2d 837 (1990)
Mississippi State Board of Nursing v. Wilson, 624 So.2nd 486 (1993).
NCAA v. Tarkanian, 488 U.S. 179 (1988).
San Juan v. American Board of Psychiatry and Neurology, 40 F.3d 247 (7th Cir. 1984).
Snyderman v. Silverman, 701 N.E.2d 791 (Ill. App. 4 Dist. 1998).
Virginia Professional Standards Review Foundation v. Blumenthal, 466 F. Supp. 1164
    (1979).

7

The Role that Licensure Plays in Society

Benjamin Shimberg

The Chauncey Group International, Lawrenceville, New Jersey, and Citizen Advocacy Center, Washington, D.C.

The credentialing system in the United States and Canada is based on the premise that the general public lacks the information and expertise necessary to determine by itself which practitioners in certain occupations and professions have the necessary qualifications and character to provide competent and trustworthy services. Over time, two principal credentialing systems have evolved. One of them (licensure) is based on governmental action. The other (certification) is based on voluntary action by nongovernmental organizations, such as professional societies.

I. Licensure and Certification Defined

Governmentally sanctioned credentialing is called *licensure* and is based on the legal concept of the police power of the state. This power holds that the state has the right to pass laws and to take such other actions, as it may deem necessary to protect the health, safety and welfare of its citizens. Once a governmental body, such as a state legislature, has passed a licensure law, it becomes illegal for any individual who is not licensed by the state to engage in the activities of the licensed occupation. Violators are subject to fines and/or imprisonment.

The nongovernmental approach, usually referred to as *certification*, is based on the voluntary action on the part of an occupational or professional group to institute a system by which it can grant recognition to those practitioners who have met some stated level of training and experience. Such individuals are granted a certificate or diploma attesting to the fact that they have met the standards of the credentialing organization and are entitled to make the public aware of their credentialed status. Violators cannot be prosecuted for practicing without certification, since there is no specific law covering voluntary certification. In some instances, the certification agency may copyright its symbol, thereby enabling it to prosecute violators for unauthorized use of the protected symbol. However, adverse publicity and other forms of peer pressure are usually sufficient to discourage a noncertified practitioner from making unwarranted claims about his or her certified status.

To further clarify each of these credentialing strategies, it is useful to discuss each one from its historical perspective.

II. Some Historical Perspective on Licensure

Licensing in the United States emerged in the aftermath of Jacksonian democracy, when virtually all forms of occupational regulation were scrapped in the belief that there was something inherently undemocratic in placing restrictions on how a person could earn his or her livelihood. One result of such deregulation was the emergence of diploma mills, which granted papers (diplomas), to individuals with little or no training in such professional fields as medicine and dentistry. The proliferation of these untrained and unqualified physicians disturbed the physicians who had been trained at the more traditional institutions of higher learning, such as Harvard or Johns Hopkins. These traditionally trained doctors considered the "diploma mill" graduates not only as unqualified interlopers, but also as a menace to the public.

In an initial attempt to set themselves apart from those they considered to be "quacks" and charlatans, the traditionally trained doctors established local and state medical societies and set admission standards, which effectively excluded those who had not received training at recognized (traditional) medical schools. These medical societies adopted strict codes of conduct and standards of practice so that any member of a medical society who failed to adhere to those standards could be ejected from the society. The public was advised that if they wanted a qualified physician, they would do well to restrict their choices to members of the medical society. To do otherwise was to risk choosing a poorly-trained "diploma mill" graduate, who could not qualify for membership in the medical society, or someone who had been kicked out of the society for ethical lapses or perhaps for failure to adhere to practice standards.

While the medical society "seal of approval" gave the public useful information about who the "good guys" were, it failed to do anything about getting rid of the "bad guys," who were still out there offering their services to the public and making all sorts of undocumented claims about their qualifications and miracle cures. In desperation, leaders of the state medical societies appealed to their state legislators for help. They argued that the unqualified doctors were a menace to society and that they should be prevented from practicing. Compliant legislators invoked the doctrine of the police power of the state to justify licensure as the most practical way to safeguard the health, safety, and welfare of the citizenry.

A. Origin of Self-Regulatory Boards

Since the legislators who had passed the laws realized they lacked the knowledge and experience to set entry qualifications, practice standards, or ethical guidelines called for by the law, they decided to create boards made up of physicians to implement the law. To the legislators, it seemed only logical that the best persons to implement the law would be the leaders of the state medical societies, who had been the main advocates for the law in the first place. Indeed, many early licensing laws stipulated that board appointments—to be made by the governor—were to be drawn from lists of candidates nominated by the medical society. Thus was born the tradition of professional self-regulation—a tradition that would later give rise to many of the problems that were to beset licensing boards over most of the century.

Boards were given the power not only to set entry qualifications and test applicants, but also to decide on practice standards and what constituted acceptable conduct. They were given the power to adopt rules and regulations that would have the force of law. They could also conduct investigations of complaints against licensed physicians and hold disciplinary hearings to determine whether or not a licensee had violated any of the board's rules and regulations. Those who were found guilty could be disciplined with such sanctions as monetary fines, restrictions on their practice, and, as a last resort, the suspension or revocation of their right to practice altogether.

In entrusting boards with such extraordinary powers, legislators were counting on board members to use them exclusively in the public interest; that is, to make sure that only qualified individuals were granted licenses and that incompetent or dishonest practitioners would be removed, so that the public would not be harmed. They clearly did not intend these powers to be used to promote the economic interests of the licensed profession. From this, it should be clear that the primary mission every licensing board must focus on public protection, not on serving the interests of the occupational or professional group.

B. Origins of Certification

The origin of certification is far less dramatic. Certification grew out of a desire by a group of ophthalmologists (already licensed as physicians) to set themselves apart from other physicians, who also had a legal right to diagnose and treat diseases of the eye and to prescribe eyeglasses where appropriate. The ophthalmologists wanted to make it clear to the public that they had been specially trained in care of the eyes and, thus, were better equipped than general practitioners to provide eye-care services.

To make a convincing case as to their superiority, the ophthalmologists decided to establish a national board to certify physicians who had met specified standards of training and experience and who had passed a rigorous qualifying examination. Those who met these standards were awarded diplomas and had the right to display the diploma as evidence that they had demonstrated a high level of competence in this area of medical practice. In following years, many other physician groups followed this pattern. Today there are 24 such medical boards that grant diplomas to individuals who can meet their standards. These boards operate under the aegis of the American Boards of Medical Specialties located in Evanston, Illinois.

The term *certification* began to lose its special meaning—connoting excellence in a specialty area—when a number of allied health associations mounted an effort to gain licensure for their members in the belief that licensure would facilitate their eligibility for reimbursement by Medicare and by private insurance companies. The insurance companies knowingly or unknowingly encouraged this trend by adopting the position that licensure was evidence of competence, hence justifying their refusal to pay for services by unlicensed providers. The mounting pressure to attain licensure became so great during the early 1970s that the Federal Department of Health, Education and Welfare [now the Department of Health and Human Services] called for a moratorium on the further licensing of allied health workers.

At about the time that the moratorium went into effect, some of the leaders of allied health groups began to consider certification as an alternative. These groups were finding that getting licensed by 50 different state legislatures required enormous effort and considerable funds to build grass-roots support to promote their case.

While still seeking licensure, a number of groups decided to establish national certification programs, which required no legislative action. It was usually the professional association representing various allied health groups that became the sponsors and major proponents of certification programs. Since they wanted the standards to be comparable to those they had incorporated in their licensing proposals, the qualifications and examinations were pitched at the minimum competency level.

III. Public Understanding

A. Some Sources of Confusion Regarding Certification

The proliferation of certification programs did nothing to reduce the public's confusion about the meaning of certification. Nobody could be sure what certification stood for. Did it connote excellence or did it convey only assurance of minimum competence?

One additional factor served to further confuse the issue. In considering requests for licensure, state legislators had come to the conclusion that not all groups seeking licensure merited such rigid controls because even the practice by incompetents was not too likely to result in serious or irreparable harm to the health, safety, or welfare of the public. As an alternative to licensure, legislators proposed an approach called *statutory certification*, by which they really meant *title control*. In short, for occupations not posing a serious threat to the public, those who met certain standards would be allowed to use a protected title. The certification process was quite similar to that used for licensure. Applicants had to show that they had the requisite training and experience and pass a test of competency.

However, unlike licensing, noncertified individuals would still be allowed to practice, but could not use the *protected* title. Suppose, for example, a state passed a law certifying auto mechanics. Anyone in the state could still work as an auto mechanic, but only those who had met the requirements of a state agency could advertise themselves as certified auto mechanics.

The confusion and ambiguities surrounding the term *certification* have limited the usefulness of this term as a guide for consumers. The general public, not familiar with the nuances among the various types of certification, could never be sure if the certificate represented *excellence*—as in the case of those recognized by the American Board of Medical Specialties or if it represented *minimum competency*—as in the case of statutory certification and certification by most of the allied health groups.

B. Caution Advised in Interpreting *Certification*

Since most certification is voluntary, the public should be cautioned not to view certification in absolute terms. When there is no legal requirement that an individual must be certified in order to engage in the practice of an occupation or profession, it is quite likely that some practitioners may elect, for personal reasons, not to sit for the certification exams. Indeed, some practitioners who are not certified may, in fact, have competence equal to or greater than that of some certificate holders. Thus, there is no easy or dependable way for the public to be sure of a noncertified practitioner's level of competence. Being certified may be considered a positive indicator, but not being certified is not necessarily a negative one.

Given the importance of certification as a way of helping consumers make informed decisions regarding the qualifications of various service providers, it follows that the primary mission of the certification agency is to ensure the integrity of the certificate it issues. Boards also have an obligation to educate the public as to the meaning of the credential. Moreover, it must be sure that all those who hold themselves out to the public as certified are qualified to provide the services covered by the credential and that they are committed to doing so in an honest and ethical manner.

IV. Social Consequences of Occupational Regulation

In theory, licensing may have seemed like a good way of rectifying market failure occasioned by a lack of adequate information upon which consumers could base judgments about the competence of service providers or, even more serious, by the lack of any constraints on the practice of occupation—with the potential for danger to the health, safety, and welfare of the public—by individuals without the training and experience to perform in a safe and effective manner.

However, the manner in which licensure has functioned over the past century raises questions about how well it has actually served the public. Some would argue that the cure was worse than the condition it was supposed to ameliorate.

Much of the criticism of licensure is unfair because the sins of the few have been generalized and used to condemn the good works of the many. However, anyone seeking to understand occupational and professional licensure at the end of the 20th century must be cognizant of the abuses that have occurred, especially in situations when licensing boards have lost sight of their primary mission—that of protecting the public.

What follows are some of the perceived shortcomings of the licensure system—past and present.

A. Once Licensed, Forever Competent

As licensure programs developed, those seeking the credential had to undergo rigorous scrutiny to establish with the licensing board that their training and experience met the board's standards and that they could pass a qualifying examination given by the board. However, once the practitioners had been licensed, they were not required to pass any further exams to demonstrate that they had maintained their competence and had kept abreast of developments in their field. Nor were they required to prove that they were still in good health and fully capable of performing the critical activities required of practitioners in the occupation or profession. The motto of the licensing community seemed to be "Once Licensed, Forever Competent."

While such an attitude may have seemed appropriate in an earlier era, when the pace of technological change was slow, it seems strangely out of place today, when new knowledge keeps coming onto the professional scene at an ever-increasing pace. As far back as 1967, the National Advisory Committee on Health Manpower, established by the Department of Health, Education and Welfare, issued a report voicing concern about the dangers of medical obsolescence. The report recommended that all physicians be reexamined periodically to assure their continued competence. While the Committee favored reexamination as the best approach for assuring continued competence, it left the door open to alternative strategies, including mandatory continuing education.

Medical societies across the nation reacted negatively to the idea of reexamination, which they perceived as a threat to their members. They seized on the proposed alternative, mandatory continuing education (CE), as much less threatening—something their members could live with.

No one is likely to argue that some form of continuing education is not essential for professionals who want to keep abreast of developments in their field and who wish to enhance their skills to better serve their patients. Unfortunately, there is little evidence to support the argument that taking CE courses necessarily assures continued competence. Nevertheless, during the 1960s and into the 1970s, state after state adopted mandatory CE laws and that trend continues into the present.

Critics of mandatory CE point out that most states that require CE do not require that there be a relationship between courses taken and practice areas in which the licensee may be weak. They note that licensees may satisfy the CE requirement by taking almost any course approved by the board, even if it bears no relationship to the licensees' areas of weakness. Indeed, some of the most popular courses relate to the business aspects of the licensee's practice, not necessarily to the clinical aspects.

Recently, a reversal of the trend toward the use of mandatory education as a way of assuring continued competence occurred in the state of Colorado, where the Medical Board and the Nursing Board revoked their mandatory CE requirement, with the observation that there was no evidence of a relationship between courses taken and the competence of licensees in these fields.

The fact remains that in the 30 years since calls for ways of assuring the continued competence of physicians and other health care professionals were heard, no consensus has emerged as to the meaning of *competence* or ways to asses it. Proposals to reexamine all licensees periodically have been offered but have been quickly rejected as wasteful of resources and unlikely to be productive as a way of ferreting out the truly incompetent physicians. The Federation of State Medical Boards has proposed that questions be asked on all license renewal forms that would trigger appropriate follow-up action for physicians who may be in need of refresher training or closer scrutiny for possible health or drug-related problems. Many states have adopted the Federation's recommendations, but recently, some physicians have challenged the right of boards to ask such questions as an invasion of their privacy under the Americans with Disabilities Act.

The seriousness of this problem may be seen in a 1998 report by the Task Force on Health Care Workforce Regulation of the Pew Health Professions Commission. The recommendation reads as follows:

> States should require that their regulated health care practitioners demonstrate their competence in the knowledge, judgment, technical skills, and interpersonal skills relevant to their jobs throughout their careers.

The Pew report discusses this issue in great detail and offers a number of suggestions for dealing with the topic. Any health board member who takes his or her job seriously will find the Pew report a gold mine of information and ideas. It should be on every board member's "must read" list. The report will help board members and others understand by defining what is meant by "competency." Developing ways of assessing competency is probably the most critical issue facing the licensing community.

B. Misuse of Board Powers

Self-regulatory boards have been called a source of many problems over the past century. The problems stem, in large measure, from the conflicts of interest inherent in boards made up entirely or even predominantly of members drawn from the regulated occupation or profession.

To fulfill their assigned mission, board members are sworn to use their regulatory powers exclusively in the public interest—that is to protect the public from incompetent, unethical, or dishonest practitioners. That is the basis on which legislators are supposed to vote when making decisions as to the need for licensure. It was with this goal in mind that legislators gave boards broad power to adopt rules and regulations—that would have the force of law—to ensure that the purpose of the regulatory law would be carried out.

However, being appointed to a board does not work a miraculous change in the individual who is appointed. In all likelihood, the appointee continues to work in his or her occupation or profession and continues to hold on to the values associated with that profession. If the licensee has been active in the professional society, it is highly likely that he or she has interiorized the goals and values of the association. Those goals have much more to do with advancing the image and the economic benefits of the profession than they do with promoting the public interest. Indeed, committed leaders in professional societies are likely to believe that "what's good for the profession is also good for the general public."

Once legislators had decided to adopt the self-regulatory model for medical boards and given these boards broad powers, other occupational groups asked that they, too, be licensed. To move a licensure law through a state legislature is no easy task. It takes money to pay for the services of professional lobbyists, and it takes a great deal of effort to mobilize members at the grass-roots level to lobby their own legislators on behalf of the proposed law. It is hard to believe that professional groups would go to so much trouble—raising money and building grass-roots support—just for the sake of protecting the public. It's only reasonable to ask, "What's in it for them?"

It is worth recalling some of the powers that the legislators entrusted to the boards they had created; namely, the power to

- Set education, training and experience requirements,
- Prepare (or contract for) examinations and set the passing score,
- Define what constitutes acceptable practice,
- Define ethical conduct,
- Investigate complaints,
- Monitor compliance with the board's rules and regulations,
- Conduct investigations and to hold hearings, and
- Impose sanctions, including suspension or revocation of the right to practice.

These regulatory powers were an incentive to other groups to decide that gaining licensed status might provide economic as well as social benefits for their members. They realized that having the power to set entry requirements would enable an occupational group to limit the number of practitioners within a specified geographical area. If there were too many practitioners to supply the needed services, some might be tempted to charge less in order to get the available business. In an unregulated market, the law of supply and demand dictates that prices will be forced downwards as the result of competition. The obvious solution is to restrict competition. Licensing provided precisely the vehicle for accomplishing this goal. Once a group had achieved licensed status, the board could raise entry requirements and/or make the examinations more difficult so that fewer applicants would qualify for licensure. This would have the effect of reducing the supply and thereby reducing competitive pressures within the occupational group. Less competition would enable those practitioners who were licensed to charge higher prices for their services.

This may sound like a diabolical plot, but it makes perfect sense for leaders of occupational and professional groups, who are charged with promoting the interest of their members, to take advantage of any legal mechanisms that will accomplish their purpose. If doctors can have their own regulatory board, why not barbers, plumbers, and optometrists? In order to make the case for licensure, a group had to make a case to the legislature that the unregulated practice of an occupation or profession constituted a threat to the health, safety, or welfare of the public. Barbers were able to argue that lack of adequate sanitation could result in the spread of diseases of the scalp, that incompetent plumbers could contaminate a home's potable water supply, that unqualified optometrists might prescribe the wrong eyeglass prescription or fail to recognize diseases of the eye to the detriment of the patient's health.

Suffice to say that almost any group that was determined to achieve licensed status could do so, if it was willing to invest in the requisite level of lobbying and political gamesmanship. Indeed, the proliferation of licensing during the 1960s and 1970s caused so much concern among governmental agencies, notably the Federal Department of Health, Education and Welfare, that state legislators were asked to declare a moratorium on the licensing of new health occupations until the impact of such new licensing on healthcare costs and services could be determined.

The social costs of licensing were forcefully called to the public attention when the Federal Trade Commission publicized its research findings on the impact of licensing on a variety of consumer goods and services. Among it most dramatic findings were the following:

> *Pharmacy boards* across the nation were prohibiting pharmacies from advertising the cost of prescription drugs by characterizing such advertising as "unprofessional conduct." Violators were subject to sanctions by the board.
>
> In this way, consumers were prevented from finding out that, in many cases, they could purchase the identical drug at a chain pharmacy at a substantially lower price than they were currently paying at their neighborhood pharmacy.
>
> *Opticianry boards* followed a similar pattern, making it unethical for opticians to advertise the price of eyeglasses.
>
> Boards that licensed funeral directors prohibited licensees from quoting the prices of funeral services over the phone, making it difficult for consumers to do comparison shopping when faced with the need to make funeral arrangements for a loved one.
>
> *Architects* were prohibited from engaging in competitive bidding on the grounds that there was no way for the consumer to be sure that the bids covered identical services.
>
> *Lawyers* who are licensed by the state bar were also prohibited from advertising the price of services, such as drawing up a will or handling an uncontested divorce application.

Most of these abuses were subsequently declared unconstitutional by the U.S. Supreme Court on the grounds that they represented an illegal restriction on truthful speech. The court held that existing laws already prohibited untruthful and deceptive advertising and that boards had no authority to infringe on truthful advertising.

In this connection, it is worth noting that boards that adopted such anticompetitive rules were clearly abusing their regulatory powers. By no reasonable stretch of the imagination could such rules be construed as serving the public interest. Clearly, the board members who approved such Rules had lost sight of their basic mission of protecting the public. Instead, they were using their powers to advance the economic interests of themselves and of fellow practitioners.

The public disclosure of the extent to which certain boards had engaged in these and other anticompetitive practices brought much discredit to the institution of licensure. From being perceived as consumer protection agencies, boards were reviled as tools of the occupational groups they were supposed to regulate. Many conscientious, hardworking boards members expressed great bitterness over the cloud that these disclosures cast over the entire regulatory landscape. One hoped-for benefit, however, is the possibility that in the future board members will examine, critically, proposals emanating from industry sources. For example, certain groups (e.g., cosmetologists) often seek to increase the length of schooling required for licensure. Such requests usually come from school owners, who stand to benefit from the higher tuition and from fees paid by clients who obtain hair care services from students at the school. Board members should ask the proponents of such proposals to justify the need for more training. *More* is not necessarily *better*. Unless they are convinced that the existing requirements are clearly inadequate, they should be cautious about increasing the current requirement. One thing is certain: if students are required to spend more hours in schooling, the cost of hair care services is very likely to increase. Will the consumer necessarily benefit from the additional training for which he or she is being charged a higher fee? That's the sort of questions board members should be asking whenever new regulatory changes are proposed. To do otherwise would represent a betrayal of their primary mission and, in the long run, the likelihood of bringing further discredit on the entire institution of licensure.

C. Failure of Boards to Enforce Practice and Conduct

Although licensing boards generally conduct their business "in the sunshine," that is, at meetings that are open to the public, it is rare for the public or the press to attend or to report on what went on unless, of course, the board is dealing with a sensational case that has attracted public attention. Lobbyists from the regulated group may be present, but not the public. This means that the public is unaware of the extent to which boards are disciplining licensees who have been charged with incompetence or unprofessional conduct. It may, therefore, come as a shock when investigative reporters publish stories about how boards have failed to take disciplinary action against "dangerous doctors" or other professionals who may bring discredit on their professions for failing to adhere to standards of practice or conduct required by the board.

The Federation of State Medical Boards, the umbrella organization to which all state boards belong, reports that the number of disciplinary actions against doctors has been increasing steadily in recent years. This sounds like good news. Unfortunately, disciplinary actions showing the greatest increase have nothing to do with a physician's competence, but a great deal to do with such matters as Medicaid fraud, sexual abuse of patients, or unlawful diversion of narcotics and other controlled substances.

How is one to explain the lack of zeal on the part of boards to fulfill their disciplinary responsibilities? Lack of adequate resources to conduct thorough investigation may be part of the answer, but a more likely one is the fact that board members do not have much stomach for the onerous task of disciplining fellow practitioners. They know that finding a doctor, dentist, or other licensee guilty of serious charges may have unfortunate consequences for the individuals involved. It could mean the send of his or her career. This is known as the "There, but for the grace of God go I" syndrome. Another factor may reflect the ability of those charged with serious violations to hire the best available legal talent and the ability of defendants to spend as much as it takes to avoid the loss of his or her license to practice. Boards are often advised by their own attorneys not to get involved in civil lawsuits involving licensees who appeal a board's decision, because such suits may put a heavy strain on the board's limited resources. Under such circumstances, one can sympathize with the board member who may feel trapped between the desire to do the right thing (i.e., take disciplinary action) and the awareness that the board lacks the resources to win what is likely to be an unequal contest.

V. Building Better Boards

A. Understanding the Role of a Board Member

From the foregoing, it should be evident that good board members, whether drawn from the public or from the occupational group, are not born to the role but get that way as the result of proper orientation, education, and experience.

Most members of a regulated group know little about the nature of the regulatory process beyond what they, themselves, may have experienced when they were licensed, probably many years ago. If they have been involved in the governance of their trade or professional association, they may have some understanding of the role that the regulatory board plays in setting ground rules for their group. They may have participated in discussions, which leave them with some sense of how regulatory changes might further enhance the status and economic well-being of the group. When they are appointed to serve on the board that regulates their profession, there may be an understandable tendency to surmise that the board's major function is to look out for the interests of the regulated group. Protecting the public interest is *not* a concept that comes naturally. A board member is more likely to think, *After all, we are just a bunch of hardworking stiffs trying to earn a living; it's ridiculous to think that the public needs protection from us.*

The new board member from the occupational group needs to learn that as a board member his or her responsibility must be to the public, not to the group from whence he or she came. That concept may take time to sink in. Members of various occupational and professional groups have been heard to refer to the regulatory board as "our board" as if to let others know that it was their money and their efforts that made the board a reality. And, by their attitude, they imply that the board exists to serve the interests of the group. Why else would we have worked so hard to pass the needed legislation? The notion that the mission of the board is to protect the public may not come readily to someone accustomed to thinking another way.

The new public member may also have difficulty grasping what he or she is supposed to do as a board member. Some may seek such an appointment because they have a private or personal agenda to pursue, such as the frustrated builder who could not pass the architectural licensing exam. This member of a California board acknowledged that he actively sought the appointment because he wanted to inject some realism into the board's screening process. After all, he had built dozens of homes and commercial buildings and had frequently advised architects on ways to improve their designs. How could the board fail to recognize his qualifications? As a member he would do his darndest to make sure that such discrimination was eliminated. Needless to say, this board member was a disruptive force throughout his term.

Fortunately, most public member appointees do not carry such baggage. However, their lack of a personal agenda does not automatically qualify them to be an effective board member. Most public member appointees do not have the foggiest notion of what they are supposed to do. Are they on the board to serve a sounding board and to express what they believe to be consumer concerns or are they there to serve as watchdogs to make sure that the occupational members on the board do not try to put something over on the public? From the earliest conception of having public members serve on boards, their role has never been clearly delineated, and this has been the cause of many problems. For example, should they vote on disciplinary matters? Should they be involved in standard setting? What role, if any, should they play in the examination process?

B. Selection of Board Members

Clearly, the board-building process must begin with the selection of potential members. While professional and trade associations can usually provide helpful input, it is probably not a good idea to allow them to dominate the process as if they own the board and can dictate who will serve. Such appointments leave the door wide open for the occupational group to use the licensing board to serve its own purposes. Unfortunately, and all too often, board appointments are made as a form of patronage, thanks to financial or political support during a campaign. While this approach is deeply entrenched in the American political psyche, other approaches have been tried. For example, several years ago Governor (now U.S. Senator) Graham of Florida invited citizens of the state to nominate professionals who they felt would make good licensing board members. The Governor also invited interested professionals to nominate themselves and to explain whey they thought they should be appointed. After a screening board had culled the list, the Governor personally interviewed the finalists in order to ascertain their views on a number of regulatory issues of concern.

No matter how board members are chosen, it is critical that they receive a thorough orientation regarding their roles and responsibilities. This is the time to disabuse occupational members of the notion that they are on the board to look after the interests of the occupational group. It is the time to reinforce the concept that all board members are there to protect the public and to make sure that all consumers receive competent and trustworthy services. When asked what types of information they need to do their jobs, board members are quite specific regarding what they would find most helpful. The following topics are drawn from two studies, one conducted by the Council on Licensure, Enforcement and Regulation (CLEAR) and the other by the American Association of Retired Persons (AARP). While neither survey purports to be completely scientific, they nevertheless provide useful insights into what board members feel they need to know.

The CLEAR survey, which was directed at members of health boards, yielded the following results:

- The public significance of the board's functions
- Leadership skills
- Topical issues confronting health professionals
- Regulation and access to quality health care

The AARP survey, restricted to public members, yielded the following list of "needs":

- What it means to be an effective public member
- The roles and responsibilities pubic members have that are different from those of professional members
- Greater support for all board members by providing such items as a newsletter, objective background papers relating to the profession being regulated, informal meetings with other public members to exchange ideas, name of community leaders, and a mentor," who would occasionally contact the board members to find out how they were doing and offer support

C. Improving Communication

Board members need to reach out to the community to let citizens know that they exist and what their mission is. They should make themselves accessible to community groups, not only to report on what their board is doing, but also to invite citizens to come forward with complaints or concerns related to the occupation or profession they are regulating. True, consumers can look up the phone number of a board in the phone book if they have a problem or want to lodge a complaint. However, they are more likely to take such an action if they have heard first hand from a board member who assures them that he or she is not only willing to listen, but that the problems or concerns will be called to the attention of the full board, as appropriate.

Failure to communicate with the public is probably the most significant mistake that many boards make. Failure to keep the public informed means that there is no reservoir of goodwill on which to draw on those occasions when the board may have a problem or make a mistake. The public and the press are far less likely to go after a board that has been up front with them than with a board that has conducted all of its business close to its chest.

Board members who have a clear understanding of the central purpose of licensing and who are committed to fulfilling the mission of the board should be able to derive great satisfaction from their board service. But it is not a job that the faint hearted or popularity seekers should undertake. Board members have an obligation to the community to ensure that those who hold licenses are competent to deliver quality services in an honest and ethical manner. They may not shrink from the responsibility of ferreting out incompetents and wrongdoers. Some of those subjected to disciplinary action may be salvaged or rehabilitated through prescribed remedial courses or through treatment programs designed to overcome alcohol or other drug abuse patterns.

VI. Conclusion

It is difficult to conceive of a society in which so many matters of enormous consequence—matters of life and death, financial security, and personal happiness—are safeguarded by the work of thousands of unpaid volunteers who make up the regulatory boards of our nation. Licensure and certification, despite their many imperfections, continue to be marvelous institutions serving the public interest. There is cetainly room for improvement, which will come even though all such institutions are the creations of mere mortals, who must do the best they can despite their own shortcomings and imperfections.

Recommended Reading

American Board of Medical Specialties. (1999) *1999 annual report and reference handbook.* Evanston, IL: ABMS, Research and Education Foundation.

Bateman, R. H. (1971). *Regulating occupations and professions.* New Jersey Professional and Occupational Licensing Study Commission, Report submitted to the Governor and legislature of the State of New Jersey.

Bates v. State Bar of Arizona, 433 U.S. 350[53:ed2d 810,97SC2691] (1977).

Baughcum, A. (1970). Occupational licensing boards: Benefactors of their licensees or protectors of the public? Paper presented at Southern Economic Association, Raleigh, NC.

Bertram, D. A., & Brooks-Bertram, P. A. (1977). The evaluation of continuing medical education: A literature review. *Health Education Monographs,* winter, 1977.

Cramer, A. L. (Chair), et al. (April 1995). *Making informed choices about doctors: A report by the advisory committee on public disclosure of physician information.* Submitted by the Secretary of Consumer and Business Affairs, Commonwealth of Massachusetts, Boston, MA.

Federal Trade Commission, Bureau of Economics. Staff report on the effects of restrictions on advertising and commercial practice in the professions: The case of optometry" Washington, DC, April, 1980.

Finocchio, L. J., Dower, C. M., Black, N. T., Gragnola, C. M., & the Taskforce on Health Taskforce on Health Care Workforce Regulation. (1998). *Strengthening consumer protection: Priorities for health care workforce regulation.* San Francisco, CA: Pew Health Professions Comission.

Finocchio, L., J., Dower, C. M., McMahon, T., Gragnola, C. M., & the Taskforce on Health Care Workforce Regulation. (1995). *Reforming health care workforce regulation: Policy considerations.* San Francisco, CA: Pew Health Professions Commission.

Gellhorn, W. (1976). The abuse of occupational licensing. *University of Chicago Law Review, 44.*

Hershey, N. (March 1969). An alternative to mandatory licensing of health Professionals. *Hospital Progress.*

Hogan, D. B. (1979). *The regulation of psychotherapists, Volume 1: A study in the philosophy and practice of professional regulation.* Cambridge, MA: Ballinger.

Houle, C. O. (August 1975). The nature of continuing professional education. *Journal of the American Pharmaceutical Association.*

Jost, T. S. (Fall, 1995). Oversight of the quality of medical care: Regulation, management, or the market? *Arizona Law Review, 37*(3) 825–868.

Kany, J. (June 30, 1995). *Toward a more rational state licensure system for Maine's health professionals.* Augusta ME: Medical Care Development.

Morrison, R. D. (1993). Continuing education requirements: Suggested guidelines" *Research Briefs* 93–103. Lexington, KY: The Council on Licensure, Enforcement and Regulation.

Office of Health Services. (June 1995). *Leading Washington's health care workforce into the 21st century.* Olympia, WA.

Roederer, D., & and Shimberg, B. (1980). *Occupational licensing: Centralizing state licensing functions:* Lexington, KY, Council of State Governments.

Schmitt, K., & Shimberg, B. (1996). *Demystifying occupational and professional regulation: Answers to questions you may have been afraid to ask.* Lexington, KY: Council on Licensure, Enforcement and Regulation.

Shimberg, B. (1980). *Occupational licensure: A public perspective.* Princeton, NJ: Educational Testing Service.

Shimberg, B., Esser, B., & Krueger, D. (1972). *Occupational licensing: Policies and practices.* Washington, DC: Public Affairs Press.

Shimberg, B. (1990). Social considerations in the validation of licensing and certification exams. *Educational Measurement: Issues and Practice,* Winter, pp. 11–14.

Shimberg, B. (1984). The relationship among accreditation, certification, and licensure. *The Federation Bulletin,* April, pp. 99–115.

Shimberg, B. (1991). *Regulation in the public interest: Myth or reality?* Lexington, KY: Council on Licensure, Enforcement and Regulation.

Shimberg, B., & Roederer, D. (1978, Revised 1986). *Occupational licensure: Questions a legislator should ask.* Lexington, KY. Council on Licensing, Enforcement and Regulation.

Shimberg, B. (1987). Assuring the continued competence of health professionals. *The Federation Bulletin*, June.

Thain, G. (1978). Occupational licensing: Protecting the public or the licensed profession? Paper delivered at second annual conference on enforcement, Chicago, IL, May 19, 1978.

U.S. Department of Health, Education and Welfare. (1967). Report of the national advisory committee on health manpower. Washington, DC: Government Printing Office.

U.S. Department of Health, Education and Welfare. (1971). Report on licensure and related health personnel credentialing. Washington, DC: Government Printing Office.

U.S. Department of Health, Education and Welfare, Public Health Service. (1977). Credentaling health manpower. Washington, DC: Government Printing Office.

8

Missions of Organizations Involved in Licensure

The Mission of the American Institute of Certified Public Accountants and the Certified Public Accountants License

James D. Blum

American Institute of Certified Public Accountants, Jersey City, New Jersey

The American Institute of Certified Public Accountants (AICPA) is the national professional organization for all Certified Public Accountants (CPAs), with more than 330,000 members in public practice, business and industry, government, and education. The AICPA is incorporated as a not-for-profit organization—a 501(c)(6) entity.

The CPA license is issued by one of 54 jurisdictions: the 50 states, the District of Columbia, Guam, Puerto Rico, and the U.S. Virgin Islands. To become a licensed CPA, one must meet the education, experience, and examination requirements of a Board of Accountancy, which is generally part of the administrative branch of a jurisdiction's government. The requirements for the designation include experience, education, and passing the Uniform CPA Examination. Currently, passing the Uniform CPA Examination is the only uniform requirement, as types of experience and required course credits vary among the jurisdictions. However, the AICPA and the National Association of State Boards of Accountancy (NASBA) are working toward true uniformity in creating the Uniform Accountancy Act.[1]

I. The AICPA's Role in Protecting the Public

The AICPA has long been involved in the regulation of the profession. In fact, the AICPA and many within the profession and the public believe that a strong partnership between self-regulation and government regulation provides the greatest protection against substandard accounting work. The AICPA assists Boards of Accountancy and state CPA societies in fulfilling their missions—regulation of the profession and the protection of the public—through setting auditing, attestation, and accounting standards; maintaining a liaison with the Securities and Exchange Commission, including overseeing the Independence Standards Board; issuing comments on the pronouncements of the Financial Accounting Standards Board and the Governmental Accounting Standards Board; operating the Joint Trial Board for the enforcement of professional standards; developing, with NASBA, regulatory resources such as the Uniform Accountancy Act and Rules; developing and enforcing rules of conduct, to which AICPA members must adhere (many Boards of Accountancy have adopted and incorporated the AICPA rules of conduct into their own statues or rules); providing AICPA members and the profession with the highest quality continuing professional education (CPE) programs; and preparing and grading the Uniform CPA Examination.

The AICPA is a unique professional organization committed to the protection of the public and the pooling of resources of both the public regulators, at the state and federal levels, and the self-regulators (such as the AICPA). In this way, the public receives the best protection against substandard work within the accounting profession. The AICPA's mission statement recognizes the public as an important constituent:

> The American Institute of Certified Public Accountants is the national, professional organization for all Certified Public Accountants. Its mission is to

---

[1] The Uniform Accountancy Act is a model act prepared by the AICPA and NASBA. Its requirements for initial licensure include 150 hours of university credit, one year of professional experience, and passing the Uniform CPA Examination.

provide members with the resources, information, and leadership that enable them to provide valuable services in the highest professional manner to benefit the public as well as employers and clients.

In fulfilling its mission, the AICPA works with state CPA organizations and gives priority to those areas where public reliance on CPA skills is most significant.

The key stakeholders within the accountancy profession are the public; the public regulators who must answer to their legislators, e.g., through sunset review; the profession itself, whose image of integrity and objectivity is tarnished when any member does not uphold all of the professional standards; the business world, especially the financial markets, which relies on CPAs to ensure that fair information is provided to investors; the academic community training future CPAs; and those aspiring to enter the profession.

The AICPA is committed to establishing entry-level requirements that assure that a person becoming a CPA has the minimum knowledge and skills necessary, and to ensuring that that person, having received the CPA license, maintains his/her competency to protect the public. The Appendix at the end of this chapter contains more information on AICPA objectives and strategic initiatives.

II. Entry into the Profession: The Uniform CPA Examination

One major role the AICPA plays in the licensing of CPAs is the preparation and grading of the Uniform CPA Examination. The AICPA Board of Examiners is responsible for overseeing the preparation and grading of the Examination (AICPA, 1997). The Examination, which lasts for 15½ hours, comprises four separately graded sections, administered over two days. The Examination is administered every May and November, with more than 120,000 candidates taking it annually.

III. AICPA Board of Examiners and Uniform CPA Examination: Mission, Scope, and Objective

The Board of Examiners' mission, scope, and objective are as follows.

The Board of Examiners of the American Institute of Certified Public Accountants is the entity within the CPA profession that is responsible for the preparation and grading of the Uniform Certified Public Accountant examination. In carrying out its mission, the Board of Examiners provides to the fifty-four American jurisdictions (Boards of Accountancy) that license Certified Public Accountants a high-quality, reliable standard examination. The Uniform CPA Examination assures each board of accountancy that CPAs entering the profession have passed an Examination that has uniform (1) content coverage, (2) level of difficulty, and (3) grading methodology and practices. The Uniform CPA Examination provides the entry-level uniformity that is essential to ensuring interjurisdictional mobility for the CPA license holder.

The scope of the Uniform CPA Examination encompasses entry-level knowledge and skills that bear a reasonable relationship to the audit and attestation, taxation, and other functions normally performed by Certified Public Accountants that affect the public interest and for which CPAs possess particular professional expertise.

The objective of the Uniform CPA Examination is to provide reasonable assurance to boards of accountancy that candidates passing the Uniform CPA Examination possess the level of technical knowledge, skills, and abilities necessary for initial licensure to protect the public interest (AICPA, 1998).

IV. Boards of Accountancy

As the state agencies that license CPAs, the Boards of Accountancy have the primary responsibility to set entry-level requirements and to ensure that CPAs maintain continued competency. In this respect, all major policy changes to the Uniform CPA Examination proposed by the Board of Examiners must be exposed to Boards of Accountancy for approval. Generally, the Board of Examiners will issue an Invitation to Comment or Briefing Paper and ask the Boards of Accountancy for their comments. To make the change, the Board of Examiners needs a consensus from the 54 Boards of Accountancy.

V. After Entry: Continuing Competence Assurance

The AICPA assists Boards of Accountancy and the profession in ensuring that CPAs, especially those in public practice, continue to perform competently by offering services such as developing rules of conduct and ethics standards, operating practice-monitoring programs, overseeing the Joint Trial Board, and providing continuing education programs for its members.

A. AICPA Professional Ethics Division

One objective of the AICPA is to promote and maintain high professional standards of practice by its members, thereby ensuring that the public interest is protected. In furtherance of this objective, the AICPA's Bylaws and Code of Professional Conduct set forth the criteria that a member is expected to observe as a condition of continued membership (AICPA, 1996). The Bylaws also describe how a member who may have departed from the criteria for continued membership will be investigated and judged, and, if found guilty, expelled or suspended from membership and/or required to take certain remedial or corrective action. The AICPA cannot suspend or revoke a member's license to practice accounting, since this remains under the jurisdiction of the Board of Accountancy. However, the AICPA does report in its newsletter (The CPA Letter) the names of all CPAs expelled or suspended from membership, from which Boards of Accountancy can obtain information to further investigate the situation.

The accounting profession has long supported self-regulation and has enjoyed the benefits of being a self-regulated profession. The profession has been granted the right to self-regulate itself by the public, who relies on the expertise that the CPA provides. The profession continues to earn that right through its continuous reassessment of its activities and the introduction of new initiatives, and the recurring success it has had in protecting the public interest.

B. Practice Monitoring: Peer Review

Peer review is one of the cornerstones of the AICPA's efforts to maintain and improve the quality of its members' practices. Peer review involves an independent, rigorous examination of a firm's system of quality control (including independence, integrity, objectivity, engagement performance, personnel management, acceptance, and continuance of clients and engagements and monitoring) with respect to its accounting and auditing practice. The peer review process also encompasses reviewing reports, financial statements, and relevant working papers for a representative sample of accounting and auditing engagements. The peer reviewer issues a written opinion and, if necessary, a letter of comments reporting on findings when there is more than a remote possibility that the firm will not conform to professional standards. The firm is required to respond to any findings noted in the peer reviewer's letter of comments. Published standards and extensive guidelines assist reviewers in conducting and reporting on peer reviews.

More than half the Boards of Accountancy require peer review of licensed CPAs. All boards accept the AICPA peer review program. This program ensures the continuing competency of CPAs and CPA firms with the professional standards and thereby protects the public by reducing the likelihood of substandard work within the profession.

C. Continuing Professional Education

Fifty-three of the 54 Boards of Accountancy require licensed CPAs to take continuing professional education (CPE) courses to retain their licenses. Each of these jurisdictions has separate rules regarding CPE. The AICPA itself requires members in public practice to complete 120 hours of CPE for each three-year reporting period, with a minimum of 20 hours every year. Members not in public practice must complete 90 hours of CPE for each three-year reporting period, with a minimum of 15 hours every year. The purpose of the AICPA's CPE requirement is to increase the professional competence of each member. Members maintain the high standards of the profession by selecting quality education programs to fulfill their continuing education requirements.

The AICPA and NASBA issue jointly the Statement on Standards for Continuing Professional Education Programs. These standards establish a framework for the development, presentation, measurement, and reporting of CPE programs and thereby help to ensure that accounting professionals receive the quality CPE necessary to satisfy their obligations to serve the public interest. The Boards of Accountancy have not universally adopted the Statement, but it is a step toward harmonization.

The AICPA is the major source of CPE courses for CPAs. It publishes hundreds of courses in the fields of accounting and auditing, consulting services, management, specialized industries, and taxation. AICPA courses are prepared by authorities in those fields, technically reviewed by other authorities, and edited in the Institute's Professional Development Division.

VI. CPA Vision Elements

To ensure the CPA profession meets the market needs of the future, the AICPA has developed a vision for 2011 and beyond. The core purpose defines the CPA profession's reason for being. The Vision Statement is the profession speaking to itself about the mandates for a successful future. Besides stating each of the top five core competencies and services, it states the following top five core values:

Core Purpose: CPAs . . . making sense of a changing and complex world.

Vision Statement: CPAs are the trusted professionals who enable people and organizations to shape their future. Combining insight with integrity, CPAs deliver value by:

- Communicating the total picture with clarity and objectivity,
- Translating complex information into critical knowledge,
- Anticipating and creating opportunities, and
- Designing pathways that transform vision into reality.

Top 5 Core Values:

- *Continuing Education and Life-Long Learning*—CPAs highly value continuing education beyond certification and believe it is important to continuously acquire new skills and knowledge.
- *Competence*—CPAs are able to perform high-quality work in a capable, efficient, and appropriate manner.
- *Integrity*—CPAs conduct themselves with honesty and professional ethics.
- *Attuned to Broad Business Issues*—CPAs are in tune with the overall realities of the business environment.
- *Objectivity*—CPAs are able to deal with information free of distortions, personal bias, or conflicts of interest.

VII. A Unique and Different Way

The partnership among the professional association, the AICPA, the Boards of Accountancy, and NASBA is truly a case where the whole is greater than the sum of its parts. The arrangement offers many checks and balances not seen in the normal regulation model. With the CPA Examination, it allows the profession to prepare and grade the examination and the Boards of Accountancy to administrate the examination, and includes the participation of NASBA both as an auditor and oversight body for the Boards of Accountancy. The resources of the AICPA are used to ensure that the entrance examination is up to date, that grading is done with technical accuracy, and that funding is available for future examination changes in policies and procedures, such as the computerization of the Examination, and not dependent on the state governmental appropriation process. The openness of obtaining the Boards of Accountancy consensus before policies and procedures are changed and the audit by NASBA that approved policies and procedures are adhered to ensures that the public is protected in all 54 jurisdictions that use the AICPA's Uniform CPA Examination as a licensing examination. Most other professions do not have the luxury of this kind of partnership.

For more information on the AICPA, visit its Web site at http://www.aicpa.org; for information on the Uniform CPA Examination, go directly to http://www.aicpa.org/exams.

References

AICPA. (1997). *Information for Uniform CPA Examination Candidates,* 15th ed. New York: Author.

AICPA Board of Examiners. (1998). *Uniform CPA Examination—Annual Report, 1997,* (p. 17). New York: AICPA.

AICPA. (1996). Bylaws of the American Institute of Certified Public Accountants, as amended June 17, 1996, and Code of Professional Conduct, as amended January 14, 1992, AICPA, New York: Author

Appendix: AICPA Objectives and Strategic Initiatives

AICPA Objectives

The following are the major areas of activity to pursue in carrying out the Institute's mission. To achieve its mission, the Institute:

A. Advocacy

- Serves as the national representative of CPAs before governments, regulatory bodies and other organizations in protecting and promoting members' interests.

B. Certification and Licensing

- Seeks the highest possible level of uniform certification and licensing standards and promotes and protects the CPA designation.

C. Communications

- Promotes public awareness and confidence in the integrity, objectivity, competence and professionalism of CPAs and monitors the needs and views of CPAs.

D. Recruiting and Education

- Encourages highly qualified individuals to become CPAs and supports the development of outstanding academic programs.

E. Standards and Performance

- Establishes professional standards; assist members in continually improving their professional conduct, performance and expertise; and monitors such performance to enforce current standards and requirements.

Strategic Initiatives (as of April 1, 1998)

The activities of highest priority to pursue in order to help achieve the Institute's mission and objectives are as follows:

- Form new and strengthen existing alliances with appropriate organizations where they would enhance the Institute's and other organizations' capacity to fulfill their respective missions.
- Develop a shared, comprehensive vision for the future of the accounting profession.
- Develop an improved means for formally recognizing, advocating, and supporting specialization within the accounting profession for informing, educating and assisting members.
- Identify changes and trends affecting the accounting profession, including the impact and application of technology, and inform the members about their implications.
- Assist members in identifying and expanding assurance services to new types of information and promote the value of these services when provided by CPAs.
- Influence the extent to which financial and business information is relevant, understandable and beneficial to users.

- Enhance the effectiveness of communications with members, the public, the business community and other stakeholders about the unique competencies, responsibilities and professionalism of CPAs (i.e., promote the value of the CPA designation).
- Work towards uniform awarding of the CPA designation and uniform regulation of the profession.
- Encourage and support the recruitment and retention of talented people in the profession, the AICPA and state CPA organizations.
- Improve the quality, appropriateness and value of the education of accountants (including achieving the 150-hour education requirement in all jurisdictions).
- Align the Institute's committee structure so as to continually improve and accelerate the decision-making processes used to develop and bring products and services to members and to achieve the Institute's mission.
- Reengineer CPE to improve the appropriateness, quality, value, availability and delivery of lifelong education for CPAs.
- Strengthen collaborative relationships with state CPA organizations to improve the planning, development and delivery of services including support of advocacy efforts at the federal and state levels.

The Mission of the National Association of State Boards of Accountancy

David A. Costello

National Association of State Boards of Accountancy, Nashville, Tennessee

The National Association of State Boards of Accountancy (NASBA) coordinates the activities of the nation's state boards of accountancy, which administer the Uniform CPA Examination, license certified public accountants, and regulate the practice of public accountancy in the United States. On behalf of state boards, NASBA has also been influential in international trade agreements and has implemented a number of programs and services that assist state boards of accountancy yet are used by many parties outside the boards' purview.

NASBA's mission is to enhance the effectiveness of state boards of accountancy. Our goals are to provide high-quality, effective programs and services; identify, research, and analyze major current and emerging issues affecting state boards of accountancy; strengthen and maintain communications with member boards to facilitate the exchange of ideas and opinions; and develop and foster relationships with organizations that impact the regulation of public accounting.

Every three years, NASBA undergoes a comprehensive review of its strategic plan, typically with the assistance of an outside consultant. During the process, the mission is reviewed for relevancy, and we take the time to formally ask, "What are the current needs of state boards and how can we address those needs?" and "What role should NASBA play with regard to each issue and need?" Once we have confirmed our mission, we develop our strategic plan and map out our goals, objectives, strategies, and actions. This document then becomes our map for the next few years; it gives us direction and helps steer our decision making. This process is particularly important for NASBA because of the high turnover of delegates (one-third of the individuals who serve on the state boards are replaced each year) and the annual election of volunteer officers and directors.

To achieve our goals, NASBA has established a number of objectives. Primarily, the board of directors is regularly reminded to focus on our mission statement and to proceed in accordance with it. When appointing committees, the chairman-elect attempts to create a foundation with NASBA's goals in mind by creating new committees where necessary and disbanding committees whose charges are no longer appropriate.

Most of NASBA's programs and services are developed through the efforts of the volunteer force. However, a number of programs are developed by staff, and all programs are implemented and managed by staff. To meet our goal of providing high-quality programs and services, staff is trained to be professional and very responsive to the needs of members, clients, and the public. Upper management is encouraged to be motivators and to provide leadership. All staff is given the opportunity to attend seminars and continuing education courses to improve their skills. In addition, all types of incentives are employed to keep staff morale high and maintain a positive atmosphere.

Some of NASBA's programs are not geared directly to the state boards yet provide them with very valuable services. Professional Credential Services, Inc., NASBA's newly created for-profit corporation, was established to allow NASBA to share the expertise it has achieved through its CPA Examination Services (CPAES) program with other professions. Many state boards of accountancy could not take advantage of CPAES's proficiency and competitive fees because CPAES only administers the Uniform CPA Examination. Many boards are required to contract their examination administration to a vendor that can administer all of the state's credentialing examinations. With the advent of Professional Credential Services, all state boards of accountancy can become NASBA client states.

CredentialNet, a credentials verification service available to accountants and accounting firms, gathers and verifies an accountant's professional portfolio of information, stores it in a centralized location, and makes it easily accessible for future needs. CredentialNet facilitates the licensure process for both accountants and state boards by streamlining information gathering and eliminating duplication of effort.

Accountants save time and money by submitting credentials information one time. Likewise, state boards benefit by obtaining verified information from one source, which reduces workload, lessens administrative time, and provides time for more productive activities.

To identify emerging issues, committees such as NASBA's New Horizons Committee are appointed to ensure that state boards are prepared for the regulatory implications of the significant changes occurring in the accounting profession. Currently, this committee is studying the impact of the borderless economy; who and what should be regulated; and what boards of accountancy should look like in 2008. To elicit input from the boards of accountancy, a discussion forum related to these issues has been posted on NASBA's Web site (www.NASBA.org). The responses to this discussion forum will assist the Committee in determining if they are proceeding appropriately.

Communicating with boards, soliciting their input, and building consensus on issues are NASBA's top priorities. To strengthen and maintain communications with member boards, NASBA sponsors a monthly newsletter, regular conferences, educational meetings, publications, videotapes and electronic discussion forums, and chat rooms. Additionally, on a quarterly basis, Regional Directors poll each of the boards within their regions on a specific set of questions related to current issues. The results of this poll are disseminated to all boards, and staff responds in writing to any board that has made a request or suggestion. Each year a comprehensive annual report is issued which details all of the activities undertaken by the organization throughout the year. Typically, when a new program is about to be implemented or when NASBA is developing a position on an issue, an "exposure draft" or "invitation to comment" paper is distributed for the board's comments. The comments are then compiled, distributed, and discussed at NASBA's June Regional meetings or fall Annual Meeting. In the future, most of these activities will be conducted electronically.

Most recently, operation Café, i.e., *C*onstant *a*nd *F*requent *E*xchange, was established. This program has the Chairman and President telephoning each state board administrator and president to discuss their concerns and seek input on current activities. Notes are kept on the conversations and appropriate follow-up is delegated to staff. Although future requests for input will be managed electronically, this program was specifically created to establish more personal relationships with NASBA's top leadership and state boards.

An important aspect of NASBA's successful achievement of its mission is developing and fostering relationships with relative organizations. Additionally, to be most effective, on some issues NASBA must work closely with other organizations within the profession. For instance, the Uniform Accountancy Act (UAA), a model statute developed to promote uniformity among boards, has been developed jointly by NASBA and the American Institute of Certified Public Accountants (the largest voluntary association in the accounting profession, which has no regulatory authority). Although at times burdensome, this collaboration creates a balanced product, which is more readily accepted by the regulators and members of the profession. Through this process, the joint committee working on the UAA developed a uniform system for evaluating the credentials of individual certified public accountants (CPAs) by including the newly coined phrase "substantial equivalence" in the UAA. The phrase suggests that boards of accountancy should issue reciprocal licenses to individuals whose credentials are "substantially equivalent" to the requirements outlined in their statutes. Substantial equivalence was developed to encourage reciprocity among states and allow for interstate commerce.

Spurred by the U.S.–Canada Free Trade Agreement and the North American Free Trade Agreement, NASBA has been actively involved in assessing the international market for recognition for CPAs, promoting the CPA designation as the global standard for professional accountants, and developing mutual recognition among countries. NASBA has established an International Qualifications Appraisal Board (IQAB) to assess the entry requirements of equivalent licenses of other countries. An important aspect of IQAB's work is to seek mutual recognition agreements with other countries to ease the ability of CPAs to practice internationally.

NASBA is unique because it is the only accounting association dedicated to the protection of the public. In this role, NASBA must represent and support all of its 54 member boards, even though at times boards hold dissenting viewpoints. Proceeding in accordance with its mission is imperative for NASBA's successful continuation.

The Mission of a State Licensing Board

Lynda Farrar

Optometrist, Oregon, and Wisconsin Department of Regulation and Licensing, Madison, Wisconsin

The mission of a state licensing board is to protect and safeguard the general well-being of the people of the state for the use of state-regulated occupational and professional services. Being a member of a state licensing board and part of the mission of the licensing board is an honor. The mission is accomplished by establishing appropriate eligibility requirements, setting practice parameters and standards of conduct, and the enforcement of the requirements, parameters, and standards.

The rules regulating the mission are found in the state statutes and administrative codes. The rules allow the people of the state to know the minimum standards necessary for safe and effective practice of the regulated occupational or professional services. They also allow the regulated occupation to know the minimum standard necessary for safe and effective practice. Therefore, both the receiver and the provider of the state-regulated occupational and professional services are on the same playing field by having to follow the rules regulating the mission of the licensing board.

I have found that the people of my state and those providing the services that are regulated do not always understand, read, or know about the state statutes and administrative codes. Many do not know or care about these regulations until they perceive they have a problem. The providers of the regulated services many times do not know that the statutes or rules have been updated. The public and the providers of regulated services must stay aware of and understand their statues and administrative codes to best benefit from safe and effective services.

I. Establishing Appropriate Eligibility Requirements to Provide a Regulated Service

The licensing board sets objective measurable minimum standards necessary for effective and practical provision of state regulated services. The minimum standards may change as the rules of the regulated profession or occupational service change. This allows for the most up-to-date provision of regulated services to the people of the state. The licensing board and the testing unit of the licensing department keep abreast of modern examinations, modem examination technology, secure and better access to examinations at an affordable cost, precredentialing examinations, and continuing education involvement. The appropriate eligibility requirements and continued competency requirements for regulated occupational and professional services are periodically monitored and evaluated to ensure consistency and effectiveness of the licensing board objectives. The monitoring and evaluating provide for minimal but essential standards for public protection and communicate the results of these processes to the public, professionals, occupations, schools, and agencies involved in the regulated services.

I have found in my state that the state board examinations for licensing are fair and test minimum competency. They test what the regulated service provider would actually do in providing the regulated service. In consideration of the phenomenon that some candidates perform poorly on examinations because of nervousness, the licensing board and state testing unit provide retake examinations in a timely sequence. Candidates in this category generally pass upon retaking the exam.

The testing unit that works with the licensing board provides valuable assistance in writing the examinations and arranging the actual physical location of the examination. It also helps the licensing board review the examination questions. After the examination, it helps the licensing board review the results to eliminate poor or psychometrically deficient questions. The testing unit and the licensing board work together closely and efficiently to provide a modern, fair, high-quality licensing examination.

The examination that measures the minimum standards necessary for the safe and effective practice is a learning device as well as a testing device. By allowing candidates in the regulated occupation or profession to see their weaknesses and improve in that area, the examination furthers candidates' knowledge of the rules and minimum standards of practice in their state.

II. Setting the Practice Parameters and Standards of Conduct to Achieve Safe and Effective Practice

The rules regulating the parameters and standards of conduct are reviewed to maintain current practices in the regulated profession or occupation in order to set and maintain minimal, essential practice standards to provide for safe and effective services. These standards are constantly changing with improvements in technology, procedures, and medications. Review must be timely and must fairly consider such aspects as the effects on small business and other state agencies. Information regarding the practice parameters and standards of conduct is available for the public and the regulated professions and occupations through public relations efforts via articles in newspapers, regulatory digest, letters, the Internet, and other consumer education initiatives.

The public and the providers of regulated services sometimes object to the amount of time taken to change the parameters and standards of conduct. Consumer education needs to emphasize that the steps that must he followed ultimately protect both the public and the provider so that inappropriate changes do not occur. The public and the service provider must be reminded that cutting corners to save money must never compromise the provision of safe service. This does not always make the licensing board popular with either group.

III. Enforcing the Mission of the State Licensing Board

The state licensing board and the division of enforcement unit are responsible for the enforcement of rules relating to the protection of the public. They must identify and appropriately discipline those in the regulated occupation who exhibit incompetence or do not adhere to professional practice standards. The discipline must be fair and timely fashion and always guided by the interest of protecting the public. The licensing board relies on the advice of legal counsel to ensure that enforcement adheres to due process and the careful adherence to applicable statutes and rules.

The Mission of the National Conference of Bar Examiners

Erica Moeser

National Conference of Bar Examiners, Chicago, Illinois

The National Conference of Bar Examiners (National Conference) is incorporated in Illinois as a 501(c)(3) nonprofit corporation. Its mission from its beginnings in the 1930s has been to promote better quality in the process of qualifying lawyers for practice.

The bar examination is conducted by a public agency in each jurisdiction, ordinarily under the auspices of each state's highest court. Since bar examiners are therefore isolated from their counterparts within the jurisdiction who regulate the other vocations and professions, the need for an organization at the crossroads of admission was perceived as acute and potentially valuable.

Initially, the work of the National Conference took the form of publications and educational gatherings. In addition, the Conference launched an investigative service whereby jurisdictions referred applications filed by candidates for law licenses for background checks. The investigative service exists today and has steadily improved through the introduction of technology.

In the early 1970s, the National Conference developed its first of four licensing examinations, which have become the evaluation instruments of choice by a majority of American jurisdictions. The mission of the National Conference remains to serve the state boards of bar examiners in their quest to use fair and defensible tests and to achieve an acceptable degree of consumer protection in the review of applications prior to licensure.

The National Conference differs from other credentialing organizations in that it does not confer licenses to practice. In 1931, the organizers of the Conference described their purpose and mission as being to "increase the efficiency of the state boards in admitting to the bar only those candidates who are fully equipped both from a standpoint of knowledge and of character to serve as lawyers, and also to study and cooperate with the other branches of the bar in dealing with problems of legal education."

The National Conference devotes considerable resources to activities and outreach efforts geared to enhance the competence of bar examiners and to foster positive interactions with other entities, such as the legal academic community, that build a stronger profession. The enormous strides that have been taken in the development and administration of examination measures is due in no small part to the combined volunteer strength that has made the National Conference an important servant of the bar admissions community.

For more information about the National Conference, visit its Web site: www. ncbex.org.

The Mission of the National Association of Boards of Examiners of Long Term Care Administrators

John H. Hogan

National Association of Boards of Examiners of Long Term Care Administrators, Portland, Oregon

The National Association of Boards of Examiners of Long Term Care Administrators (NAB) is a 501(c)(6) nonprofit corporation comprised of state boards or agencies responsible for licensing long-term care administrators.

I. Mission and Objectives

The mission of NAB is to enhance the effectiveness of state boards of examiners and/or licensing authorities of long-term care administrators in meeting their statutory and regulatory duties and responsibilities to protect the health, safety, and welfare of the public. The objectives of the Association (NAB, 1998a) are:

1. To conduct research and make recommendations on questions of common interest to the long term care administrators examinations and boards of examiners and/or licensing authorities of the states, commonwealths, and territories of the United States of America, and the District of Columbia.

2. To study and recommend professional and educational standards for long term care administrators in order to promote and protect public health and welfare.
3. To cooperate in obtaining uniformity of the laws, rules, regulations, and procedures concerning state boards of examiners and/or licensing authorities in order to create efficiency for those receiving licenses as long term care administrators.
4. To consider, establish, and maintain a uniform code of ethics and standards of professional conduct and practice for Boards of Examiners and/or licensing authorities of long term care administrators.
5. To work toward reciprocal endorsement and/or recognition of long term care administrator licenses by the boards, authorities of the states, commonwealths, and territories of the United States of America and the District of Columbia.

NAB strives to meet its mission through a number of organizational mechanisms and related activities, including its membership structure. NAB has four membership categories: regular, associate, subscribing, and distinguished service (NAB, 1998a).

Regular membership status relates to members of the applicable board or licensing authority for each jurisdiction. These members are eligible to name a delegate to the Board of Governors, NAB's governing body, and to participate fully in organizational activities. Associate member status refers to board members whose term of service for their respective jurisdiction has expired. These individuals may elect to continue to participate in NAB and can hold office and serve on committees but are ineligible to vote or serve as a state delegate. Subscribing membership is for representatives of academic institutions whose course of instruction has been approved by the respective board and/or licensing authority. In addition, representatives of business or professional organizations may join through this membership category. Subscribing members can serve on all committees except the examination committee and are not eligible to vote, serve on the Board of Governors, or hold office. Distinguished Service membership is for members who have served the association with distinction for the past five years and made contributions to NAB or for individuals who have made significant contributions to the profession.

The Board of Governors consists of one delegate for each regular member. It oversees the direction and control of the association.

Guided by this mission and structure, NAB seeks to fulfill its objectives through service of critical activities. One key example is the development of licensing and/or competency examinations for nursing home and residential care/assisted living administrators. These examinations enable NAB to meet its mission by enhancing the effectiveness of the individual state boards and/or licensing authorities through a collaborative effort to create a fair, defensible examination.

NAB serves as a focal point of information and provides a forum for discussion, cooperation, and collaboration for members relative to new laws or regulations, professional standards, and issues of common concern. Through these efforts, NAB meets the challenge of its mission and continues to provide support for its members as they serve to meet applicable statutory responsibilities.

References

National Association of Boards of Examiners of Long Term Care Administrators. (1998a). Bylaws, Article III, p. 1, Washington, DC: Author.
National Association of Boards of Examiners of Long Term Care Administrators. (1998b). Bylaws, Article IV, p. 1, Washington, DC: Author.

The Mission of a State Testing Unit

Barbara A. Showers
Wisconsin Department of Regulation and Licensing, Madison, Wisconsin

In a number of states, professional regulation is organized within a state agency that provides centralized administrative services to regulatory authorities. The central state agency that provides these services in Wisconsin is the Wisconsin Department of Regulation and Licensing. The Office of Examinations within the Department is responsible for providing and administering examinations for all regulated professions.

The mission of the Office stems from the mission of the Department, which is stated in the Department's Strategic Business Plan:

> Our mission is to safeguard the general well being of Wisconsin consumers of state regulated occupational and professional services. The mission will be accomplished by:
>
> 1. Establishing appropriate eligibility requirements and ensuring professional competence by establishing evaluation procedures clearly related to safe and effective practice.
> 2. Setting the practice parameters and standards of conduct to achieve safe and effective practice.
> 3. Enforcement of standards.

The Office of Examinations carries out goals related to part 1 of the mission. These goals are articulated in the Department's Plan as follows:

- Credentialing authorities will set objective, measurable minimum standards necessary for safe and effective practice.
- The Department will be the source of quality technical expertise, fairness and service capabilities in examinations, recredential education, continuing education, experience requirements, and evaluation.
- The Department will provide courteous, accurate, and efficient processing of all applications in compliance with federal and state requirements, fully utilizing information technology.

To carry out these goals, a number of specific objectives were identified in the Plan. Those specifically related to the testing function are as follows:

- Create and administer valid and reliable examinations that fairly assess the competencies necessary for safe and effective practice.
- Provide direction, consultation, and assistance on all matters regarding . . . examinations.
- Assure that Wisconsin interests are represented in the decisions of national examination providers related to examination content and fairness and in the provision of other national services, such as national databases for sharing credentialing information.
- Keep abreast of developing technology in examinations and utilize this technology to improve efficiency, effectiveness, and service, such as providing better access to examinations at an affordable cost with quicker score results.
- Provide accessible, affordable, and secure automated examinations.
- Increase public access to Wisconsin credentialing information requirements and application processes by expanding Internet capabilities.
- Preserve the right of candidates, credential holders, and the public concerning access to information contained in electronic databases held by the Department and national examination providers.

The Office's primary key stakeholder is the public, which is to be protected by state regulation of the profession. The Office's more direct customers, who are also stakeholders, are the candidates for credentials and the regulatory authorities.

The Office's philosophy and core values have been summed up in this guiding statement:

The Office of Examinations stands for quality in testing, fairness to candidates, and excellence in service.

Each year, specific goals are established for the year's activities. The goals include specific state test development projects performed in-house, as well as monitoring of examination service providers by means of audits, committee participation, and other information-gathering efforts. The goals also include issuing requests for proposals for examination services and contract renewals.

Examination policy making is carried out by suggesting and reviewing administrative code for credentialing authorities, and implementing internal policies and procedures relating to the examination function.

More information about the Office may be obtained from its Web site: badger.state.wi.us/agencies/drl. The Office also maintains physical facilities for administering and scoring examinations, hires and trains proctors and examiners, evaluates requests for modifications of examinations for persons with disabilities, and conducts candidate satisfaction surveys.

The Mission of the National Council of State Boards of Nursing

Anthony Zara

National Council of State Boards of Nursing, Chicago, Illinois

The National Council of State Boards of Nursing, Inc. (National Council) is a 501(c)(3) not-for-profit association whose membership is composed of the 61 regulatory boards of nursing in the United States and its territories (U.S. Virgin Islands, Puerto Rico, Guam, Northern Marianas, and American Samoa). Each member board of nursing is the governmental agency empowered through action taken by its jurisdiction's legislature to protect the public's health, safety, and welfare by licensing and regulating nursing practice. Licensing laws are enacted to protect the public by defining the qualifications of those eligible to practice a profession, appropriate quality standards for practice, and the legal scope of practice of the licensed professionals. Boards also monitor nurses' compliance with laws and regulations and take action against those practitioners who have demonstrated unsafe practice.

Incorporated in 1978, the mission of the National Council is to lead in nursing regulation by assisting member boards, collectively and individually, to promote safe and effective nursing practice in the interest of protecting public health and welfare. The purpose of the National Council is to provide an organization through which state boards of nursing act and counsel together on matters of common interest and concern affecting the public health, safety, and welfare, including the development of licensing examinations in nursing.

I. National Council Structure

The structure of the National Council is a bit more complicated than a standard for-profit organization. Both the governance and the operational structures were developed to assure that boards of nursing would have a high degree of control over the direction of the organization.

A. Delegate Assembly

The Delegate Assembly provides the highest level of decisions and policy direction for the National Council. It is composed of two delegates from each member board of nursing. Once a year, delegates from the member boards convene as the Delegate Assembly to determine the direction and policies of the National Council and to elect individuals to the National Council's board of directors.

B. Board of Directors

Between the annual meetings of the Delegate Assembly, a nine-member, elected Board of Directors composed of officers and representatives from each geographic region of the National Council is charged with overseeing the implementation of policy and directing the activities of the National Council. The Board also develops potential strategic suggestions for decision by the Delegate Assembly and monitors the work of National Council committees.

C. Committees and Task Forces

Many of the National Council's operational objectives are accomplished through the efforts of volunteer committees and task forces. Committee/task force membership is available to current members and staff of National Council's member boards of nursing. When assigning volunteers to committee projects, the Board attempts to select people with appropriate expertise for the project, balance geographic representation, and include staff and board members, registered and licensed practical/vocational nurses, and consumers. Committee and task force activity is monitored throughout the year by the Board and reported to the Delegate Assembly at the National Council's annual meeting.

D. Staff

A professional staff provides the in-house expertise to execute and support all National Council activities, projects, and programs. Current staff experience includes nursing regulation, psychometrics, nursing education, nursing practice, business, accounting, and communications.

E. Contractors

Given the National Council's many diverse programs and limited number of staff, a significant part of the available resources are provided by outside contractors and consultants. Some of National Council's most important functions are accomplished with the contribution of outside personnel as "staff extenders." The National Council currently contracts for professional testing services, legal services, web site hosting services, research support, and human resources consulting.

II. National Council Products and Services

The major activities of the National Council are directly related to its mission to lead in nursing regulation by assisting boards of nursing. The most significant programs include developing the national licensure examinations for nurses, performing policy analysis and promoting uniformity in the regulation of nursing practice, disseminating nurse licensure data, conducting regulatory research, and serving as a forum for information exchange for boards of nursing.

The National Council has extensive experience in developing examinations used for regulatory purposes. The primary product and service provided to nursing boards is the national licensure examinations for nurses (NCLEX-RN® and NCLEX-PN®). For their regulatory purposes, boards need information for determining whether or not to grant legal authority to practice, based on each jurisdiction's laws and administrative rules. This "police power" exercised by boards as agents of government is a powerful authority and thus carries strict constitutional responsibilities related to due process, property rights, and other rights of citizens. The key issue in developing examinations for regulatory purposes is each examination's rational relationship to performing the essential functions of the entry-level professional position. Regulatory examinations must:

1. Be targeted to entry-level practice;

2. Measure only job-related knowledge, skills, and abilities;
3. Require demonstration of competence at the minimum level necessary for safety and effectiveness; and
4. Be psychometrically sound.

The demonstration of minimum competence requires that the passing standard be set at the lowest level of mastery that is safe and effective. Considerations of professional excellence are tangential and not directly related to setting this type of standard.

Every board of nursing in the United States contracts with the National Council to provide its licensure examinations. The NCLEX program is one of the preeminent licensure examination programs in the country, testing over 170,000 nurse candidates per year. The National Council is ultimately responsible for the development and delivery of the NCLEX. These functions (accomplished using committees, staff resources, and service vendors) include conducting the required job analyses, developing NCLEX test plans, recruiting item writers and reviewers, specifying the NCLEX item style, approving item pools, developing all NCLEX-related policies and procedures, and continually monitoring NCLEX performance. Along with the NCLEX, the National Council is the developer of the National Nurse Aide Assessment Program (NNAAP; formerly NACEP) and the Certification Examination Program for LPNs (licensed practical nurses) in Long-Term Care (CEPN-LTC).

Other National Council programs also serve the goal of the mission. For example, the Computerized Clinical Simulation Testing (CST®) program is researching a new testing methodology along two lines: (1) for individual board of nursing use and (2) as a potential component of the NCLEX examination. The Nurse Information System (Nur*sys*) project is currently progressing by building a database with the goal of housing data on all the nurses licensed in the United States. The National Council also provides a central clearinghouse service for research conducted by boards of nursing and for other information about nursing regulation. Educational conferences and regional meetings are conducted throughout the year.

The National Council maintains a national disciplinary data bank that contains information about nurses who have had disciplinary action taken against their licenses. Boards of nursing utilize this service during the licensing process to ensure that the safety of the public is protected. The National Council's staff and committees continually monitor and analyze issues and trends in public policy, nursing practice, and nursing education to inform and assist boards of nursing as they respond to the rapidly changing healthcare environment. Additionally, the National Council develops and disseminates position papers and models related to the regulation of nursing practice and education to promote uniformity in standards and expected outcomes, aiding boards in their role to protect the public health, safety, and welfare.

The National Council publishes much material about its mission, program, and services. The best resource for an overview about the National Council can be found at its Web site: http://www.ncsbn.org.

9

The Mission of Stakeholder Organizations in Licensure

The Mission of the Council on Licensure, Enforcement and Regulation

Pam Brinegar

Council on Licensure, Enforcement and Regulation, Lexington, Kentucky

In 1980, a group of professional and occupational regulators, along with a few private sector representatives, met in New Orleans to discuss their need to share information on issues of common concern. The goal of this proposed cooperation was to help professional regulation stakeholders carry out their shared mission of consumer protection. The outgrowth of that initial discussion was the formation of a new association, The Council on Licensure, Enforcement and Regulation (CLEAR). Supported by seed money from state regulatory agencies, and staff support contributed by The Council of State Governments,[1] CLEAR's leaders rapidly designed and implemented many of the programs and projects that CLEAR continues today.

---

[1]The Council of State Governments (CSG), with which CLEAR retains an affiliation, is a national organization in service to state governments and U.S. territories. Headquartered in Lexington, Kentucky, CSG has regional offices in Atlanta, Chicago, New York, and San Francisco, as well as a headquarters branch in Washington, DC.

194

From CLEAR's beginning, its founders decided that the kind of organization they would find most useful was one in service to representatives of all three governmental sectors as well as the private sector and others with an interest in the field of professional and occupational regulation. The organization would thus be a resource to anyone involved in the licensure, certification, or registration of the hundreds of regulated occupations and professions, both related and unrelated to health. This holistic approach worked well for CLEAR's members and continues as an excellent vehicle for responding to a necessarily diverse constituency.

I. CLEAR's Membership

CLEAR has two membership categories that define its constituency. *Regular CLEAR membership* is open to governmental agencies concerned with professional and occupational regulation, other approved governmental jurisdictions, individual employees or officials of government agencies concerned with professional and occupational regulation; and officers and directors of national associations of state professional and occupational licensing boards. *Associate CLEAR membership* is open to approved nongovernmental organizations, individuals representing an organization not eligible for regular membership, and private individuals who have a personal interest in professional and occupational regulation.

Within a few years of its founding, CLEAR's leaders began to recruit international members. This ongoing initiative has enriched the texture of CLEAR's organizational culture as first Canadian, then European, and most recently, South American members joined CLEAR's far-ranging conversation. Recently, CLEAR established an Office of International Affairs based in England that will provide assistance to all non–North American constituencies. By establishing this office, CLEAR is now positioned to bring the benefits of global cooperation to its membership.

II. CLEAR's Mission

CLEAR is a 501(c)(3) not-for-profit organization whose primary purpose is therefore educational. The organizational mission statement, as amended in 1997, states that

> CLEAR is an association of individuals, agencies and organizations that comprise the international community of professional and occupational

regulation. CLEAR is a dynamic forum for improving the quality and understanding of regulation in order to enhance public protection.

CLEAR's bylaws supplement the mission statement with the association's purpose, which is to:

- Bring together government officials and agencies involved in or affected by professional and occupational regulation,
- Encourage and provide for the exchange of information and ideas,
- Provide education and training to government officials and other interested parties concerned with professional and occupational regulation,
- Provide a central clearinghouse of information pertinent to professional and occupational regulation, and
- Improve the administrative regulatory practices of government officials and agencies concerned with professional and occupational regulation.

III. How CLEAR Accomplishes Its Mission

Through conferences, publications, training, inquiry, and other services, CLEAR provides a resource for sharing of regulatory licensure issues among all groups involved or interested in the field. CLEAR does not lobby, nor does it adopt resolutions or take stands on policy issues that cannot reflect the collective viewpoint of its extremely diverse constituency. CLEAR does identify on an ongoing basis significant issues affecting the field of professional and occupational regulation, providing a forum for the presentation of all viewpoints on these issues to its constituency. CLEAR also identifies and highlights good practices among regulators.

Much of CLEAR's work is carried out through various standing committees and special interest groups. Usually, between 125 and 150 individuals serve on these committees, which meet at least twice a year to conduct business. It is primarily through the extraordinary contribution of its many highly involved volunteer members that CLEAR accomplishes its mission. Typical active participants include agency administrators and other staff members, board members, legislators, legislative staffers, and individuals, as well as representatives of offices of attorneys general, examination companies, national professional associations, national associations of state boards, and federal government agencies.

IV. Areas of Substantive Inquiry

There are four distinct areas of substantive inquiry that CLEAR supports on an ongoing basis. In fact, its annual conference program committee is organized into four subcommittees named for the following inquiry areas. Each of these areas depends on the advice and guidance of the International Relations Subcommittee of the Education and Training Committee, a body that works to help CLEAR provide a balanced approach in its educational offerings and publications.

A. Professional Discipline

The percentage of their budgets that most state and provincial agencies must spend on professional discipline activities is quite high. Since 1984, to meet the critical need for skilled investigative staff members, CLEAR has provided certification training in investigation and inspection techniques and procedures. The National Certified Investigator/Inspector Training (NCIT) program holds training programs several times during the year at locations throughout North America. Each training session is coordinated between CLEAR and a host agency. The sessions, which include lectures, role playing, and video presentations, conclude with an examination that can lead to certification. Training is available on two levels, basic and specialized. This training is a project of the NCIT Subcommittee of the Education and Training Committee.

B. Credentialing and Exam Issues

The area of candidate entry into professions and occupations is critical to the regulatory process. CLEAR is fortunate to have in its membership key representatives of the regulatory psychometric community at large. Topics that come under the purview of this area of inquiry are the Americans with Disabilities Act, computerized testing, and a host of other testing and measurement issues. A significant project of the Exam Resources and Advisory Committee is *CLEAR Exam Review* (CER), a semi-annual part-newsletter, part-journal of useful information on licensing examination issues intended for all audiences.

C. Legislative and Policy Issues

Each regulatory jurisdiction is the result of legislative action. Beyond that, each jurisdiction is responsible for interpreting its legislative mandate through regulations and public policies. Current areas of particular significance to the field are barriers to professional mobility, overlapping or overly restricted scopes of practice, continued professional competence, and the impact of technological change on geographical boundaries. A special interest group on regulatory issues focuses specifically on legal issues for regulatory attorneys.

D. Management and Administration

Agencies of every size confront the same or similar issues of how to effectively run their operations. Particularly through its annual conference and publications, CLEAR makes available new, useful information that managers and administrators can add to their "tool kits." CLEAR also hosts two special interest groups, one for autonomous board administrators and one for central agency administrators, both of which provide ongoing guidance for management and administration issues.

E. The General Audience

Some of CLEAR's products are intended for general use by all those interested in the field and therefore cut across all areas of inquiry. These include

- *CLEAR News,* a quarterly newsletter, the purpose of which is to provide timely information relative to the CLEAR organization and general issues of interest regarding professional and occupational regulation. *CLEAR News* is free to professional and occupational licensing community members.
- *Resource Briefs,* an occasional papers series, and a project of the Publications Subcommittee of the Education and Training Committee. The series' primary purpose is to provide brief overviews of topical issues as defined annually by CLEAR members.

CLEAR sponsors an annual international conference, offering the most comprehensive and substantive agenda in the field, regional conferences, board member training, and stand-alone seminars in specialized areas of current interest to the constituent community. Recent offerings include symposia on the healthcare workforce and preparing for the 21st century as well as identifying and building bridges to partners in professional regulation. A current project is the development of a summit on strengthening consumer protection that will reach beyond regulatory stakeholders, to include the educational and private accreditation communities as well. Board member training and other specialized educational offerings are projects of the Training and Development Subcommittee of the Education and Training Committee.

CLEAR provides an inquiry and referral service in substantive areas involving the regulated professions. This service relies in large part on CLEAR's resource library of topical and historical materials. CLEAR members and staff also make themselves available to provide expert testimony to legislative committees and others upon invitation.

Finally, CLEAR operates the CLEAR Consulting Service (CCS), which draws on the experience and talent of member consultants who provide clients with practical solutions in several areas of expertise.

V. What Makes CLEAR Unique?

As is true of associations everywhere, it is CLEAR's philosophy and core values that distinguish it from all other groups in service to segments of the professional and occupational regulatory community. CLEAR is unique among credentialing stakeholders in offering neutral ground to all those interested in professional and occupational regulation. In brief, CLEAR's hallmark is its inclusiveness. Although there is a perception to the contrary, CLEAR does not license, enforce, or regulate anything. Rather, it is in service to those whose responsibility it is to carry out these important consumer protection functions as well as to those with complementary missions. CLEAR has defined its role as proactively identifying critical issues, providing a dynamic, interactive forum for those interested in these issues, and collecting and disseminating information on various issue perspectives as well as on excellent regulatory practices.

Recommended Reading

Brinegar, P., & McGinley, M. (1998). *Telepractice & Professional Licensing: A Guide for Legislators.* Lexington, KY: The Council on Licensure, Enforcement and Regulation.

Council on Licensure, Enforcement and Regulation. (1998). Internet Web site: www.clearhq.org.

Shimberg, B., & Roederer, D. (1994). *Questions A Legislator Should Ask* (2nd ed.). Lexington, KY: The Council on Licensure, Enforcement and Regulation.

The Role of Mission Statements in the Work of the Pew Health Professions Commission

Catherine Dower

University of California, San Francisco, San Francisco, California

Crafting and adhering to a mission statement has been key to the work of the Pew Health Professions Commission at several levels. First has been the work and mission of the initiative of the Commission itself. More targeted has been the work of the Commission's Taskforce on Regulation, with its own more specific mission. Finally, with its two reports and several years worth of efforts, the Taskforce and the Commission together have highlighted the apparent tension in regulation between trying to serve both the public and the professions. To address this conflict, a set of principles has been offered to better inform the mission of health professions regulation. The role of the mission within each of these efforts is explored in more detail below.

I. History

The Pew Health Professions Commission was created in 1989 with funds from The Pew Charitable Trusts to focus on the people who make up the healthcare workforce.[1] This was at a time when considerable attention was being paid to health care, but that attention was largely directed to patient needs, delivery systems, and financing of health care. Policy development in the arena of healthcare professionals—how they are trained, how many the country has and needs, how they are regulated—was limited. Efforts to address health professions issues were often done at the local or state level, and almost exclusively within single professions. The concept behind the creation of the Pew Health Professions Commission was to look at the health professions together, not as separate and unconnected entities, and to do so from a national perspective.

During its decade-long tenure, the profile of the Commission has varied somewhat in size and membership during each of its three consecutive phases. The Commission as a group has represented leaders from a variety of fields, including health professional education, accreditation, insurance, delivery systems and institutions, and practice. Professions represented include medicine, nursing, physician assistants, dentistry, allied health, pharmacy, osteopathy, and public health. Commissioners from the private sector, elected office, law, consumer interest, organized labor and economics have served. This interprofessional, interdisciplinary, and interstate composition reflects a conscious effort to bring a wealth of perspectives to the table.

II. The Mission of the Pew Health Professions Commission

The Pew Health Professions Commission works to help policy makers and educators produce health care professionals who meet the changing needs of the American healthcare system.

Implicit in this mission is the assumption that because healthcare professionals play such pivotal roles in the delivery of health care, any efforts to improve health care must include the people who ultimately provide that care. Thus, changes in

---

[1]The Pew Health Professions Commission is a program of The Pew Charitable Trusts. The Pew Charitable Trusts supports nonprofit activities in the areas of culture, education, the environment, health and human services, public policy, and religion. Based in Philadelphia, the Trusts make strategic investments that encourage and support citizen participation in addressing critical issues and effecting social change. In 1997, with more than $4.5 billion in assets, the Trusts awarded $181 million to 320 nonprofit organizations.

healthcare financing, delivery structures, or research processes that are not accompanied by corresponding changes in the way healthcare professionals are educated, trained, regulated, and managed will create ultimately unworkable systems. Working within this framework, the most significant goal of the Commission has been raising the awareness of the role of healthcare professionals—as distinguished, for example, from issues of delivery organization or universal access—in the larger healthcare environment.

The Commission was inspired by the belief that the education and training, regulation, utilization, and distribution of health professionals are out of step with the evolving healthcare needs of the American people. The Commission believes that the nation's 11 million healthcare providers have a tremendous impact on the cost, quality, and accessibility of the healthcare system. With the appropriate skills, attitudes, and values, these practitioners can become the foundation for an efficient, high-quality, accessible, and equitable new system.

A. Strategies and Activities

The Commission has worked at the federal, state, institutional, and association levels to promote change and has employed several strategies in pursuit of its mission and goals. These include high-profile conferences and forums, an awards program for primary care providers, a speakers' bureau, subgranting programs, expert analysis and policy recommendations on specific topics such as graduate medical education financing, press conferences, and testimony.

Perhaps primary among the Commission's activities has been the publication of a series of reports that seek to make sense of the chaos and change in health care generally and offer recommendations for the professions to best respond to the trends and developments. Some of the reports have been broad, covering a wide range of issues relevant to the health professions; others have been more focused on a single topic.

B. The Focus on Health Professions Regulation

One of the Commission's areas of focus has been the regulation of healthcare professionals. In its early work on health professional education, the Commission noted the link between educational programs and regulatory systems. Some proposed changes in health professions education could not be accomplished without changes in state regulation. Examples include efforts to change curriculum content or length of study programs that were written into state regulation.

Despite this close tie, the credentials offered by educational programs, such as diplomas or certificates, and the credentials (usually licenses) granted by state regulatory agencies were not always in accord. For example, a nurse practitioner might be educated, trained, and tested on how to prescribe pharmaceuticals but might not have prescriptive authority under the legal scope of practice act for nurse practitioners in her state. Regulatory credentials meant something to the public, but it was far from clear whether licenses and the regulatory systems that revolved around them were operating optimally.

C. The Taskforce on Health Care Workforce Regulation

The Taskforce on Health Care Workforce Regulation was first convened in 1994. The Pew Health Professions Commission, recognizing that healthcare workforce reform must include regulatory reform, charged the Taskforce with identifying and exploring how regulation protects the public's health and proposing new approaches to healthcare workforce regulation to better serve the public's interest. Based on the research, analysis, and discussions of the Taskforce, the Commission released *Reforming Health Care Workforce Regulation: Policy Considerations for the 21st Century* in late 1995 (Finocchio et al., 1995). The report covered 10 issue areas[2] and was intended to provoke discussion, debate, and dialogue about the state of health professions regulation in America.

Following release of the 1995 report, Commissioners, Taskforce members, and staff participated in hundreds of discussions, conferences, and hearings about the role and meaning of health professions regulation. Formal and informal responses were collected and summarized in a 1997 report (Gragnola & Stone, 1997). In addition, the Center for the Health Professions, where the Pew Health Professions Commission was administered, distributed 14 grants to individuals and organizations to discuss, research, and plan for regulatory reform in the 10 issue areas of the 1995 report. Overall, the report generated considerable interest; although far from everyone involved in health professions regulation agreed with all of the proposed recommendations, most agreed that the regulatory system had at least some shortcomings worthy of reform.

---

[2]The 10 issue areas were regulatory language and terms; entry-to-practice requirements; scopes of practice authority; structure and function of regulatory boards; information dissemination; data collection; continuing competency; complaint and disciplinary processes; regulatory evaluation; coordination between regulation and other systems.

In 1997, the second phase of the Taskforce on Health Care Workforce Regulation was convened to take a closer look at the topic. As noted in the subsequent report, the Pew Health Professions Commission charged this phase of the Taskforce to be "bold and visionary, producing work that would be a catalyst for change." To that end, the Commission charged this Taskforce to "envision a future health professions regulatory system that meets consumers' reasonable expectations of access to comprehensive, appropriate, cost-effective and high quality health services and to explore ways to move the current system toward this future system."

The final findings and recommendations of the Commission and its Taskforce on Health Professions Regulation are contained in the 1998 report *Strengthening Consumer Protection: Priorities for Health Care Workforce Regulation* (Finocchio et al., 1998). This policy document targets three priority areas that present the most challenges to, and promise for, improving professional regulation: health professions boards and governance structures, scopes of practice authority, and continuing competence.

The way scope of practice authority decisions are made and whether healthcare professionals should demonstrate their competence throughout their careers are examples of the link between credentialing (in this case via initial licensure and licensure renewal) and health care. The Commission's work in this area has highlighted that a professional's license to provide care may cover more than the individual is competent to provide; alternatively, the license may be overly restrictive, thus hindering access to, and increasing the costs of, health care. This may happen when regulation unreasonably limits the categories of people who provide certain services or unnecessarily restricts competition.

III. The Mission of Health Professions Regulation

From its earliest work on health professions regulation, the Taskforce emphasized the need to identify and understand the mission behind regulation. This was more challenging than it first appeared. It was quickly apparent that, although the concept of a guiding mission statement is not new, the term has not always been part of the legislative language defining regulation. Legislative declarations and statements of purpose, which can be found at the beginning of statutes authorizing professional practice acts, are often the closest we can get to a written "mission." While they spell out the legal authority of the state to regulate the profession at hand on the grounds of protecting the public's health, safety and welfare, these statements rarely offer much more. Moreover, not every professional practice act is accompanied by one of these minimalist declarations about public protection from unsafe practitioners.

In addition to the limited legislative attention to the mission of regulatory efforts was the notion found repeatedly in the literature that health professions regulation might be serving an unstated goal or mission of protecting professional interests instead of, or in addition to, the interests of the public.[3]

In its research, the Taskforce found one notable exception to the dearth of details about the purpose and mission of health professions regulation. During its decade-long regulatory reform process, policy makers in Ontario, Canada, explored the system's goals, objectives, inherent contradictions, and underlying themes in depth (Bohnen, 1994).

The Pew Health Professions Commission Taskforce on Health Care Workforce Regulation focused its initial efforts on the development of a list of principles. These principles were seen as the future guidelines for health professions regulation. They were also the backbone of the work of the Taskforce itself. It was against these principles that the group's recommendations were held before publication and release.

The Pew Commission believes that state-based health care workforce regulation will best serve the public by:

- Promoting effective health outcomes and protecting the public from harm;
- Holding regulatory bodies accountable to the public;
- Respecting consumers' rights to choose their healthcare providers from a range of safe options;
- Encouraging a flexible, rational, and cost-effective healthcare system that allows effective working relationships among healthcare providers; and
- Facilitating professional and geographic mobility of competent providers.

These five principles help clarify what we mean when we say that the mission of health professions regulation is to protect the public's health, safety, and welfare. They provide guidance to legislators and regulators charged with the responsibility to protect the public's interest but faced with competing interests and proposals from the various professions.

In the eyes of the Commission, the licensing of professionals plays several

---

[3]For a long, though not exhaustive, list of reports, books, and articles discussing the strengths and weaknesses of professional regulation, see the bibliography in Finocchio et al., 1998.

roles. It serves as one element of a complex system to help ensure the public that health care is safe and of high quality. It also serves as a barometer to gauge the state of the healthcare professions. That is, we can look to licensure requirements when we compare different professions or when we compare individual professions across state or national borders. Finally, in light of the mission of the Pew Health Professions Commission, licensure can serve as a lever for reform. For example, through appropriate and relevant licensure requirements, we can improve quality of care; by ensuring that boards are properly staffed and structured, we can improve consumers' satisfaction when they file complaints about incompetent practitioners; and by making sure that scopes of practice authority are not unnecessarily narrow, we can improve both access to health care and the costs of that care.

Using its own mission statement as a starting point, the Pew Health Professions Commission has emphasized the need to reform health professions regulation within a framework of prioritizing the public's interest over the professions'. A framework, while necessary, is insufficient alone. Action in line with such a stated mission must follow. Whether regulatory efforts are actually meeting the stated mission of protecting the public should be evaluated and corrected as necessary. The principles offered by the Commission provide a more detailed approach to the regulatory mission. It is this sort of comprehensive and integrated approach the Pew Health Professions Commission trusts legislators, regulators, and policy makers will embrace so that healthcare professionals can truly meet the needs of the American public.

References

Bohnen, L. S. (1994). *Regulated health professions act: A practical guide.* Aurora, Ontario, Canada: Canada Law Book Inc.

Finocchio, L. J., Dower, C. M., McMahon, T., Gragnola, C. M., & the Taskforce on Health Care Workforce Regulation. (1995). *Reforming health care workforce regulation: Policy considerations for the 21st Century.* San Francisco, CA: Pew Health Professions Commission.

Finocchio, L. J., Dower, C. M., Blick, N. T., Gragnola, C. M., & the Taskforce on Health Care Workforce Regulation. (1998). *Strengthening Consumer Protection: Priorities for Health Care Workforce Regulation.* San Francisco, CA: Pew Health Professions Commission.

Gragnola, C. M., & Stone, E. (1997). *Considering the future of health care workforce regulation.* San Francisco, CA: UCSF Center for the Health Professions.

The Mission of the Federation of Associations of Regulatory Boards

Randolph P. Reaves

Association of State and Provincial Psychology Boards, Montgomery, Alabama

T he Federation of Associations of Regulatory Boards is known throughout the licensure and credentialing community as FARB. The organization has been in existence for approximately a quarter century and has played an important role in the education of licensure board members, staff, and attorneys throughout the United States and Canada.

I. The Evolution of FARB

FARB was founded in the early 1970s. Its original purpose was to provide a means for those interested in professional licensing to gather to discuss mutual issues of concern and learn not only from formal presentations but also from interaction with others interested in the same issues.

Initially, FARB had only one class of member—full membership—and those members were associations of regulatory boards. Its founders were all from the healthcare professions, and it originally restricted membership to those associations of boards that regulated certain healthcare professions. When FARB was founded, it was known as FAHRB, the Federation of Associations of Health Regulatory Boards.

The original full members were the associations of regulatory boards in the fields of chiropractic, dentistry, medicine, nursing, optometry, osteopathy, pharmacy, podiatry, psychology, and veterinary medicine. Some of the individual founders were Fred Mahaffey of the National Association of Pharmacy Boards, John Robinson of the International Association of Optometry Boards, and Ed Loveland of the American Association of State Psychology Boards. According to Robinson, Fred Mahaffey pulled the group together. Naturally, he was FARB's first president. Both Robinson and Loveland later served as President, as did Eileen Dvorack of the National Council of State Boards of Nursing.

In its early days, FARB was fortunate to have the advice and assistance of John "Jack" Atkinson, the dean of all professional regulatory lawyers. A practitioner in Chicago, Jack's hard work resulted in 50l(c)(3) tax-exempt status—very important to organizations such as FARB.

Since its purpose was to provide a means for professionals to gather and discuss mutual issues of concern, its annual meeting was called the FARB Forum. The early events were well attended since there was widespread concern among the professions regarding the threats from the Federal Trade Commission, which took issue with many prohibitions on licensed professionals, particularly those that involved advertising. As Robinson recalls, FARB was founded before the Council on Licensure, Enforcement and Regulation. For the first few years, there were no other sponsors of meetings devoted to issues involving professional regulation.

A. The Forums

FARB still sponsors an annual Forum. The 24th such event will be held February 18–20 in Memphis, Tennessee. Forums have themes involving various regulatory issues and feature plenary and small group sessions. A typical Forum attracts a substantial number of the best-known experts in administration, assessment, and professional discipline. Most Forums are 2½ days in length. Participants in the most recent Forum represented 30 different professions.

B. FAHRB Becomes FARB

In the early 1980s, those most involved in the organization decided that a broader base existed within professional regulation and that FAHRB should open its full membership to associations that regulate professionals in non-healthcare fields. Once this decision was made, the organization changed its name to FARB, and several non–health-related organizations joined, including the National Association of State Boards of Accountancy (NASBA) and the National Council of Architectural Registration Boards (NCARB). The Forums went almost unchanged since the issues remained the same; that is, administration, assessment, and professional discipline. Sam Balen, the Executive Director of NCARB, was the first President of FARB from a non–health-related profession. Later, James Thomashower of NASBA served as President.

Over the years, there has always been one characteristic that distinguished FARB from other similar organizations: its long-standing position that professionals, not bureaucrats, should regulate professionals. This position is hardly surprising since full membership is restricted to associations of regulatory boards, whose member boards are, for the most part, made up of licensed professionals. At any FARB Forum, while there are administrators, attorneys, and investigators present, the majority of attendees are regulatory board members. Some of these participants are public members, but most are licensed professionals.

II. FARB in the 1990s

In 1990, FARB underwent another reorganization and hired its first part-time Executive Director, Randolph P. Reaves, the Executive Officer and General Counsel to the Association of State and Provincial Psychology Boards (ASPPB) and the author of *The Law of Professional Licensing and Certification* (Reaves, 1982). Under his leadership, membership in the organization was expanded to include individuals and other entities involved in professional regulation such as attorneys, board members, investigators, staff, and testing companies. The individual members were called associate members, while those involved as vendors were named affiliates. Later, a contributing membership category was established. In 1998, the names of the categories were modified, but the concept to include more members of the regulatory community stayed the same.

As the 1990s began, FARB began to grow, not only in terms of new classes of membership, but also as the size of its full membership expanded from 5 associations of regulatory boards in 1989 to 12 such entities in 1998. Currently there are 11 full members:

American Association of State Counseling Boards
American Association of State Social Work Boards

American Association of Veterinary State Boards
Association of State and Provincial Psychology Boards
Federation of Chiropractic Licensing Boards
International Association of Boards of Examiners in Optometry, Inc.
National Association of Boards of Examiners of Long Term Care Administrators
National Association of State Boards of Accountancy
National Council of Architectural Registration Boards
National Council of Examiners of Engineering and Surveying
National Council of State Boards of Nursing

A. Expansion of FARB Services

In the 1990s, the services offered to the licensure community also expanded. The FARB newsletter, originally dubbed the *FAHRB Wire*, was re-instituted under the name *FARB Facts*. It is now distributed to all members and others within the licensure community three times a year. Each issue contains articles on professional licensing issues, summaries of important judicial decisions, and news of coming events of interest to those involved in professional licensing.

During its growing years, FARB was fortunate to have excellent leaders. Dr. Jerald Jorgensen, representing ASPPB, served as president for several years. Under Jorgensen's leadership, ASPPB supplemented FARB's resources and even contributed the professional services of Emily Bentley, the ASPPB Director of Publications. Bentley's talents made FARB meetings and publications as professional as any in the regulatory community. Jorgensen was followed as President by Doris Nay of the National Council of State Boards of Nursing, and she shepherded the organization during three more years of success before handing the reins to Dr. Greg Gormanous, also from ASPPB.

In 1993, FARB offered its first Attorney Certification Course. The three-day meeting is a continuing legal education seminar for attorneys who work in professional regulation. It was a success from the very beginning. Over the years, it has drawn large numbers of regulatory lawyers to plenary and small group discussions on the law that regulates professionals and the boards that license those professionals.

Beginning in1996, FARB offered a leadership course for those individuals involved in professional regulatory matters at the national or international level. The meeting gives those individuals the opportunity to interact on issues that are different from those working at the regulatory board level, such as managing a national or international testing program.

During its quarter century of existence, FARB has tried to recognize those who contributed the most to its ongoing operations. Jack Atkinson was one of the first to receive FARB's Distinguished Service Award. Later, Marsha Kelly, a board member from the National Council of State Boards of Nursing, was also recognized. Marsha served tirelessly for year as head of FARB's program committee. Patricia S. Bizzell, a board member from ASPPB, serviced as Secretary Treasurer for many years, and she too was honored with a Distinguished Service Award in 1995.

B. FARB Objectives

Today, FARB maintains the following objectives:

- Exchange information and engage in programs and joint activities relating to the licensing of professionals.
- Provide a forum for cooperation in solving the mutual problems of participating associations
- Engage in activities to improve the standards of the professions, the delivery of services, and the services of regulatory licensing agencies for the welfare and protection of the public
- Provide educational opportunities and legal updates for lawyers who represent regulatory boards
- Share information and processes on the education of professionals, including accreditation of schools, colleges, and continuing education programs
- Foster communication and discussion regarding the latest assessment techniques for associations of regulatory boards and their members

C. FARB Accomplishments

Since FARB Forums and Leadership Conferences attract board members, administrators, and attorneys from diverse professions, these meetings provide unique opportunities to discuss issues and formulate viewpoints that span all professional regulation. This began as early as 1975, when FARB became a vocal critic of the Federal Trade Commission's intrusion into state regulatory matters. More recently, FARB joined the fray over the very pointed findings and recommendations of the PEW Commission which strongly critized the current state of professional regulation.

Recently, FARB began to consider the feasibility and desirability of a Code of Conduct for board members. At the 23rd Annual Forum, participants were divided into small groups and asked to define the elements of such a code. Although the results were wide ranging, there was consensus on the areas that such a code should cover and the language that should be used:

Public Protection and Impartiality

- Board members shall act fairly, be non-partisan and unbiased in their role of protecting the public.
- The bases/foundation of all board member decisions shall be in the interest of public protection and board members should be aware of potential conflicts of interest.

Participation

- A board member shall not neglect his or her responsibilities to the board, including regular attendance, preparedness and committee assignments.
- Board members shall not participate in board decisions in which they will realize direct or indirect financial benefit. Board members shall not participate in board decisions in which their personal bias compromises their objectivity or where an appearance of bias jeopardizes the credibility of the board's decision in the matter.

Participation in Professional Association Activities

- Board members shall not hold an office in a professional or trade organization of the regulated profession.
- A board member shall not serve as an officer or committee chair in the association of professionals he/she regulates while still a board member, unless authorized by statute.

Speaking for the Board

- Board members shall not speak or act for the board without proper authorization.

Board Member Conduct

- Board members shall conduct themselves in a manner that respects the integrity of the board, its processes, and all participants, including board members, staff, licensees, and the public.

- Board members shall recognize the equal role/responsibility of all board members.

Appropriate Roles

- A board member shall not be involved in the day-to-day management and personnel issues of the board unless required by statute, rule or policy.
- Board members shall make policy; staff shall implement said policy.

Confidentiality

- Board members and staff shall maintain the confidentiality of confidential documents and information.
- Board members shall protect the confidentiality of board matters.

Dealing with Conflicts of Interest

- Board members shall reveal actual or perceived conflicts of interest.
- Upon realization of a conflict of interest or the appearance of a conflict of interest or upon a loss of objectivity, a board member shall immediately excuse himself or herself from board decision-making in the matter.

III. Conclusion

FARB has now been in existence for a quarter of a century. Just as professional licensing has seen change, so has the organization. It has seen growth and a broad expansion of service to the professional regulatory community. If one thing remains unchanged about FARB, it is the continuing belief that professionals must be heavily involved in the regulation of the professions.

Reference

Reaves, R. P. (1982). *The law of professional licensing and certification.* Montgomery, AL: Publications for Professionals.

THREE: *Implications and Conclusions*

The Meaning and Implications of the Credentialing Mission

Craig G. Schoon and I. Leon Smith

Professional Examination Service, New York, New York

We have examined the mission of licensure and certification organizations with respect to their legal, social, and political foundations. In this chapter, we will review the licensure and certification mission from these perspectives, emphasizing the meaning and implications of the credentialing mission for licensure and certification stakeholders and for the organizations that conduct credentialing activities.

I. The Legal Foundation of Licensure and Certification

The mission of the U.S. Constitution is the promotion of the public welfare. The Constitution provides the legal basis for the regulation of professions, which is carried out by the states. The states' charge to protect the public through licensure of professional practice has one and only one legitimate goal: the protection of the pub-

214

lic. The state's power to regulate professional practice is backed by the police power of the state. Furthermore, a license is recognized as the property right of the individual, and this property right is protected under the due process laws of the Constitution. Atkinson's chapter (Chapter 6) gives a full and detailed analysis of the legal basis for licensure and the implications of this legal foundation for the mission of licensure boards.

The legal basis for licensure extends to the realm of nonprofit organizations. State boards often join together in associations or federations of boards of licensure, which are incorporated as nonprofit entities. Nonprofit corporations exist on the basis of the government's recognition that private sector organizations that promote the public welfare should be exempt from taxation. The two common types of nonprofit organizations in the credentialing area are the 501(c)(3) and the 501(c)(6) corporations, as designated by the IRS. 501(c)(3) corporations are known as "charitable" organizations; their mission is to directly benefit the public welfare through a variety of activities, including education and research. The 501(c) (6) designation, on the other hand, is often given to membership and/or certification associations. Such corporations are known as "business leagues," and their primary mission is to promote the business interests of their members, which indirectly benefits the public welfare. According to Hopkins (1992, p. 12), "For example, while charitable and social welfare organizations operate to promote the general welfare, trade associations and other forms of business leagues act to promote the welfare of the business and industrial community. Thus, exemption from federal income tax is accorded 'business leagues' under IRC 501(c)(6), presumably on the theory that a healthy business climate advances the public welfare."

Certification organizations are almost always incorporated as 501(c)(6) corporations, as are many associations of boards of licensure. Atkinson (Chapter 6) believes that associations of boards of licensure, and any stakeholder organization dealing with licensure activities, should be incorporated as 501(c)(3) entities. This is because the (c)(3) designation is given to organizations whose mission is directly involved with promotion of the public welfare, which is consistent with the mission of licensure as described above. The promotion of professional interests, a primary mission of (c)(6) organizations, may be incompatible with a primary mission of public protection. Atkinson writes:

> Organizations classified as exempt from taxation under 501(c)(6) of the Internal Revenue Code are free to undertake activities that individual member boards could not undertake based on their status as a governmental agency.

Based on this potential to deviate from the public protection element as the primary purpose, and irrespective of whether the association provides limitations in its mission, regulatory boards would likely be prohibited from membership in section 501(c)(6) entities based on a legal analysis.

This conclusion is based on the fact that a 501(c)(6) entity may, under its tax classification, undertake activities that would clearly violate the authority granted to a regulatory board in its enabling legislation. These activities include lobbying efforts and other programs primarily designed to impact the economics of the profession. (p. 143)

The importance of Atkinson's analysis becomes clear when confronted with the common criticism that licensure appears to promote the economic interests of the licensed profession rather than the protection of the public (see Shimberg, Chapter 7, and Dower, Chapter 9).

Nevertheless, several authors (e.g., Blum, Costello, and Hogan, Chapter 8) indicate that their associations are incorporated as (c)(6) entities. In each case, however, these organizations have mission statements stating their primary mission as the protection of the public. Atkinson's point, on the other hand, is that, even if a (c)(6) entity states that its primary mission is public protection, the (c)(6) designation allows for activities whose goal is the promotion of the broader interests of the profession. To the extent that board members are concerned with this argument and are concerned about the criticism that their board activities have as their "real" motive the advancement of professional interests, we would suggest that an open discussion of the organization's tax status and its meaning be considered as a primary agenda item.

We have seen that the organizational structures of those associations of boards incorporated as (c)(3)'s differ from those incorporated as (c)(6) entities. The National Council of State Boards of Nursing (Zara, Chapter 8), incorporated as a 501(c)(3) entity, has a membership consisting only of state boards of licensure. On the other hand, the National Association of Boards of Examiners of Long Term Care Administrators (NAB) (Hogan, Chapter 8), a (c)(6) entity, has several categories of membership, with "regular" membership status reserved only to state board members. In addition to regular members, NAB has categories of membership called *Associate*, *Subscribing*, and *Distinguished Service*. The right to vote on motions at the delegates' assembly is reserved to regular members. The subscribing member, according to Hogan, is for

representatives of academic institutions whose course of instruction has been approved by the respective board and/or licensing authority. In addition representatives of business or professional organizations may join through this membership category. Subscribing members can serve on all committees except the examination committee and are not eligible to vote, serve on the Board of Governors, or hold office. (p. 184)

Thus, NAB's membership structure allows for the participation of professional interests other than those of board members, but does not allow these members to vote or to hold office on the Board of Governors or the examination committee. We can see, then, that the (c)(6) designation allows for the participation of those with interests that are primarily professional. The mission of the NAB, on the other hand, is clearly the protection of the public; it is "to enhance the effectiveness of state boards of examiners and/or licensing authority of long-term care administrators in meeting their statutory and regulatory duties and responsibilities to protect the health, safety, and welfare of the public" (Hogan, Chapter 8, p. 183). Thus, although the primary mission of the NAB is public protection, it has an incidental mission which allows input from the professional perspective. We have seen that this approach to public protection has a long political history and that our system of government allows maximum leeway in the mingling of public and private interests in meeting the needs of the public (Schoon, 1998).

Hopkins (Chapter 1) and Atkinson (Chapter 6) stress that the legal foundation of certification lies in private sector nonprofit organizations, most usually 501(c)(6) corporations. The IRS has taken the position that the primary purpose of certification activities is to promote the common business interests of those so certified. Hopkins provides several examples of IRS decisions holding that certification organizations' primary purpose is the promotion of their members' business interests rather than public protection. Although public protection is a stated mission of many certification organizations, the IRS has held that a public service mission is incidental to the furtherance of the business interests of the profession if the primary activity of the organization is certification. For example, Hopkins presents the case of a medical specialty certification organization where the IRS ruled that the organization was a business league and not a charitable organization. The IRS ruled that "Although some public benefit may be derived from promoting high professional standards in a particular medical specialty, the activities of the board were held to be directed primarily to serving the interest of the medical profession" (Hopkins, Chapter 1, p. 23). Hopkins gives several examples of such rulings. Hopkins also gives examples of associations classified as "charitable," 501(c)(3) entities, as does Dorn.[1] In particular, if the organization's mission is charitable (e.g., educational or scientific), such a designation may be granted. Hopkins gives the example of an engineering society engaged primarily in scientific research on the public health effects of air conditioning, to which the IRS awarded (c)(3) status.

The certification organizations described in Chapter 4 (Biel, Bertin, Brent,

---

[1] Additional examples of organizations conducting certification programs and receiving recognition as charitable readily exist. In technical advice, the IRS stated that a charitable organization did not jeopardize its exempt status by conducting two certification programs for government personnel who met certain skill and experience standards (*Tech. Adv. Mem.* 99-12-035, Dec. 17, 1998, holding that the primary purpose of the certification programs was to lessen the burdens of government). Similarly, the United States Tax Court ruled that an organization certifying crop seed which met minimum standards established by Indiana and Federal law was charitable (*Tech. Adv. Mem.* 99-12-035, Dec. 17, 1998, holding that the primary purpose of the certification programs was to lessen the burdens of government). The IRS also ruled that an organization certifying products intended for use in pleasure boating, and that met certain safety standards, was properly characterized as charitable (Rev. Ruling 65-61, holding that primary purpose of the certification program was to test for public safety). In each of these situations, the main purpose of the certification program was found to be for the benefit of the general public rather than for the benefit of a specific trade or profession. While true that many of these situations did result in a benefit to the underlying profession, such benefit was only incidental when compared with the greater public benefit conferred. Thus, it appears that as long as the benefit of certification to the profession is only an incidental by-product while the primary befit is to the public at large, the administration of a certification program will not jeopardize or preclude classification as a charity.

The vast majority of certification organizations are properly characterized as business leagues, because most truly are organized for the primary purpose of advancing the interests of a trade or profession. However, the IRS has been clear in ruling that where the primary purpose of the organization (and the certification program) is for the benefit of the general public, classification as a charitable organization can be proper. Such classification is only appropriate, however, when the actual purpose of the organization, as indicated by the governance structure of the organization, the composition of the membership, and the noncertification activities of the organization is to benefit the general public rather than the members of the trade or profession. As most certification organizations do not choose a governing body and structure drawn from those outside the profession, classification as a business league is usually the appropriate classification (Dorn, personal communication).

LaBranche, Murer, and Wooldridge) are all incorporated as 501(c)(6) entities. Many of these certification organizations state that their mission is to recognize and promote competent practice, and that their program, to the extent it is successful, promotes the protection of the public. Atkinson (Chapter 6) and Shimberg (Chapter 7), on the other hand, point out that the public protection features of certification should not be confused with the public protection features of licensure. As Atkinson states,

> A major reason certification programs exist is to enhance the economic opportunities of the individual professional and provide benefits to the individual practitioner—not the public. Any public protection element to certification programs is incidental. As a result, the legal issues, parameters and protections recognized by the judiciary through the interpretation of state and federal constitutions, statutes, and regulations as applied to private sector certifying entities are generally much less stringent than those applied to state and federal agencies. Courts are reluctant to interfere with the decision making of a private sector group involved in the certification process. Judicial decisions have determined that the denial or removal of certification is not an impediment to practice and, thus, not subject to heightened legal scrutiny and constitutional protections. (pp. 126–127).

The government, therefore, is involved with both licensure and certification activities. It is involved directly with licensure activities in that states conduct regulatory activities; it is involved with certification activities to the extent that nonprofit associations, which must obtain their exemption from taxation from the government, conduct these activities. Licensure, therefore, may be defined as a government-directed activity whose direct purpose is to protect the welfare of the public. Certification is, for the most part, a private sector, nonprofit activity whose purpose is to promote the business interests of professions and thereby indirectly benefit the public welfare. In terms of their stakeholders, licensure's sole stakeholder is the public; certification's primary stakeholder is the members of the profession, and incidentally members of the public.

Hamm (Chapter 2) gives a comprehensive description of the means by which a certification organization establishes and demonstrates the value of its certification program. The very act of promoting the credential is an act that would be prohibited for an association of boards or a board of licensure. Hamm makes clear that certification programs have a very strong public protection element and that their success may depend on convincing their stakeholders of this public protection feature. Indeed, many certification programs have features that could be emulated by licensure groups, such as rigorous programs of accreditation, recredentialing by examination, the maintenance of practitioner databases, and the maintenance of disciplinary databases. The programs described herein all have an exemplary commitment to competency assessment and competency assurance, programs that could be emulated by licensure programs. But, because certification is voluntary and private, it cannot be depended upon by the public as a public protection device, even though the public may correctly infer that the use of certified practitioners will increase the probability that it will receive competent care and service.

II. The Social and Political Foundations of Licensure and Certification: Implications for Stakeholders

We have emphasized that governmental and nonprofit organizations exist to meet the needs of their stakeholders. If they misidentify their stakeholders, or if they do not meet their expressed needs, the stakeholders will eventually demand a change in management and/or mission, or will cease to use the organization's services and products (Bryson, 1988). Locke (1690/1952) in his *Second Treatise of Government*, states:

> The legislative being only a fiduciary power to act for certain ends, there remains still in the people a supreme power to remove or alter the legislative when they find the legislative act contrary to the trust reposed in them; for all power given with trust for the attaining an end being limited by that end; whenever that end is manifestly neglected or opposed, the trust must necessarily be forfeited and the power devolve into the hands of those that gave it, who may place it anew where they shall think best for their safety and security. (p. 84)

The primary stakeholder of licensure activities is the public, and the only legitimate goal of licensure is to protect the public. By stating that the public is the primary stakeholder of licensure activities, we must also state who or what is not a stakeholder. Included in this group are the members of the licensed profession; the schools that prepare and train these professionals, the companies that provide resources to the profession, and any other group that has an interest in the practice of the profession other than public protection. By asserting that the members of the licensed profession are not stakeholders of the licensure activities of their boards, we mean that a licensure board's activity must be directed solely to those issues that affect the welfare of the public, and not the welfare of the profession. Licensed professionals constitute the majority of membership of most licensure boards. Their duties, however, as expressed in the public service mission of boards, are exclusively to make decisions that are in the best interest of the public that they serve.

The mission of licensure boards may not be as clear as we might assume, and the board's perception of who its stakeholders are may be at the core of this confusion. Board members may believe that the profession is a primary stakeholder. This perception is common among critics of licensure. For example, Shimberg (Chapter 7) states that licensed professions use their power to restrict entry into the profession, affect pricing of their services, ensure that currently licensed practitioners can retain their ability to practice without having to demonstrate continuing competence, and make it difficult to remove current practitioners from practice despite complaints regarding their ability to practice safely and competently. Shimberg places the primary blame for these problems on the legislators' choice of board members from those practitioners who are active in their professional associations or have political influence with politicians in their state or for reasons other than that they are best qualified to protect the public. As Shimberg (Chapter 7) states,

> In entrusting boards with such extraordinary powers, legislators were counting on board members to use them exclusively in the public interest; that is, to make sure that only qualified individuals were granted licenses and that incompetent or dishonest practitioners would be removed, so that the public would not be harmed. They clearly did not intend these powers to be used to promote the economic interests of the licensed profession. From this, it should be clear that the primary mission of every licensing board must focus on public protection, not on serving the interests of the occupational or professional group. (p. 148)

The primary stakeholder of a certification organization, on the other hand, is the certified practitioner in the profession. Other stakeholders may be their employers, the communities in which they reside, the institutions at which they work, the educational institutions at which they receive their training, and, to an extent that should be specified, the public, which may view the credential as information relevant to the selection of health and other services. Hamm (Chapter 2), Early (Chapter 4), and Dorn (Chapter 3) have described how certification organizations should base their programs on a thorough stakeholder analysis. In the case of certification organizations, the stakeholder analysis should lead to boards and committees that represent stakeholder needs. In the case of licensure boards, since the public constitutes the sole stakeholder, public membership should receive serious consideration (Dower, Chapter 9; Gragnola & Stone, 1997; Finocchio, Dower, McMahon, & Gragnola, 1995; Swankin & Cohen, 1996).

Complex stakeholder issues may arise when certification and licensure programs have overlapping social and political goals. For example, certification programs take on a strong regulatory cast when either a certification is perceived as necessary for employment, or certification examination scores are used by state boards as a component in the licensure decision. In such a situation, the scores from a certification examination may be used for licensure purposes by state boards. In such cases, the public assumes the role of a primary, but not the sole, stakeholder for the certification organization. The resulting question that certification organizations must address is the degree to which the organization has an obligation to meet the public protection needs of the licensure boards, and the extent to which, if any, the certification organization should conduct other activities in place of or in support of normal licensure board functions.

One clear example of such an activity is a certification examination that is also used for licensure purposes. Because the examination is used by boards for licensure, the examination's focus must be on public protection, and not on the assessment of professional activities that do not relate to public protection. For example, a certification organization whose examination is not used for licensure might assess knowledge of professional activities unrelated to public protection. However, certification examinations used for the purpose of licensure should restrict all questions on the examination to items with a direct relation to the protection of the public. Less clear would be the conduct of activities that would normally be undertaken by an association of boards of licensure, such as the establishment and maintenance of disciplinary databases, the formulation of practice acts, continuing education required for maintenance of licensure status, and the study of regulatory issues. Of particular importance in cooperative mission activity of this nature would be the clear understanding of where missions diverge and therefore where the mission activities of one organization may be antithetical to those of the other.

Following our discussion, the most important issue would be for a definite demarcation between activities of the certification organization that promote the interests of the profession, and those that protect the public. All stakeholders of certification other than the public (i.e., the members of the profession, educators, employers, providers of technology, etc.) should not have their needs met in any way that would conflict or compete with public protection needs. We have seen from our analysis that the social and political needs of licensure and certification stakeholders are distinct; when they overlap, it can be difficult to meet the needs of one stakeholder group without neglecting or conflicting with the needs of another. The reader is directed to Wooldridge's chapter (Chapter 4) for a presentation of the mission of a certification agency whose certification program also must meet the public protection needs of licensure boards. In regard to the regulatory implications of certification and licensure of occupational therapists and occupational therapy assistants, Wooldridge (personal communication) confirms that, in those states where licensure is not in effect for these professionals, certification is voluntary; those choosing to practice without being certified are free to do so, even though such a choice may affect the job opportunities of those making the choice not to be certified.

III. The Missions of Credentialing Organizations

The mission statement of an organization is a statement of its purpose. For example, the mission statements in this book address questions such as the following:

- Who are we?
- How are we incorporated?
- Who are our stakeholders, and what social and political needs of theirs do we exist to meet, or what social or political problems do we exist to address?
- What do we do to recognize and meet these needs and/or problems?
- What is our philosophy and what are our core values?
- What makes us distinctive or unique?

The mission statement is the credentialing organization's face to its stakeholders. Stakeholders can read a mission statement and assess whether an organization intends to meet their needs. The mission statement encapsulates the *raison d'être* of the organization; it places the organization firmly in the social and political context of our society and indicates what needs and/or problems of the society or political context it exists to serve. Thus, a certification organization should indicate in its mission statement how its certification program would advance the interests of the profession; a licensure organization should specify how its program would protect the public health, safety, and welfare. Guidelines for generating credentialing mission statements are given in the publication "Guidelines for the Development, Use, and Evaluation of Licensure and Certification Programs" (PES, 1996) and in "Guidelines for Credentialing Programs (Schoon & Smith, 1996).

A. The Licensure Mission

1. The Mission of Boards of Licensure

The mission of a licensure board is contained in its practice act. According to Atkinson (Chapter 6), the practice act should contain a legislative declaration and/or a statement of purpose that clearly indicates that the purpose of the licensure is to protect the public. Atkinson gave examples of such legislative declarations and statements of purpose:

> Section ____. Legislative Declaration
>
> The practice of _____ in the state of _____ is declared a professional practice affecting the public health, safety, and welfare and is subject to regulation and control in the public interest. It is further declared to be a matter of public interest and concern that the practice of _____, as defined in the Act, merit and receive the confidence of the public and that only qualified persons be permitted to engage in the practice of _____ in this state. This Act shall be liberally construed to carry out these objectives and purposes.
>
> Section ____. Statement of Purpose
>
> It is the purpose of this Act to promote, preserve, and protect the public health, safety, and welfare by and through the effective control and regulation of the practice of _____; the licensure of _____, the license, control, and regulation of persons, in or out of this state, who practice _____ within this state. (p. 128).

Atkinson (Chapter 6) says that such explicit statements of purpose within a practice act "not only establish the mission of the board, but also help shape judicial interpretation through an analysis of this important language that can be cited to support board decisions in the event of a legal challenge" (p. 129). The absence of such statements in some practice acts exacerbates the criticisms against licensure boards that their purpose is not public protection. Dower (Chapter 9) indicates that in the PEW review of licensure acts, few statements of mission were found.

Showers (Chapter 8) presents the mission statement of the Wisconsin Department of Regulation and Licensing. This statement of purpose is for agencies within a state that provide centralized administrative services to licensure boards. Showers' mission statement is an excellent example of a complete mission statement that addresses not only the purpose of the department, but also how the mission will be accomplished, the goals and objectives of the mission, a stakeholder analysis, and the philosophy and core values of the Department. The statement of mission of the Department is as follows (Showers, Chapter 8):

> Our mission is to safeguard the general well being of Wisconsin consumers of state regulated occupational and professional services. The mission will be accomplished by:
>
> 1. Establishing appropriate eligibility requirements and ensuring professional competence by establishing evaluation procedures clearly related to safe and effective practice.
> 2. Setting the practice parameters and standards of conduct to achieve safe and effective practice.
> 3. Enforcement of standards. (p. 186)

Farrar (Chapter 8) presents a more personal statement of the mission of a board from the inside, as a public member of a licensure board. Farrar has also served as a board secretary and a board Chair, and is a licensed member of a profession. Farrar indicates at several points in her chapter that perhaps the major problem with a board's mission is a lack of understanding of the board's purpose by the board's members, the candidates for licensure, and the public that is to be served by the license. Board members often are not familiar with state statutes and administrative codes, and the public as well as board members are often less than fully aware of the procedures for establishing practice parameters and standards of conduct or of the procedures of due process that must be followed in disciplinary hearings. Farrar gives the perspective, from the inside, of the demanding nature of board membership and the challenges of educating the board members, candidates for licensure, and the public on the mission of the board. Farrar's description of the problems boards encounter in serving the public points to the overriding importance of a clear mission statement as an educational tool and guide for stakeholders of licensure activities.

2. *The Mission of Associations/Federations/Councils of Boards of Licensure*

Atkinson emphasizes that the mission of an association of boards should be identical to the mission of the boards that are its members. Thus, the primary mission of an association of boards should be the facilitation of its member boards' ability to advance the public health, safety, and welfare. Atkinson (Chapter 6) describes other appropriate goals and objectives of associations of licensure boards as (a) contracting and evaluating licensure examinations used by the boards, (b) disciplinary data banks, (c) model licensure legislation, (d) compilations of licensure statutes and regulations, (e) practitioner data banks, (f) clearinghouses for licensure transfers, (g) general publications, and (h) board member training. Zara (Chapter 8) presents the mission of the National Council of State Boards of Nursing as follows:

> [The Council's mission is] to lead in nursing regulation by assisting member boards, collectively and individually, to promote safe and effective nursing practice in the interest of protecting public health and welfare. The purpose of the National Council is to provide an organization through which state boards of nursing act and counsel together on matters of common interest and concern affecting the public health, safety, and welfare, including the development of licensing examinations in nursing. (p. 189)

Hogan (Chapter 8) presents the mission of the National Association of Boards of Long Term Care Administrators. It is "to enhance the effectiveness of state boards of examiners and/or licensing authority of long-term care administrators in meeting their statutory and regulatory duties and responsibilities to protect the health, safety, and welfare of the public" (p. 183). The NAB is an example of as association of boards incorporated as a 501(c)(6) nonprofit corporation, as we have seen.

The NASBA (Costello, Chapter 8) and the AICPA (Blum, Chapter 8) are both incorporated as (c)(6) entities. The mission of the NASBA, whose membership is composed of state board members, is to

> enhance the effectiveness of state boards of accountancy. Our goals are to provide high-quality, effective programs and services; identify, research, and analyze major current and emerging issues affecting state boards of accountancy; strengthen and maintain communications with member boards to facilitate the exchange of ideas and opinion; and develop and foster relationships with organizations that impact the regulation of public accounting. (p. 174)

Costello goes on the say that "NASBA is unique because it is the only accounting association dedicated to the protection of the public" (p. 177). On the other hand, and in accordance with NASBA's status as a (c)(6) nonprofit entity, the association "has been actively involved in assessing the international market for recognition for CPAs, promoting the CPA designation as the global standard for professional accountants, and developing mutual recognition among countries" (p. 177).

The AICPA (Blum, Chapter 8) is the professional association for accountants. It has a mission to "provide members with the resources, information, and leadership that enable them to provide valuable services in the highest professional manner to benefit the public as well as employers and clients" (p. 166). In accord with its (c)(6) status, the stakeholders of AICPA are both the public and the members of the profession. Blum reports that

> The key stakeholders within the accountancy profession are the public; the public regulators who must answer to their legislators, e.g., through sunset review; the profession itself, whose image of integrity and objectivity is tarnished when any member does not uphold all of the professional standards; the business world, especially the financial markets, which relies on CPAs to ensure that fair information is provided to investors; the academic community training future CPAs; and those aspiring to enter the profession. (p. 166)

The mission of AICPA, then, is to serve both the public and the profession.

3. The Mission of Stakeholder Organizations

The field of licensure has stakeholder organizations that provide services to state boards. Organizations such as CLEAR (Brinegar, Chapter 9) and FARB (Reaves, Chapter 9) exist to provide such services. Brinegar gives an exemplary statement of the mission of CLEAR.

> CLEAR is a 501(c)(3) not-for-profit organization whose primary purpose is therefore educational. . . . CLEAR is an association of individuals, agencies and organizations that comprise the international community of professional and occupational regulation. CLEAR is a dynamic forum for improving the quality and understanding of regulation in order to enhance public protection. (pp. 195–196)

Brinegar goes on to describe how CLEAR accomplishes its mission and what makes CLEAR unique in the credentialing field. Brinegar's chapter contains a model of a mission statement that specifies (a) tax-exempt status, (b) stakeholder analysis, (c) mission statement and objectives, and (d) what makes CLEAR unique in the field.

Reaves (Chapter 9) describes the purpose of FARB, a (c)(3) entity, as being to "provide a means for those interested in professional licensing to gather to discuss mutual issues of concern and learn, not only from formal presentations, but from interaction with others interested in the same issues" (p. 207). Reaves indicates that full membership in FARB is restricted to associations of regulatory boards.

As an example of the service FARB provides its member boards, Reaves describes discussions regarding a Code of Conduct for board members. Given the criticism that licensure board members tend to serve the interests of the profession rather than the public, the Code of Conduct provides an outstanding example of a possible code that any licensure board could use to ensure the recognition of board members that public protection is their role duty. For example, conflict of interest between board membership and membership in a professional association is squarely addressed. The Code recommends that "Board members shall not hold an office in a professional or trade organization of its regulated profession" (p. 212). If adopted by licensure boards, the Code of Conduct would go far in educating board members as to their duty to serve the public and to address the criticisms of many stakeholders.

B. The Certification Mission

1. The Mission of Certification Organizations

Many certification organizations in the health professions state as their mission the assessment of competence, which implies a benefit to the public safety, health, and welfare. For example, Bertin (Chapter 4) reports that "The mission of the Board of Pharmaceutical Specialties is to improve public health through recognition and promotion of specialized training, knowledge, and skills in pharmacy by certification of pharmacist specialists" (p. 78). The mission of the AACN is "to be a leader in providing comprehensive credentialing programs that contribute to the desired health outcomes for individuals" (Biel, Chapter 4, p. 87). Wooldridge (Chapter 4) states that "Above all else, the mission of NBCOT is to serve the public interest" (p. 100). And Murer (Chapter 4) reports that "The PTCB mission is to certify pharmacy technicians to enable them to work more effectively with pharmacists to improve patient care" (p. 93).

In accomplishing their missions, certification organizations can conduct activities that licensing boards and associations cannot. Thus, they can lobby on behalf of the profession and promote the economic and social benefits of certification to the profession. They can lobby employers to hire certified professionals and promulgate codes of conduct and codes of ethical conduct, and, in general, they have objectives and goals involving the promotion of the business interests of the profession. Hamm

(Chapter 3) presents an excellent discussion on how certification programs can promote their credential through such activities and goals as those mentioned here.

Certification organizations have a broader range of stakeholders than licensure organizations. Their stakeholders encompass not only the public, but also, and most importantly, the members of the profession, employers and educators, legislators, and businesses selling goods and services to certified professionals. The missions and mission objectives of certification organizations, accordingly, can go beyond protection of the public to advancement of the profession. Accordingly, whereas licensure necessarily implies the obligation to protect the public, certification can have a focus on competence not correlated with public protection. For example, the mission of the ASAE Certification program, as reported by LaBranche (Chapter 4), is "to promote and support excellence and professionalism among association executives, and to work diligently to increase the effectiveness, image and impact of associations to better serve their members and society" (p. 110). There are hundreds of private certification programs for professionals that have little or nothing to do with protection of the public (Pare, 1996). For example, there are Certified Professional Resume Writers, Certified Customer Service Specialists, Certified Professional Tennis Instructors, and Certified Economic Developers. In general, certification programs that lie outside of the health-related professions have missions that focus exclusively on the advancement of the business interests of the professional. Certification programs in the health professions, on the other hand, of necessity also have a focus on the assessment of competencies that involve a benefit to the public.

2. The Mission of Stakeholder Organizations

NOCA/NCCA, 501(c)(3) entity, is the primary stakeholder organization for certification organizations. The chapter on the mission and objectives of NOCA/NCCA (Early, Chapter 5) describes the efforts made to enhance the effectiveness of certification activities, particularly in the health-related professions. Early reports its mission, vision statement, and function as follows:

> NOCA promotes excellence in competency assurance for practitioners in all occupations and professions. According to its vision statement, NOCA will be the international leader in advancing the theory and practice of competency assurance through education, research, and the promulgation of standards in the public interest.
>
> NOCA's functions include:

- Developing standards and accredits organizations that meet them through the NCCA
- Evaluating methods for assuring competency
- Disseminating findings of competency assurance research
- Helping employers make informed hiring decisions
- Establishing standards, recommending policies, and defining roles for certifying organizations
- Assisting consumers to make informed decisions about qualified providers. (pp. 116–117)

NOCA offers an outstanding example of the mission of a stakeholder organization for certification agencies. Its mission focus on competency assurance stems from its founding as an organization dedicated to finding an alternative to licensure for the allied health professions. NOCA's program of accreditation of certification programs offers an excellent model for any credentialing program whose aim is to protect the public through the identification of competent practitioners.

IV. Summary and Conclusions

Mission statements are a hallmark of governmental and private, nonprofit organizations. The government's mission is to fulfill the Constitution, whose purpose is to promote the welfare of the public. Licensure and certification are activities conducted by governmental and private, nonprofit entities to promote the health, safety, and welfare of the public. Licensure and certification, together called credentialing, are activities whose mission is based on the constitutional directive to promote the public welfare. In the case of licensure, this directive is given to states, and their sole mission is to promote the public health, safety, and welfare. Many licensure boards join together in associations, federations, or councils of boards of licensure that are incorporated as private, nonprofit organizations. Such nonprofit associations of boards must have as their primary mission the mission of the boards that are their members.

The government recognizes that the private sector may also conduct activities that promote the public welfare. This recognition takes the form of allowing tax exemption to those private sector entities that have a mission to promote the public welfare. It is clear, then, that nonprofit organizations also have a mission based on the Constitution of the United States to promote the public health, safety, and welfare. The government grants tax exemption for such entities because, in the absence of these entities, the government itself would likely have to conduct the activity. Accordingly, certification is conducted by private sector, nonprofit organizations, and licensure is conducted by the government with the support of nonprofit entities.

Nonprofit entities must submit their mission statements to the government, and the government, through the IRS, decides whether to grant tax exemption to the entity, and what kind of tax-exempt entity it is, based on the entity's purpose. The primary types of tax-exempt organizations involved with credentialing are 501(c)(3) entities, called "charitable" organizations, and 501(c)(6) entities, called "business leagues." Charitable, (c)(3) organizations often have an education- or research-based mission that directly benefits the public welfare. Business leagues, as (c)(6) organizations, have missions that primarily promote the business interests of the members of the organization and incidentally benefit the public welfare. Associations, federations, and councils of state boards of licensure are incorporated as either (c)(3) or (c)(6) entities, with the recommendation that the (c)(3) status may in many cases be appropriate, given the primacy of the public protection mission. Certification organizations are incorporated primarily as (c)(6) entities, although they may be incorporated as (c)(3) entities if their primary mission is charitable (e.g., educational or scientific). For the most part, if an organizations primary activity is certification, the IRS has ruled that this activity primarily benefits the business interests of the profession, and is therefore a (c)(6) entity.

The mission statements of credentialing organizations are necessary in order to obtain their tax-exempt status from the government and to state whether their primary mission is to benefit the public welfare or the business interests of the profession. They are also necessary in order to state how the organization will meet the needs of its stakeholders. If the stakeholders of an organization do not believe in, or have credence in, the mission of the organization, the organization may founder through lack of support. Mission statements change with the changing needs of stakeholders. As the demands and challenges of credentialed professionals change, mission statements change to meet their needs. Clear and effective mission statements are especially imperative in today's rapidly changing healthcare environment.

Although it may seem that the mission of licensure and certification organizations is clear, with little need for explicit statement, there are stakeholders who challenge their missions. Many stakeholders in the licensure area believe that the primary mission of licensure is actually to promote the business interests of the licensed professions rather than protect the public. The mission of many certification organizations incorporated as (c)(6) entities is stated as promotion of the public welfare rather than promotion of the interests of the profession. In the area of licensure, in order to meet this criticism, associations of boards may consider incorporation as (c)(3) entities, which would directly address their primary mission of public protection. In the area of certification, organizations that have public protection as their primary stated mission should make a clear distinction between the protection offered by "competency assessment" and that offered by statutory licensure, and that they conduct a stakeholder analysis so that their mission can serve their broad range of stakeholders in addition to the public. Clear and effective mission statements by both licensure and certification groups enhance their credence to their stakeholders and therefore increase the probability that credentialing will fulfill its social and political responsibilities to the public and to the professions.

References

Bryson, J. M. (1988). *Strategic planning for public and nonprofit organizations: A guide to strengthening and sustaining organizational achievement.* San Francisco, CA: Jossey-Bass.

Hopkins, B. R. (1992). *The law of tax-exempt organizations* (6th ed.). New York: John Wiley & Sons.

Finocchio, L. J., Dower, C. M., McMahon, T., Gragnola, C. M., & the Taskforce on Health Care Workforce Regulation. (1995). *Reforming health care workforce regulation: Policy considerations for the 21 century.* San Francisco, CA: Pew Health Professions Commission.

Gragnola, C. M., & Stone, E. (1997). *Considering the future of health care workforce regulation.* San Francisco, CA: UCSF Center for the Health Professions.

Locke, J. (1690/1952). In Peardon, T. P. (Ed.). *The second treatise of government.* New York. The Bobbs-Merrill Company.

Pare, M. A. (Ed.). (1996). *Certification and accreditation programs directory: A descriptive guide to national voluntary certification and accreditation programs for professionals and institutions.* Detroit, MI: Gale Research.

Professional Examination Service (1996). *Guidelines for the development, use, and evaluation of licensure and certification programs.* New York: Author.

Schmitt, K. (1995). What is Licensure? In J. C. Impara (Ed.), *Licensure testing: Purposes, procedures, and practices* (pp. 3–32). Lincoln, NE: Buros Institute of Mental Measurements.

Schoon, C. G. (1998). Guidelines for the development, use, and interpretation of credentialing examinations. In A. N. Wiens (Ed.), *Comprehensive clinical psychology; Vol. 2, Professional issues* (pp. 107–119). Oxford, England: Elsevier Science.

Schoon, C. G., & Smith, I. L. (1996). Guidelines for credentialing programs. *Professions Education Quarterly,* 17 (4), 6–9.

Swankin, D. A., & Cohen, R. A. (1996, November). The place of the public in the credentialing process. Paper presented at the Fifth Annual PES Invitational Seminar on The Credentialing Mission. Palm Beach, Florida.

Index

AACN. *See* American Association of Critical-Care Nurses
AACN Certification Corporation, 85
    mission statement, 87, 228
Accessibility of test sites, 43
Accreditation standard, 116, 118, 119
AICPA. *See* American Institute of Certified Public Accountants
American Association of Critical-Care Nurses
    mission of, 85
American Boards of Medical Specialties, 148
American Institute of Certified Public Accountants
    mission of, 164
    mission statement, 166, 170
American Pharmaceutical Association, 77
American Society of Association Executives
    certification program, 111
    mission of, 108, 229
    mission statement, 110
    programs, 108
Application, 43
    and due process, 131
    denial of and due process, 131
    difference between 501(c)(3) and 501(c)(6) organizations, 142

[Application]
    efficient processing of, 187
    making the process easy for applicants, 43, 44, 97, 187
    for renewal of certification, 106, 107
    review of, 69
    satisfying request for materials, 41
    screening of, 104, 115, 120, 181, 182
    standards, 122
    waiver of fee, 117
ASAE. *See* American Society of Association Executives
Associations of regulatory boards, 134 *See also* Federation of Associations of Regulatory Boards
    development of services and programs, 144
    and 501(c)(6) status, 143
    meeting of, 137
    membership, 136, 142
    mission of, 135
    services provided by, 139
    tax status, 140
Atkinson, Dale J., 4, 7, 11, 14, 124, 208, 211, 215–217, 219, 224–226

Bertin, Richard J., 77, 84, 219, 228

Biel, Melissa, 85, 87, 219, 228
Bifurcation, 28, 118
  as a structuring consideration for tax-exempt organizations, 27
Blum, James, D., 164, 216, 226, 227
Board of directors, 24, 57, 58, 73, 87, 90, 107, 175, 190 *See also* Board members; Boards
  composition of, 101
  consumer representation on, 121
  selection of, 28
Board members *See also* Board of directors; Boards
  avoidance of conflicts of interest, 63
  determination of an effective number of, 67
  determination of willingness to serve, 70
  diversity of, 69
  improving communication among, 160
  nomination of, 62
  role of, 158
  selection of, 38, 159
  term limits, 68
  training and orientation, 71
Board of Pharmaceutical Specialties
  mission of, 77, 228
  mission statement, 78
  objectives, 80
  specialty recognition and certification, 79
Boards *See also* Board of directors; Board members
  accountability of, 127
  associations of regulatory, 134
  disciplinary authority of, 130
  failure to enforce practice and conduct, 156
  improvement of, 158
  mission of, 128
  misuse of powers, 153
  primary importance of public protection of, 127

[Boards]
  role of, 125
  selection of, 67
Boards of Accountancy, 167
Boards of licensure, 9, 215
  and 501(c)(3) status, 7
  and 501(c)(6) status, 7
BPS. See Board of Pharmaceutical Specialties
Brent, Graham J., 88, 219
Brinegar, Pam, 194, 199, 227
Business leagues, 6, 18, 19, 25, 28, 142, 215 *See also* 501(c)(6) organizations

Candidate, 24, 76
  for board service, 62, 63, 68
  collection of data from, 97, 107
  concerns about failing of, 66
  definition of, 18
  facilitating application process for, 97
  fairness to, 188
  Internal Revenue Service decisions rulings regarding, 21
  notification of, 70
  providing information to, 139
  requirements of, 26, 89, 112, 182
  retesting of unsuccessful, 179
  screening of, 23, 79, 102–104, 106, 138, 181
  for specialty areas, 80
  as stakeholders, 187
  surveying of, 188
  volume of, 41
CCO. *See* National Commission for the Certification of Crane Operators
Center for Quality Assurance in International Education, 118
Certificants, importance of providing special recognition for, 44
Certification
  argument in favor of over licensure, 11

[Certification]
  definition, 2, 126, 146, 219
  distinction between public and private
    sectors, 127
  legal foundation of, 7, 214
  origins of, 3, 148
  purpose, 1
  social and political foundations of, 10
Certification board, 37, 38, 56, 57, 63, 65,
  66, 69, 70, 93, 99, 102
  public representation on, 66
Certification organizations, 4, 5, 7, 8, 10, 12–
  14, 16, 17, 26, 29, 32, 33, 38, 41–47, 49,
  50, 54, 55, 116, 118–120, 122, 222, 228,
  229
  classification of, as tax-exempt entities,
    26
  demarcation between activities of, 222
  and 501(c)(6) status, 7, 10
  goal of, 11
  mission of, 228, 229, 232
  need for funding marketing and public
    relations, 45
  questions for evaluating value of creden-
    tial, 49
  rationale for tax-exempt status, 16
  and tax-exempt status, 16
Certification programs, 87, 126, 222
  of American Society of Association Ex-
    ecutives, 111
  anatomy of, 24
  Internal Revenue Service rulings regard-
    ing, 24
  management and operation of, 38
  motives for developing, 33
  reason for, 33, 126
  voluntary, 115
Certification renewal, 104–107
Charitable organizations, 7, 17, 19, 24, 29,
  215 *See also* 501(c)(3) organizations
  and private inurement doctrine, 20

Charitable organizations, 19, 215, 216
  categories of, 19
  Internal Revenue Service rulings regard-
    ing, 19
Choosing an effective board, 67
CLEAR. *See* Council on Licensure, En-
    forcement and Regulation. code of eth-
    ics, 26
Code of standards of conduct, of American
    Society of Association Executives, 112
Communication plan/strategy, development
    of for marketing a credential, 44
Competence, 36, 51, 58, 101, 119, 126, 148,
    150, 151, 153, 157, 169, 172, 180, 186,
    192, 198, 204, 225, 229
  continuing, 43, 46, 121, 125, 151, 152,
    204, 221
  definition of, 118, 170
  indicators of, 100
  measure of, 11, 32, 54, 55, 118, 119, 228
  minimum, 129, 138, 142, 149, 150, 192
  promotion of, 86, 182
Conflict of Interests Statement, 63
Conflicts of interest, preemptive recognition
    of, 63
Constitution, U.S., 3, 128, 131, 144, 214
  mission of, 214
  promotion and protection of public wel-
    fare, 5
Continuing competence, 36, 43, 46, 125, 167,
    204, 221
Continuing education, 59, 81, 94, 96, 97,
    113, 125, 151, 168, 169, 170, 175, 179,
    187, 211
Continuing professional education. See Con-
    tinuing education
Costello, David A., 174, 216, 226
Council on Licensure, Enforcement and
    Regulation, 38, 118, 160, 208, 227
  membership, 195
  mission of, 194

[Council on Licensure, Enforcement and Regulation]
  mission statement, 195, 227
  programs and services, 197
Council of State Governments, 194
Credential, 2, 4, 12, 31, 33, 34, 35, 36, 37, 38, 42, 43, 45, 46, 48, 50, 51, 54, 59, 60, 81, 85, 99, 131, 136, 150, 151, 175, 187 *See also* Credentialing
  definition, 2
  developing a strategy to establish and demonstrate the value of, 37
  establishing and demonstrating the value of, 31
  evaluating an organization's success in developing the value of, 46, 49
  legal foundations, 12
  motivations for seeking, 81
  origin of term, 2
  promoting the merits of, 43
  scope of, 51
  social and political foundations of, 12
  importance of reputation of certification body, 33
Credentialing, 2, 4, 5, 7, 12, 13, 31, 32, 34–40, 41, 43–45, 47, 48, 51, 53–55, 57–60, 62–64, 66–69, 71, 72, 73, 78, 83, 84, 87, 92, 93, 101, 114–116, 118, 120, 121, 122, 126, 127, 145, 146, 163, 175, 182, 187, 188, 197, 204, 207, 214, 215, 220, 223, 224, 227, 228, 230–232 *See also* Credential
  basis for, 5
  goals of, 53
  governance structure of, 53
  purpose of, 12
  social and political foundations, 7
  use of information from stakeholders for evaluation, 48
Credentialing board, 37, 38, 52, 53, 69

Credentialing mission, meanings and implications, 214–232
Credentialing organizations, 12, 51, 52, 54, 59, 65, 223
  addressing value enhancement, 35
  characteristics of a good governing board, 55
  importance of mission statement in distinction of National Conference of Bar Examiners, 182
  importance of independence of certification body, 37
  missions of, 223, 231
  need for high-quality assessment and examination services, 39
  selection criteria for public members, 71
  survey instrument for studying, 54
Credentialing program, 38, 51, 52, 53, 55, 56, 58, 59, 62–65, 67, 68, 72, 83
  legal segregation from professional association, 56
  responsiveness to the public, 64
Criticisms of licensure activities, 7, 221
Cultivation of leadership
  of board members, 69

Data
  collection of by National Board for Certification in Occupational Therapy, 107
  collection of by Pharmacy Technician Certification Board, 97, 98
  collection of through surveys and questionnaires, 97
  creation of certificant database by Board of Pharmaceutical Specialties, 80
  database containing disciplinary information, 137, 138
  database containing practitioner information, 139
  database of the American Society of Association Executives, 108

[Data]
  determining adequacy of applicant database, 41
  ensuring integrity of, 112
  importance of marketing data for credentialing effort, 35
  importance off developing database for marketing strategy, 41
  market research, 47
Data bank. *See* Data
Database. *See* Data
Delegation, and legal authority of board, 133
Disciplinary actions, 56, 90, 102, 104, 105, 121, 125, 130, 131, 137–139, 147, 157, 159, 161, 180, 192, 197, 208, 220, 225
Disciplinary committees, 69
Disciplinary data, 138, 226
Disciplinary reasons, 131
Diversity, of board members, 69
Dorn, Susan, 13, 53, 218, 221, 218
Dower, Catherine, 8, 200, 206, 216, 222, 224, 232
Due process, 6, 127, 128, 131, 132, 180, 191, 215, 225

Early, Larry Allan, 13, 14, 114, 221, 229
Educational entities, 19
  as charitable organizations, 19
  examination process
  importance of, 39
Examination program, 24, 39, 102, 107, 137, 142, 192

FARB. *See* Federation of Associations of Regulatory Boards
Farrar, Lynda, 178, 225
Federation of Associations of Regulatory Boards *See also* Associations of regulatory boards
  Code of Conduct, 211
  history, 207

[Federation of Associations of Regulatory Boards]
  membership, 207
  mission of, 207, 228
  programs and services, 209
Federation of State Medical Boards, 157
501(c)(3) organizations, 6, 7, 14, 17, 18, 20, 30, 73, 117, 140, 142, 143, 181, 189, 195, 215–223, 231 *See also* Charitable organizations
  deductibility of gifts to, 18
  definition of, 18
  as distinguished from 501(c)(6) organizations, 6, 215
  mission of, 231
  requirements of, 7
501(c)(6) organizations, 6, 7, 10, 13, 14, 18, 21, 30, 73, 77, 85, 88, 93, 100, 108, 142, 143, 164, 183, 215–223, 231 *See also* Business leagues
  and associations of regulatory boards, 143
  as distinguished from 501(c)(3) organizations, 6, 215
  membership, 143
  mission of, 6, 231
  requirements of, 7, 217
Focus groups, 35, 42
Formal review timetable for evaluating an organization's performance, 46
Foundations for the development of certification examinations, 103
Foundations of licensure and certification, 1

Governance structure, 13, 59, 60, 72, 73
  of credentialing organizations, 53, 55
Government
  representation of a profession in affairs of, 27
  role of in certification and licensure, 11, 219, 231

[Government]
role of in licensure and certification, 12, 219, 231

Hamm, Michael S., 13, 31, 219, 221, 228
Health professions regulation, mission of, 204
Hogan, John H., 183, 216, 217, 226
Hopkins, Bruce R., 4, 6, 7, 10, 13, 15–19, 21, 23, 30, 117, 146, 215, 217, 218, 232

Improving communication among board members, 160
Institute of Public Administration, 115
Internal Revenue Service, 4–7, 17–19, 21, 22, 24, 27–29, 117, 140, 142, 143, 217
determination of tax-exempt status, 17, 26
filing requirements, 18
interpretation of public service mission, 7
requirement of statement of mission for tax-exempt status, 4
IRS. *See* Internal Revenue Service

LaBranche, Gary A., 108, 219, 229
Leadership, cultivation of in board members, 69
Legal foundation of certification, 7, 214
Legal foundation of licensure and certification, 5, 214, 215
Legal issues in licensure policy, 124, 214
License, definition, 126
Licensed professionals, duties of, 8
Licensure
authority of governing body (board), 125
criteria for eligibility, 125
definition, 2, 3, 145, 219
goal of, 8
grounds for disciplinary action, 125
history, 146
legal foundation, 5, 214
legal issues, 124

[Licensure]
mission of stakeholder organizations, 194
missions of organizations involved in, 164
political nature, 10
and policy, 124
purpose, 1
requirements of, 125
role in society, 145
social and political foundations of, 8
standards for renewal and removal, 125
Licensure board, 6, 8, 10, 14
mission of, 9
Licensure organization, 10, 14, 119
mission of, 10, 232
Licensure program, 38, 128, 151, 222

Market research information, as a key to establishing the value of a credential, 34
Marketing
budgetary concerns, 45
developing a communication plan/strategy, 44
by Pharmacy Technician Certification Board, 97
Member boards, 135–138, 142–144, 176, 177, 189, 190, 215, 226
communication among, 174
cooperation among, 139
definition of, 136
and disciplinary actions, 138
importance of uniform examination program, 137
limitations of, 142
and practice act, 138
Mentoring program for new board members, 71
Mission *See also* Mission statement
achievement of objectives as means of evaluation, 47
of American Institute of Certified Public Accountants, 164

[Mission]
  of associations of regulatory boards, 135
  of boards, 128, 221
  of certification organizations, 228
  of Constitution (U.S.), 214
  of Council on Licensure, Enforcement and Regulation, 194
  of credentialing organizations, 223 adhering to, 46
  evaluating an organization's success in adhering to, 46
  of Federation of Associations of Regulatory Boards, 207
  of health professions regulation, 204
  of licensure boards, 221, 224
  of National Association of Boards of Examiners of Long Term Care Administrators, 183
  of National Association of State Boards of Accountancy, 174
  of National Conference of Bar Examiners, 181
  of National Council of State Boards of Nursing, 189
  of National Organization for Competency Assurance, 229
  of Pew Health Professions Commission, 200
  of stakeholder organizations, 227, 229
  of a state licensing board, 178
  of a state testing unit, 186
Mission statement, 1–4, 7, 10, 12–14, 35, 36, 37, 78, 86, 116, 134, 136, 143, 165, 175, 195, 196, 200, 215–231 *See also* Mission
  of AACN Certification Corporation, 86
  of the American Association of State Social Work Boards, 135
  of American Institute of Certified Public Accountants, 166, 170, 227

[Mission statement]
  of American Society of Association Executives, 110
  of Board of Pharmaceutical Specialties, 78
  of Council on Licensure, Enforcement and Regulation, 195
  definition, 3
  importance, 1, 3, 5
  legal, social, and political foundations, 4
  as means of establishing value of a credential, 35
  of National Association of Boards of Examiners of Long Term Care Administrators, 183, 226
  of National Board for Certification in Occupational Therapy, 100
  of National Commission for Certifying Agencies, 118
  of National Council of State Boards of Nursing, 189, 226
  of National Organization for Competency Assurance, 116
  periodic review of, 37
  purpose of, 12
  requirements of, 4, 8
  of a state testing unit, 186, 225
Misuse of board powers, 153
Model legislation for member boards, 138
Moeser, Erica, 181
Murer, Melissa M., 93, 219, 228

NAB. *See* National Association of Boards of Examiners of Long Term Care Administrators
NASBA. *See* National Association of State Boards of Accountancy. See National Association of State Boards of Accountancy
National Advisory Committee on Health Manpower, 151

National Association of Boards of Examiners of Long Term Care Administrators
  membership, 184, 216
  mission of, 183
  mission statement, 183
National Association of State Boards of Accountancy, 165
  mission, 174
  programs and services. *See* National Board for Certification in Occupational Therapy
  mission of, 100, 228
  mission statement, 100
  programs, 102
National Commission for Certifying Agencies, 38, 54, 114, 116
  history, 115
  mission of, 114
  mission statement, 118
National Commission for Health Certifying Agencies, 114
National Commission for the Certification of Crane Operators
  committee structure, 90
  examination, 89
  key components of certification program, 89
  mission of, 88
National Conference of Bar Examiners, mission of, 181
National Council of State Boards of Nursing
  mission, 189, 216
  National Council structure, 190
  products and services, 191
National Organization for Competency Assurance, 11, 54, 114, 229, 230
  history, 115
  mission of, 114
  mission statement, 116
National Skill Standards Board, 91

NBCOT. *See* National Board for Certification in Occupational Therapy
NCCA. *See* National Commission for Certifying Agencies. See National Commission for Certifying Agencies
NCCA Standards. See Standards for Accreditation of National Certification Organizations
NCHCA. *See* National Commission for Health Certifying Agencies
NOCA. *See* National Organization for Competency Assurance. See National Organization for Competency Assurance
NOCA Guidelines, 69
Nominations process of board members, 62
Nonprofit organization, 4–6, 7, 15, 17, 27, 28, 73, 86, 87, 117
  legal basis for, 6, 7
  recognition by the government, 4
Not-for-profit organizations. See Nonprofit organizations

Occupational Safety and Health Administration, 91
Operational test, application of by Internal Revenue Service, 26
  satisfaction of for tax-exempt status, 17
Organizational audit. *See* Organizational test
Organizational test
  satisfaction of for tax-exempt status, 17
  as a tool for evaluating credentialing effort, 48

Parent–subsidiary relationship, as example of bifurcation, 27
Payment options, importance of making easy for applicants, 43
Pew Health Professions Commission, 53, 72, 152, 162, 200, 201, 203–206, 232
  history, 200

[Pew Health Professions Commission]
  mission, 200
  mission statement, 201
  programs and activities, 202
Pharmacy Technician Certification Board
  data collection, 97
  examination, 94
  marketing by, 97
  milestones, 93
  mission, 93, 228
  recertification, 96
  task analysis, 98
Police power, 128, 144, 145, 147, 191, 215
  role in protection of the public, 6
Practice act, 128, 129
  challenges to, 132
  parameters of, 129
  requirements of, 129
Practice standards. *See* Standards of practice
Pretesting of examination items, 137
Private inurement doctrine
  applicability to business leagues, 22
  applicability to social welfare organizations, 23
  as applied to charitable organizations, 20
Professional association, 2, 9, 10, 14, 28, 36, 56, 69, 72, 149, 158, 170, 196
  governance structure considerations, 55
  legal segregation from credentialing organization, 56
  reason for tax-exempt status, 9
Professional Examination Service, 38
Professional membership societies. *See* Professional associations
Protection of the public. *See* Public protection
PTCB. *See* Pharmacy Technician Certification Board
Public member
  on credentialing boards, 60, 61, 65–67, 70, 71, 79, 105, 158–160, 225

[Public member]
  selection of, 70
Public Member Declaration, 65
Public protection, 33, 127, 128, 135, 219 *See also* Public welfare
  mission of American Institute of Certified Public Accountants, 165
  mission of National Board for Certification in Occupational Therapy, 101
  as primary goal of state licensing board, 1
  and professional associations, 9
  role of licensure and certification, 1
Public relations
  avoiding misinformation and abuse, 46
  budgeting for, 45
Public welfare, 4, 219
  as goal of licensure, 10, 219
  promotion and protection of by Constitution, 5
  protection and promotion of by U.S. Constitution, 5
  and role of certification organizations, 11

Reaves, Randolph P., 207, 209, 227, 228
Recertification, 50, 59, 69, 79, 80, 90, 93, 94, 95, 97, 121
  of Board or Pharmaceutical Specialties certificants, 80
  by Pharmacy Technician Certification Board, 96
Recognition, importance of providing for certificants, 44
Registration, definition, 2, 126
Regulatory boards. *See* Boards
Reputation of credentialing organization, significance of, 33
Retaking of examinations, 179
Revocation
  of certification, reasons for by Pharmacy Technician Certification Board, 95
  of right to practice, 148, 154

[Revocation]
of tax-exempt status, 17

Safety, as primary motivation for certification of crane operators, 88
Schoon, Craig G., 1, 14, 214, 217, 224, 233
Scientific entities, as charitable organizations, 19
Screening. *See* Application, screening of; Candidate, screening of
Self-perpetuation of boards, 61
Self-regulation, 53, 120, 147, 165, 168
Shimberg, Benjamin, 9, 11, 14, 145, 162, 163, 199, 216, 219, 221
Showers, Barbara A., 186, 224, 225
Smith, 1, 14, 121, 123, 214, 224, 233
Social and political foundations
of certification, 10, 220
of credentialing, 7
of licensure, 8, 220
for stakeholders, 220
Social welfare organizations, definition of, 18
Internal Revenue Service rulings regarding, 23
Specialized Carriers and Rigging Association, 89
Specialty Councils, 83
Stakeholders, 1, 2, 4, 5, 7, 8, 10–14, 31–38, 40, 44, 45, 47, 48, 52, 55, 58, 62, 64, 72, 94, 97, 106, 114, 116, 117, 121, 122, 166, 173, 187, 194, 198, 199, 219–223, 227, 229, 230
importance of, 4, 5, 31
as information source for evaluating credentialing effort, 48
methods of communicating information to, 97
mission of stakeholder organizations in licensure and certification, 194, 220, 229
needs for organization to identify, 8

[Stakeholders]
role of, 5, 8
significance of addressing needs of in certification programs, 33, 220
surveying of to assess value of a credential, 35
Standards for Accreditation of National Certification Organizations, 62, 65, 120
requirements of a public member, 65
Standards of practice, 130, 146, 157, 168, 180
State income tax status, relationship to federal income tax status, 17
State licensing board
enforcement of mission, 180
mission of, 178
State testing unit
mission of, 186
mission statement, 186
Statutory certification, 149, 150
Structuring considerations, for determination of tax-exempt status, 27
Subsidiary organization, as a structuring consideration for certification organizations, 29
Survey, for board selection, 73

Task analysis, 79
by Pharmacy Technician Certification Board, 98
Taskforce on Health Care Workforce Regulation, 203, 205
Tax status. *See also* Tax-exempt status
of an association of regulatory boards, 140
bifurcation of, 27
definitions of and distinctions among categories, 18
structuring considerations, 27
tax-exempt organizations
Tax-exempt status, 4, 11, 14, 16–18, 20, 21, 25, 29, 54, 143. *See also* Tax status

[Tax-exempt status]
    determination of by organization's primary
       purpose, 17
    and Internal Revenue Service, 4
    meaning of for certification organizations,
       16
    recognition of by Internal Revenue Serv-
       ice, 17
Term limits of board members, 68
Title control, 149
Training and orientation of board members,
    71

Uniform CPA Examination, 166

Vagueness, as challenge to practice act,
    132

Willingness to serve, requirement of board
    members, 70
Wooldridge, Edna Q., 100, 219, 223, 228

Zara, Anthony, 189, 216, 226
Zero-Based Standards Review Study,
    121